THEATER
IN THE
AMERICAS

A Series from
Southern
Illinois
University
Press
ROBERT A.
SCHANKE
Series Editor

Teaching
Performance
Studies

Teaching Performance Studies

Edited by Nathan Stucky and Cynthia Wimmer

With a Foreword by Richard Schechner

Southern
Illinois
University
Press
Carbondale &
Edwardsville

Chapter 17, "Performance Studies, Neuroscience, and the Limits of Culture,"
copyright © John Emigh, 2001.
Portions of chapter 2, "Critical Performative Pedagogy: Fleshing Out the Politics of
Liberatory Education," by Elyse Lamm Pineau, were previously published as
"Performance Studies Across the Curriculum: Problems, Possibilities, and
Projections." *The Future of Performance Studies: Visions and Revisions.* Ed. Sheron J.
Dailey. Annandale: National Communication Assoc., 1998. 128–35.

Library of Congress Cataloging-in-Publication Data
Teaching performance studies / edited by Nathan Stucky and Cynthia Wimmer.
    p. cm.—(Theater in the Americas)
Includes bibliographical references and index.
    1. Performing arts—Study and teaching. 2. Performing arts. I. Stucky, Nathan,
1950–   II. Wimmer, Cynthia, 1946. III. Series.

PN1576. T43 2002
791'.071—dc21
ISBN 0-8093-2465-2 (cloth : alk. paper)
ISBN 0-8093-2466-0 (pbk. : alk. paper)   2002018757

Contents

Foreword

Fundamentals of Performance Studies

A happy Sisyphus, that's who an accomplished teacher of performance studies is, one whose task is never ending because the field is always changing. As soon as you think you've got it, the rock crashes to the bottom of the hill, and the work/fun begins all over again. Performance studies is not a discipline that admits yellowing lecture notes, long-stored computer files, or packaged approaches. Current events—personal, local, national, and global—are engaged and reviewed in historical and theoretical perspective; the feelings of the teacher and students are brought into play on their own and in relation to each other, not hidden under cloaks of "objectivity." Whenever I teach a course, I make sure that a significant proportion of the resources—readings, media, fieldwork—are new. I don't overprepare: The thrill of "not knowing" is extremely stimulating within the interrogative community of a seminar. I play games with myself and my students in order to better freshly engage topics. (Don't ask about lecture courses, which I do from time to time but do not love.) As for performer workshops, I step into them with as close to an empty mind as I can approach. I know that I am going to teach some yoga as preparation/relaxation/centering. But what happens after that depends on those present, what is thrown up from my storehouse of experiences, and the relationship between the hubbub of the moment and a collective search for a dilated calm.

So why does this prepared unpreparedness make the teacher of performance studies happy? Because teaching performance studies is a "repetition-of-the-never-the-same"—a fine example of restoration of behavior. The task is taken up over and over, while the particulars keep changing. An elusive, playful, embodied, multifaceted, protean operation: Teaching performance studies is very much a creative art. "Pure" academicians are uncomfortable with performance studies because it is artlike, blurring the distinctions not only between "art" and "life" but also between "scholarship" and "art making." Some artists are uncomfortable because performance studies insists on theory, on critical thought, and on rigorous historical and cultural contexts. But don't be lulled: *Blurry* does not mean "sloppy" with regard to research, trained embodied practice, and writing. Performance studies demands and engages interculturality and interdisciplinarity with precision and rigor. It goes without saying that defining performance studies once and for all is impossible. But that doesn't mean I won't give it a shot. Happy Sisyphuses we may be—but what kind of rock are we rolling up what slippery slope?

Two Fundamentals of Performance Studies

The primary fundamental of performance studies is that there is no fixed canon of works, ideas, practices, or anything else that defines or limits the field. Or to put it another way, performance studies happens at always-changing intersections of particulars, at convergences where every possible X may meet any possible Y. Whatever today's convergences, these cannot be retained once and for all. Performance studies is *fundamentally* relational, dynamic, and processual. Such rigorous indeterminacy and openness make many uncomfortable about PS.

The second fundamental is that performance studies enthusiastically borrows from other disciplines. There is nothing that inherently "really belongs to" or "really does not belong to" performance studies. Historically, these other disciplines can be specified. Especially in its present formative stage, performance studies draws on and synthesizes approaches from the social sciences, feminist studies, gender studies, history, psychoanalysis, queer theory, semiotics, ethology, cybernetics, area studies, media and popular culture theory, and cultural studies. What future borrowings may occur cannot be reliably determined.

In performance studies, texts, architecture, visual arts, or any other item or artifact of art or culture are not studied as such. When texts, architecture, visual arts, or anything else are looked at by performance studies, they are studied "as" performances. That is, they are regarded as practices, events, and behaviors, not as "objects" or "things." Thus, performance studies does not "read" an action or ask what "text" is being enacted. Rather, performance studies inquires about the "behavior" of, for example, a painting: the ways it interacts with those who view it, thus evoking different reactions and meanings, and how it changes meaning over time and in different contexts; under what circumstances it was created and exhibited; and how the gallery or building displaying it shapes its presentations. These kinds of performance studies questions can be asked of any event or material object. Of course, when performance studies deals with behavior—artistic, everyday, ritual, playful, and so on—the questions asked are closer to how performance theorists have traditionally approached theatre and the other performing arts.

What Makes Performances Studies Special?

If everything in performance studies is up for grabs, how can performance studies be itself and nothing else? The answer is in how performance studies regards actions, behavior, and practice. Performance studies takes these very seriously at two levels: Performance studies both examines actions and is itself infused with actions. Artistic practice of a particular kind is a necessary part of the performance studies curriculum. This practice privileges a living avant-garde—performance art, performance composition, performative writing, and the like. This close relationship between studying performance and doing performance is integral to performance studies.

Furthermore, performance studies' ways of studying performance emphasize activity rather than book or archival research. Participant observation—a technique adapted from anthropology but put to new uses in performance studies—is its own kind of practice. In anthropology, for the most part, the "home culture" is Western, the "other culture" is non-Western. But in performance studies, the "other" may be a part of one's own culture (non-Western or Western) or even an aspect of one's own life. The performance studies field-worker is as much, or more, a Brechtian-Boalian director as an "objective" social scientist. That means she or he is enabled to use criticism, irony, sympathetic engagement, and personal commentary. In a meaningful way, one performs one's fieldwork. It follows that those practicing performance studies are actively involved in community life, often becoming advocates for, or coactivists with, those they are studying. Performance studies does not aspire to ideological neutrality. In fact, a basic theoretical claim of performance studies is that no approach or position is "neutral." The challenge is to become as aware as possible of one's own positions in relation to the positions of others—and then to take steps to maintain or change positions.

Performances occur in many different instances and contexts and as many different kinds. *Performance* as an overall category must be construed as a "broad spectrum" or "continuum" of actions ranging from ritual, play, sports, popular entertainments, the performing arts (theatre, dance, music), and everyday life performances to the enactment of social, professional, gender, race, and class roles, to healing (from shamanism to surgery), and to the various representations and construction of actions in the media and the Internet. There is no historically fixable limit to what is or is not "performance." Along the continuum, new genres can be added, others can be dropped. The underlying theoretical claim is that any action can be framed, presented, highlighted, or displayed as a performance. Many performances belong to more than one category along the continuum. For example, a football player spiking the ball and pointing a finger in the air after scoring a touchdown is performing a dance and enacting a ritual as part of his professional role as athlete and popular entertainer.

In performance studies, questions of embodiment, action, behavior, and agency are dealt with interculturally. This approach recognizes two things. First, in today's world, cultures are always interacting—there is no group existing entirely or even largely to and with itself alone. Second, the differences among cultures are so profound that no theory of performance is universal: One-size theory does not fit all. Nor are the playing fields where cultures interact level. The current dominant means of cultural interaction—globalization—enacts extreme imbalances of power, money, access to media, and control over resources. Although globalization is reminiscent of colonialism, it is also different in key ways. Proponents of globalization promise that "free trade," the Internet, and advances in science and technology will result in a better material life for the world's peoples. However, globalization induces a sameness at the level of popular culture—"world beat" music and the proliferation of American-style fast foods and media are examples. Cultural sameness and seamless communications make it easier for transnational entities to get their messages across. The resistance to this "new world order" is extreme, as was shown in the September 11, 2001, attacks on New York's World Trade Center towers and the Pentagon.

The book you hold in your hands recounts a wide variety of teaching methods, experiences, theories, and approaches. All of it fits under the big performance studies tent. None of it is "definitive." Michelle Kisliuk in her chapter quotes her own journal of her trek across central Africa. She ends the quotation with this compelling sentence, which I find to be a most fitting invocation of performance studies: *"There we found shelter before moving on."*

Richard Schechner
Department of Performance Studies
New York University

Acknowledgments

Teaching Performance Studies grew out of the individual and collective work of innumerable students, teachers, researchers, and artists, all perhaps serving multiple roles in their explorations of performance. To these many unnamed, we offer our sincere thanks and deep gratitude. Some others have been so helpful that we hope you will join us in celebrating their contributions toward this volume.

The College of Liberal Arts and the Department of Speech Communication at Southern Illinois University have been helpful in providing resources and time as well as support for travel. We are indebted to Larry Russell, Jessica Presto, Stephanie Martinez, and Elizabeth Whitney for their extensive work with the manuscript in various stages of completion.

The support of other friends and colleagues has been invaluable. Among these, we wish to recognize Ron Pelias, Phillip Glenn, James VanOosting, Suzanne Daughton, Carol Burbank, and Tim Ruppell, all of whom provided advice, support, and encouragement at critical points in the evolution of this volume. The contributors to this collection provided conversation and feedback throughout the writing and editing process. Additionally, we are grateful for conversations with Richard Schechner, Dwight Conquergood, Sally Harrison-Pepper, Paul H. Gray, Lynn C. Miller, Ron Shields, Donna Nudd, Elizabeth Bell, Mary Frances HopKins, and the late Robert Hopper, who provided us with insight as well as inspiration.

We have had the good fortune to work with Elizabeth Brymer at Southern Illinois University Press, whose enthusiasm for the project was immediate and gratifying. We're pleased that acquisitions editor Karl Kageff pointed us in Liz's direction.

Our family members have supported, encouraged, entertained, and sustained us throughout this process. Our gratitude and profound appreciation goes to Suzanne Daughton, Michael Stucky, Evelyn Wimmer, Michael Sauri, Matthew Sauri, Wendi Sauri, and Dawn Jefferies. We dedicate this book to them.

Teaching
Performance
Studies

Introduction

The Power of Transformation

in Performance Studies Pedagogy

Nathan
Stucky
and
Cynthia
Wimmer

Beginning a book with the words *performance studies* announces at the outset "turbulence ahead." The methods and purposes of its practitioners vary, and the extent of its domain engenders disagreement.

If the term *performance studies* serves scholars with diverse aims, what does it mean to teach performance studies today? Many performance studies scholars are teachers whose classrooms, both inside and outside academic institutions, serve as sites for work beyond the familiar norms of traditional instruction, as this volume demonstrates. The heterogeneity of our contributors confirms that performance studies attracts sufficient diversity to make problematic any single definition of the field or any single overarching pedagogy. The performance turn, evident in many academic disciplines over at least the past three decades, indicates shared interests in both research methods and pedagogy among such scholars, despite their disparate disciplinary homes and individual focuses. Some of the work in performance studies has gone unnamed or is differently labeled, but it nonetheless contributes to the ongoing dialogue. As D. Soyini Madison writes, "It seems that everyone I know and don't know is thinking, speaking, and writing in the language of performance, or trying to. Performance is everywhere these days" (107). The present volume brings together for the first time scholars from diverse fields who discuss how their performance studies practices inform and/or constitute their pedagogy.

Performance studies transforms disciplines and individuals as well as curricula and departments. Over the past three decades, the record of transformations can be seen in scholarly and artistic conferences, public performances, university classrooms, the actions of tenure and promotion committees, and the archive of print and electronic materials to which this volume contributes. Performance studies has transformed formal as well as informal structures. Of course, performance studies is not a panacea for all the ills afflicting the academy, but it offers unique ways of engendering change. Broadly conceived, performance studies participates in an ongoing redefinition of cultural, social, and educational practices.

Performance Studies and the Classroom

The classroom is a charged space, a site of performance as well as a place invested in studying performances. Teachers have increasingly come to understand the special characteristics of classrooms as environments where performance holds particular power. The essays in this volume build on the dynamics of performance as a subject, as a cultural and social artifact, and as a way of knowing. In studying a range of performances, the authors seek to invest this study with the power of performance itself. Here, we do not seek to reconcile the differences our authors represent nor to assimilate diverse teaching practices into a single performance studies pedagogy. Rather, our objective is to present strategies that have been observed in the wider context of performance studies pedagogy, strategies that can be useful across the academy in humanities, social science, and even "hard" science courses. In this sense, we agree with James Winn, who seeks to forge "new interdisciplinary alliances, not only across the barriers separating the various disciplines that make up the modern humanities, but across the larger barrier separating scholars from performers" (108). Indeed, throughout this book, scholarship, performance, and teaching are treated as inseparable, sometimes indistinguishable, terms.

The teaching of performance studies challenges the traditional bifurcation of teaching and research that treats these as though separate enterprises. The linkage of research and teaching can be seen in the work of master pedagogues. For example, in his 1995 volume, *Pedagogy of Hope,* Paulo Freire asserts:

> I think it is important to bring out the fact that the moment of
> our cognition of existing knowledge is by and large the moment
> of instruction, the moment of the teaching and learning of content, while the other, the moment of the production of new
> knowledge, is in the main, that of research. But actually, all instruction involves research, and all research involves instruction.
> There is no genuine instruction in whose process no research is
> performed by way of a question, investigation, curiosity, creativity; just as there is no research in the course of which researchers
> do not learn—after all, by coming to know, they learn, and after
> having learned something, they communicate it, they teach.
> (192–93)

The innovative and interdisciplinary nature of much performance studies research has necessarily provoked innovation in curricula and in the presentation of course content. The chapters in this volume suggest a variety of pedagogical practices for performance studies classrooms that resist tendencies to press new knowledge formations only into old pedagogical forms. We encourage "conscious teaching," that is, teaching with self-reflectivity and a heightened awareness of methods, attitudes, hidden curricula, postures, and inflections.

Performance studies teachers are daily engaged in the process of studying, evaluating, interpreting, and changing the intersection between performance and pedagogy, whether it is having students learn to perform a sonnet or having them study the intricacies of the Balinese cockfight. The root of understanding lies in a felt-knowledge of human experience. In most of the essays in this volume, we see demonstrated pedagogies that have arisen from classroom interaction and thus are partly produced by students in the moment of their occurrence, rather than pedagogies developed by research trials, written in formulas for reproduction, and deposited into the classroom dynamic. We expect that this spirit of innovation will continue to be a force in the future development of pedagogies that will be useful across the curriculum.

One characteristic of performance studies pedagogy is its emphasis on embodiment. This emphasis demonstrates its concern with what happens to the bodies of teachers and students in the classroom. Coming to know another human being (as closely as one can ever accomplish such a goal) necessarily involves an embodied response to the human condition. A substantial development in performance studies pedagogy has been a consistent attention to enactment, to experiential learning in the classroom. The underlying philosophies trace back at least to John Dewey. In politicized, contemporary forms, they appear in the work of Paulo Freire, Peter McLaren, and Henry Giroux and many influenced by their thinking. For example, Elyse Lamm Pineau advocates what she calls "critical performative pedagogy" ("Performance Studies" 128). Her work articulates a move away from thinking about the bodies of teachers and students as being on display toward understanding the "'body as a medium for learning' [that] requires the rigorous, systematic, exploration-through-enactment of real and imagined experience in which learning occurs through sensory awareness and kinesthetic engagement" (132–33). Many of the essays in the second part of this volume elucidate strategies of embodiment as mediums for gaining understanding and empathy for others. McLaren's concept of *enfleshment* informs much of this thinking. For McLaren, the body is a "body/subject," that is,

> a terrain of the flesh in which meaning is inscribed, constructed, and reconstituted. In this view the body is conceived as the interface of the individual and society, as a site of embodied or "enfleshed" subjectivity which also reflects the ideological sedi-

mentations of the social structure inscribed into it. (*Critical Pedagogy* 64)

Techniques of embodiment increase students' awareness of others' ideological and social subjectivities, an awareness that can be seen in the work of a new generation of educators (McLaren, "Liberatory"). This pedagogical emphasis is political because, as Ann Cooper Albright has argued, "While issues of diversity are never confined to the physical body—they are always implicated in social contexts and representational structures—they are made present through our bodies" (45). The importance of embodiment and its relation to power in the classroom leads bell hooks to comment that:

> Significantly, those of us who are trying to critique biases in the classroom have been compelled to return to the body to speak about ourselves as subjects in history. We are all subjects in history. We must return ourselves to a state of embodiment in order to deconstruct the way power has been traditionally orchestrated in the classroom, denying subjectivity to some groups and according it to others. (139)

Another development can be seen in the family resemblance between pedagogy and ethnography. Take, for example, McLaren's introduction to *Schooling as a Ritual Performance*, where he discusses his fieldwork in a Catholic school in downtown Toronto. He was "invited there as an ethnographer who was undertaking some scholarly research in pedagogy" (1). An additional example of this juncture can be found in the work of Bryant Keith Alexander, who draws on McLaren in his study of cultural performance in the classroom to create "an autoethnographic analysis of [his] own lived experience as a Black male student and teacher" (307). Alexander comes to "know" through performing himself, then studies his own performance, and publishes his findings.

Performance's role in ethnography, especially to "interpretive ethnography," is explored in a volume of that title by Norman Denzin. While performance theory and practice is woven throughout this work, there are specific discussions of performance texts, ethnographic performance, standpoint epistemologies, and narrative. Denzin argues that "ethnography has crossed that liminal space that separates the scholarly text from its performance" (123). For Denzin, the future of ethnography, what he calls ethnography's "sixth moment," will be significantly informed by performance. In the collection you are now holding, ethnographic and performance threads intertwine in many ways, reflecting a major influence on performance pedagogy as it has developed over the past two decades.

A sense of play, experimentation, exploration, and humor also suffuses much performance studies pedagogy; this development is one of
mood or tone rather than specific strategy. McLaren concludes *Schooling as a Ritual Performance* with observations about laughter that he identifies as "a politics of refusal . . . reinvoking the fool and the itinerant clown as pedagogical agents of resistance" (287). Laughter is, of course, a particular kind of performance, imbued at once with a myriad of possibilities: appreciation, surprise, recognition, irony, sarcasm, understanding, sympathy, disgust, enjoyment, puzzlement, concern, disdain—an embodied political position, a kind of representation.

In a work that echoes some of McLaren's thinking on the performative in education, Elizabeth Ellsworth draws on her formal study of cinema to challenge contemporary conceptions of teaching. In chapters with such evocative titles as "Teaching as a Performance Suspended in the Space Between Self and Other" and "Teaching as a Performance Suspended in Time," Ellsworth refers to Peggy Phelan's discussion of representation and the fact of performance's ephemerality, arguing that "teaching is never completed or finished" (158). This indeterminacy feeds into the sense of experimentation, play, and inventiveness of this aspect of performance studies pedagogy.

Embodiment, ethnography, and play can also be seen as threads in the larger movement within performance studies utilizing such techniques to question the politics of representation through a compilation of pedagogical strategies, a movement comprised of many threads from diverse disciplinary bodies of research. This movement resonates with much recent work in education informed by cultural studies.

The rich interweaving of performance studies with cultural studies can be seen in what Giroux and Patrick Shannon call "the pedagogical as performative practice or performative pedagogy" (3). They announce an interest in analyzing

> how the intersection of the language of the pedagogical and performative might provide cultural-studies theorists and educators alike an opportunity to address the effectiveness of pedagogical practices that are not only interdisciplinary, transgressive, and oppositional but also connected to a wider public project to increase the scope of racial, economic, and social justice while expanding and deepening the imperatives of a radical democracy. (2–3)

Our sense of the place of performance studies as an interdisciplinary phenomenon resonates with Giroux's call for cultural studies in education programs. Giroux contends that "traditional academic disciplines cannot account for the great diversity of cultural and social phenomena that has come to characterize an increasingly hybridized, postindustrial world" (235). He argues for the importance of understanding the power of mass media and performance pedagogy as sites of learning and for grounding the language of theory in the practices of daily life.

The essays in the present volume are one way of addressing Giroux's challenge for cultural studies within performance studies. They are as well a demonstration of the degree to which teaching performance studies "is a cultural practice that can be understood only through considerations of history, politics, power, and culture" (233). An additional site for resonance between this framework for teaching popular culture and the pedagogies presented in this volume is David Buckingham's *Teaching Popular Culture*, in which he acknowledges the impact of Freire and McLaren, recapitulates the themes of "radical pedagogy," and offers a collection of essays that largely concern incorporating popular culture into the classroom and theorizing about pedagogy.

While performance studies pedagogy offers new subjects and methodologies, it may be helpful to locate these developments in the context of the historical educational spectrum. In general, the pedagogies discussed in this volume can be viewed as based on a "constructivist" model of education, which, as educational philosopher Nel Noddings argues, maintains "that all knowledge (and perception itself) is constructed, neither merely received nor innate" (109). One root of this current popular trend can be traced from the educational philosophy of Immanuel Kant, who emphasized "the interaction of cognitive mechanisms with the world in constructing knowledge" (Noddings 110). Building on the work of Kant, Jean Piaget and his followers defined a developmental model of education that stressed timing in education (in other words, we are ready to learn certain things at certain times, as Rousseau believed) but also accentuated subject-object interaction. Some critics of Piaget's emphasis on this interaction, however, turn to the work of L. S. Vygotsky, whose contructivism emphasizes social interaction for learning, as many of the pedagogies in this volume do. Both types of constructivist educators maintain that objects and events are not stored as exact images in memory but rather that memories are constructed and therefore affected by context, mood, and recognition of relationships with previous experience.

Educational philosophers such as Freire, Piaget, Vygotsky, and Dewey have maintained that students should be involved in constructing their own learning as well as be active pursuers in their own purposes. As Noddings has written: "Constructivist teachers deemphasize lecturing and telling and encourage instead the active engagement of students in establishing and pursuing their own learning objectives" (115). Some postmodern thinkers have argued, however, that people are not autonomous subjects; we do not simply create our own realities, nor are we able to establish learning objectives outside of our cultural contexts. Rather, we are situated knowers whose knowledge, and

therefore decision-making ability, is constructed through "weak" subject-object and social interactions as well as through "strong" constructions, such as embodiment and intensive study. Because our understandings and perceptions are constructed through both strong and weak constructive processes, we are viewed as constituted subjects who "retain some agency[;] our cognitive process may very well be constructive, but we do not construct reality" (Noddings 118). Much has been written about the constituted subject and multiple identities, and the influence of this work is evident here.

Another strain of educational philosophy clearly evident in the work of our authors derives from Aristotle's communitarian model that recognized community values and taught students to question them. The values clarification models of 1966 (Noddings 157–58) and 1975 (Chazan 48) demonstrate the beginnings of this emphasis within a postmodern environment. The current move to expose students to a variety of value structures from cultures (including their own) and to examine values in the light of concerns about race, class, gender, sexual preference, age, ability, and other facets of difference represents a further pedagogical emphasis on the development of appropriate values and ethics for functioning in this hybridized world. To understand, among other things, the values of a culture, Richard Rorty advocates a holistic approach:

> This holistic line of argument says that we shall never be able to avoid the "hermeneutic circle"—the fact that we cannot understand the parts of a strange culture, practice, theory, language, or whatever, unless we know something about how the whole thing works, whereas we cannot get a grasp on how the whole thing works until we have some understanding of its parts. (319)

Many of the pedagogies found in this volume represent a holistic approach to education. Holistic efforts to promote health demonstrate the need to take into account the interconnectedness of all circumstances impacting the health of the patient. Holistic education is education that strives to promote cultural health within its students and teachers; it takes into account not only mind, body, and spirit but cultural constructs and contexts.

The term *holistic* in the context of education has, in fact, been used in a variety of ways. In *Teaching to Transgress*, bell hooks uses the term to emphasize the need for both teachers and students to be "'whole' human beings" in the classroom and argues that this pedagogy is "more demanding than conventional critical or feminist pedagogy [because] it emphasizes well-being [and] means that teachers must be actively

8

Nathan
Stucky
and Cynthia
Wimmer

committed to a process of self-actualization" for themselves first and then their students (14–15). At the Holistic Teaching/Learning Unit of the University of Tennessee, Knoxville, education department, the term *holistic* refers to an "integrative and interdisciplinary" course of instruction "which addresses the needs of the whole person (the integration of cognitive, physical, affective, moral, and spiritual dimensions)" (Knight). Other universities that use the term in descriptions of their education programs include Stanford, Toronto, and Carnegie Mellon. Used in this way, the term seems to signal a response by the teachers of teachers to incorporate instruction that reflects the values and missions of the international movement that calls itself "Holistic Education." We quote here from a Web site originating in Tasmania, Australia:

> Holistic Education is concerned with the growth of every person's intellectual, emotional, social, physical, artistic, creative and spiritual potentials. It actively engages students in the teaching/ learning process and encourages personal and collective responsibility. . . . By introducing students to a holistic view of the planet, life on Earth, and the emerging world community, holistic strategies enable students to perceive and understand the various contexts which shape and give meaning to life. . . . [Holistic education] recognises that all knowledge is created within a cultural context and that the "facts" are seldom more than shared points of view. It encourages the transfer of learning across the chasms that have separated academic disciplines in the past. Holistic education encourages learners to critically approach the cultural, moral and political contexts of their lives. (Holistic Education)

These identifying characteristics of the holistic education movement resonate so strongly with the pedagogies found in most performance studies classrooms, and thus with those in this volume, that performance studies in both its research objectives and its pedagogies can also be termed holistic.

Scott Forbes, the contributing educator editor for the *Putman Pit*, has traced the rise of the movement known as holistic education from its beginnings in the 1960s and 1970s, a period that also saw early signs of performance studies. Forbes cites several shifts that fed into the call for reevaluation, and eventually, challenge to traditional models of education: the disillusionment with scientific thinking, the rise of new forms of psychology that moved away from the model of the mind as machine, the rise in awareness of a global ecological crisis that did/ does not respect political boundaries, and other globalizations of economy and entertainment. The movement embraces spirituality but of a "generalised and inclusive" nature, and it emphasizes social justice and equality. Arising during the 1960s, when concerns about equality for women and people of color were front-page news, these issues became part of the foundation for the grassroots holistic education movement. The movement, however, is a philosophical stance most directed toward primary education with middle and high school education receiving secondary attention, and as such, most holistic education literature does not delineate either particular pedagogical strategies or goals for students to attain specific knowledges and skills.

While the knowledge attained in performance studies courses varies widely, the skill sets taught through performance studies pedagogy as evidenced in this volume are central to college education as well as being transferable and preparatory for a wide range of career options. Students learn critical reading and critical thinking skills, and they learn print, electronic, and ethnographic research skills. Students learn to read and evaluate all kinds of performance with what William O. Beeman in his chapter in this volume calls "fine-grained observational research practices." These practices teach students to read language as heard (as well as written) and to analyze nonlinguistic media such as music, dance, gesture, facial expression, movement, graphic arts, and plastic arts.

Students in performance studies classrooms routinely develop their critical, descriptive, and analytical skills in the process of performance itself. Students learn to perform before others, both in class and without, and in a variety of modes: cabaret; storytelling; speech making; class presentations; improvisatory role-playing; dance pieces; and small and large, long and short theatre pieces. Within the performance context, students have the opportunity to increase their skills in working in community with fellow students and in ensemble. They have the opportunity to learn how to direct attention and how to communicate content as well as emotion. They learn how to evaluate speech elements of volume, pitch, tone, rhythm, and pace and movement elements of posture, pace, and spatial relations between people and between people and objects. In some performance studies courses, students are given the opportunity to learn to use, not simply evaluate, production elements in their performances as well: costumes, makeup, sets, props, lighting, music, and movement.

Performance studies pedagogy solicits the development of students' writing skills. The wide variety of writing skills developed in the performance studies courses reflected in this volume alone is quite impressive: formal paper writing; research paper writing; analytical essay writing; script writing from research on current issues; script writing through sampling auto/biographical and/or historical material; script writing for performance of self (stories to be told, sermons, speeches, presentations, reports); script (re)writing from literary texts; script writing without words, or image scripts; scenario writing; character profile writing; journal writing; performance diary/notebook writing; more formal performance autobiography writing; lesson-plan writing; journalistic writing; poetry writing; narrative writing that is poetically crafted; and ethnographic writing. Some students also have the opportunity to learn notation systems for movement and for transcription of conversation. But perhaps the most crucial skill set students have the opportunity to discover is a way of embodied thinking that encourages self-reflection and critical distance as well as empathy, concern with cultural contexts, values, and issues, and confidence in their own opinions.

Along with McLaren, we believe that "pedagogies constitute a form of social and cultural criticism" (*Critical Pedagogy* 50). The developments and philosophies discussed rather briefly here represent where performance studies pedagogy is at the dawn of the new millennium. We hope that they are but the beginning of a larger move on the part of educators across the curriculum to tap into the knowledge we now have regarding multiple intelligences and epistemologies, a move that begins to answer McLaren and Giroux's call "to engage student experience with a pedagogy that is both affirmative and critical and which offers the means for self and social transformation" (35).

Towards (Not) Defining Performance Studies

We address the question of defining performance studies in this volume through three broad themes that can be seen to characterize it: disciplinary position, epistemology and methodology (especially embodiment), and border negotiations. These themes, reflected throughout the three parts of this book, indicate sufficiently broad trends to identify major currents in the field.

Performance studies is a broad-based discipline; it takes as its subject human performance behaviors in cultural, aesthetic, and social contexts; it finds its methods in ethnography, communication, cultural studies, literary studies, theatre, anthropology, and especially, in performance itself. Performance studies is a field with a continually moving center of gravity. Any attempt at a single definition of performance studies risks falling into boundary discussions that are ultimately exhausting if not counterproductive; the very effort to circumscribe its domain is resisted by the project of performance studies itself. As Richard Schechner observes, "At the descriptive level there is no detail of performance that occurs everywhere under all circumstances. Nor is it easy to specify limitations on what is, or could be treated as, performance" ("Magnitudes" 19). Mary S. Strine, Beverly Whitaker Long, and Mary Frances HopKins argue that performance is "an essentially contested concept" (183), a notion they derive from W. B. Gallie's observation that certain concepts contain inherent disagreement. Marvin Carlson begins his book *Performance: A Critical Introduction* by citing this argument from Strine et al. and then suggesting that "recent manifestations of performance in both theory and practice, are so varied that a complete survey of them is hardly possible" (2). Strine et al. identify eight representative sites of performance: sites of aesthetic enjoyment, intellectual inquiry, affective play, cultural memory, participatory ritual, social commentary, political action, and psychological probe (185–89). Rather than create a prescriptive definition of performance, Strine et al. offer these representative sites as a way of understanding the range of performance. As Ronald Pelias and James Van-Oosting assert:

> Performance Studies calls into question the privilege of academic authority by including all members of a speech community as potential artists, all utterances as potentially aesthetic, all events as potentially theatrical, and all audiences as potentially active participants who can authorize artistic experience. (221)

Performance studies examines the continually expanding range of behaviors invented by human beings to communicate with each other, especially those which are rehearsed, replayed, or consciously constructed.

Performance studies concerns itself broadly with culture and identity; it involves a study of the human as a performing being. Humans construct performances in everyday conversational interaction, in play, and more obviously, in orchestrated rites, rituals, festivals, and theatrical shows. The array of subjects performance studies scholars have chosen to examine hints at the breadth of the field. A good deal of attention centers on performances that specifically mark cultures, such as religious rituals, formal theatre, dance, sporting events, and music. Much work in performance studies addresses formal performance as it appears in cultures around the world. However, the scholarship sometimes centers on more ordinary forms of expression, such as storytelling or everyday talk. There has also been much interest in social issues as they intersect with performance. In consequence, a number of scholars have focused on performance as it relates to gender, class, or race, as well as on an array of subjects including street theatre, performance art, staged resistance, political rallies, scrapbooks, gallery installations, political demonstrations, parades, and workplace performances. Any listing can only be suggestive of the range of performance studies, because the scope of the field emerges through ongoing exploration. Schechner observes that "performance is no longer easy to define or locate: the concept and structure has spread all over the place" (General Introduction n.pag.).

Performance studies evokes the negotiating of borders—cultural,

disciplinary, theoretical, personal, and political. Two foci may be identified here, one in which performances (broadly construed) are seen as
subjects to be studied, a second in which performance is viewed as
epistemological. Performance epistemology locates performance itself
as a site and a method of study. In practice, these two approaches "in-
teranimate" each other. In this volume, we give space to a wide range
of performance studies scholars to discuss their work and to advance
their views. One would be surprised to discover absolute agreement
over terms in a multidisciplinary field. Here we echo Dwight Conquergood's assertion that "performance studies, itself, could be a focus, or
prism, for illuminating a wide spectrum of issues, methodologies, and
perspectives" (Introductory Note 3).

The Emergence of Performance Studies

Performance studies is a field of study with multiple roots. Or, to mix
the image, there are many species in the same lawn (or field, if you
will). It is not a monoculture, all Bermuda or Augustine or clover. The
disciplinary position is not really rhizomatous either, because it does
not trace just one parent. The performance turn in fields such as anthropology and sociology reflects significant rethinking about human
nature. Victor Turner, offering an argument that people are "self-performing" and self-reflexive animals, refers to humans as essentially
performing creatures, *Homo performans* (81). The work of anthropologist Clifford Geertz, sociologist Erving Goffman, theatre director and
theorist Richard Schechner, folklorist Richard Bauman, and many
others points to a performative turn within and across disciplines. The
revolution of thinking both in and out of the academy can be seen, for
instance, in the increasing impact of qualitative research in the human
sciences and in business, government, and other organizations.

Just as the terms performance and performance studies are contested, the emergence of this work with disciplinary status and academic structures varies. One can write several disciplinary histories
for performance studies, each with its particular attributes. As Elizabeth Fine and Jean Speer explain:

> Despite the interdisciplinary origins and nature of this study,
> each discipline brings its own impress to its study of perfor-
> mance. While the anthropologist might approach performance
> studies to reveal more about the social organization and beliefs of
> a culture, those coming from speech communication tend to look
> at the structure and aesthetics of the performance itself, as it is
> embedded in and informed by its social context. (xi)

Fine and Spear identify a number of generative influences on contemporary performance studies practice including: the Prague School of
linguistics in the 1920s and 1930s (especially the work of Roman Jakob-

son), Erving Goffman's *The Presentation of Self in Everyday Life*, Kenneth Burke's theories of dramatism, Dell Hymes's work in the ethnography of speaking, and especially the work of anthropologists Clifford Geertz and Victor Turner (3–5). Schechner's contributions (as a theorist, teacher, and editor) have been noteworthy; his work with Turner proved especially valuable in developing the cross-disciplinary character of performance studies. As Ronald Pelias asserts, a complete history of performance studies would have to be "one that takes into account performance practices across cultures and examines all forms of verbal art" (*Performance Studies* 40).

In the past twenty years, three factors demonstrate the developing energy and recognition of performance studies: it has achieved standing in scholarly organizations; its presence is evidenced in scholarly publications and performances; and it increasingly can be seen in the curricula of colleges and universities both in the United States and abroad.

First, we note several institutional markers establishing performance studies within professional organizations. Following a decade of reflection and discussion, the Interpretation Division of the National Communication Association (NCA) officially changed its designation to the Performance Studies Division in 1990. In the Association for Theatre in Higher Education (ATHE), a Performance Studies Focus Group was formed in 1993. Some have argued that performance studies is not new but is already incorporated in much of the work of other disciplines. Describing the formal emergence of performance studies in ATHE, Jill Dolan argues for "a politically aligned performance studies [that] could invigorate theatre studies without eviscerating it" ("Geographies" 430). While the circumstances differ, in both NCA and ATHE the emergence of performance studies groups provoked positive and negative reaction, what Ronald Shields calls "mixed reviews" (185). Formal recognition was granted in both instances despite concerns that included questions about "disciplinary fragmentation" in the case of NCA or duplication of work conducted under the auspices of other units in the case of ATHE. A new organization dedicated solely to performance studies has recently developed. Discussions for Performance Studies International (PSI) began about 1993; the group formalized its structure in 1997. PSI conducted its first conference outside the United States in Aberystwyth, Wales, in 1999, and following that conference, the number of non-US members of PSI exceeded those from the United States. Performance studies work has also emerged in meetings of the Modern Language Association, at the Women and Theatre annual conference, at the American Association for Theatre Research, at the Performance Research Institute, at gatherings of anthropologists, sociologists, folklorists, and elsewhere.

Second, published scholarship (in addition to performed scholarship) increasingly, and explicitly, is called performance studies. In recent years, there has been a steady rise in the number of performance studies books published. Journals publishing performance studies scholarship (whether or not they identify with the label) include *Drama Review, Performance Research, Performing Arts Journal, Seagull Theatre Quarterly, Text and Performance Quarterly, Theatre Annual, Theatre Journal, Theatre Topics, Women and Theatre,* and many others in anthropology, communication, semiotics, sociology, theatre, and so forth. Intersections with feminist theory, literary theory, and cultural studies, for example, are difficult to sort out. Some sense of this may be seen in the diversity of contributors and content within a number of anthologies (e.g., Case and Reinelt; Dailey, *Future;* Diamond; Franko and Richards; Hart and Phelan; Pelias and Miller; Pollock; Reinelt and Roach; Schechner and Appel), in textbooks (e.g., Pelias, *Performance Studies;* Schechner, *Performance Studies;* Stern and Henderson; Howard; Yordon), and in other volumes (e.g., Carlson; Fuoss; Kistenberg; Harrison-Pepper; Phelan; Turner). It is virtually impossible to corral these studies and associations since the performance paradigm has been so influential, informing, and multifaceted.

Third, in colleges and universities, in the United States and elsewhere, performance studies has emerged in the form of departments, specializations within programs, new course offerings, shifting curricula, faculty hires, course restructuring, and more fundamentally, in ways of conceptualizing performance. These changes inevitably involve both personal and institutional "border negotiations." Although most discussions of performance studies pedagogy address its place in colleges and universities, it can be productively located in high schools as well. Veteran secondary school educator Bethany Girton writes, "just the words 'high school classroom' are usually enough to send shivers down one's spine, but what a fantastic setting for performance studies" (156). Girton discusses the climate of funding cutbacks in the arts and humanities and discusses strategies for educating the public about the value of performance studies in education. She points out that "utilizing performance as a pedagogical tool and publicly emphasizing process as well as product will greatly benefit participating students and audience members" (157).

While performance studies has achieved a presence in established professional organizations, in publications and performances, and in many colleges and universities, it faces continued misunderstanding, resistance, and inertia. The challenge to achieve institutional recognition may be seen, for example, in the difficulty of achieving standing as a category by the National Endowment for the Arts and the National Endowment for the Humanities. In the simplest terms, there is, as yet, in the year 2002, no performance studies box to check on the NEH application form; this work can only fit into the category labeled "inter-disciplinary."

In an introductory note on methodology, Pelias argues for a poetics of performance scholarship; he critiques the recurrent specter of positivism and invites the reader to experience a kind of scholarship that "celebrates the multivocal, multilayered, and multivalent realities of everyday life" (*Writing* x). Essentially, Pelias takes up J. L. Austin's "dare," rearticulated by Andrew Parker and Eve Kosofsky Sedgwick in a discussion of the performative and performance. Parker and Sedgwick's interest in Austin's example, "I dare you," is one of examining the performative force of such an utterance, which "requires a dim-paction of the scene, as well as the act, of utterance" (8). Performative writing emerges expressly in the present volume in essays by Joni L. Jones and Michelle Kisliuk and in more subtle fashion in others. The "performative," as it has come to be known, though, is not a new creature. There exists a long tradition of exploring performance in written texts, the performative nature of writing, especially of performance in and of literature (e.g., Bacon; Bell). A number of writers have noted the theoretical shifts referenced in discussions of "performativity," the scope of theatre and drama studies, and the expansion of performance studies (e.g., Conquergood, "Poetics"; Diamond; HopKins; Langellier; Lee; Schechner, "New Paradigm"; Worthen, "Drama"). A debate of sorts rippling through some corridors of the academy (e.g., a 1995 forum in *Drama Review:* Worthen, "Disciplines"; and responses by Dolan; Roach; Schechner; and Zarrilli; and a 1990 forum in *Text and Performance Quarterly:* Wendt; and responses by Conquergood; Dailey; Gray; Schneider; Stern; and VanOosting and Pelias) seeks to sort out the complexities of performance studies in a charged historical moment. William Worthen identifies one important distinction, that having to do with performativity and text in "the different disciplinary investments of performance studies and literary studies." As Worthen summarizes the issue,

> Literary engagements with performativity tend to focus on the performative function of language as represented in literary texts, and much performance-oriented criticism of drama, for all its invocation of the theater, similarly betrays a desire to locate the meanings of the stage in the contours of the dramatic text. Performance studies has developed a vivid account of nondramatic, non-theatrical, non-scripted, ceremonial, and everyday-life performances, performances that appear to depart from the authority of texts. ("Drama" 1093)

Worthen charges both literary studies and performance studies with misunderstanding dramatic performance (1098). Taking issue with

Parker and Sedgwick, Worthen charges them with "reducing the theater to the characteristic ideological apparatus of modern realism" (1097). Indeed, much of the work in performance studies has been to connect (or reconnect) with performance practices beyond the bounds of the conventional stage (e.g., festivals, everyday life performances, ritual). Along this divide, the place of literature in performance studies (theoretically, as reflected in discussions of text and performativity, and institutionally, as reflected in disciplinary debate) proves to be an especially provocative question.

Much of performance studies has been invested in cultural traditions associated with literature. Shannon Jackson discusses the "institutionalization of performance studies . . . in theatre departments, speech departments, and literature departments" (84). It is this tradition that concerns Paul Edwards, whose 1999 monograph "Unstoried: Teaching Literature in the Age of Performance Studies," traces the performance of literature intellectually as well as institutionally. Edwards describes his class as

> a strange hybrid, which moves among several academic traditions including traditional "English" and traditional "Theater." But in the strange department where I teach, such hybrids have their own tradition. In America's first "School of Speech," at Northwestern University, people have been studying literature by means of performance, and performance by means of literature for over a century. (1)

The distinction between performance treated as a method for studying something (e.g., literature) and as a subject itself suitable for study becomes significant because, as Edwards argues, "In the shift to performance studies, the performance of literature has survived . . . as a teaching methodology, not an academic discipline" (12). Edwards chooses particular texts for classroom study, in part because "a performance classroom, on a daily basis, is filled with people who are making art, not merely studying texts" (13).

Organization and Arrangement

This volume moves through essays designed to establish performance theoretically, to pursue issues of situated performance ethnographically, and to expand pedagogical practices and fields through personal descriptions of performance studies work. We have organized the contributions into these three parts, each of which draws support from and enlivens the others. The descriptions below seek to indicate our organizational logic and to guide the reader through the chapters.

That performance studies resists easy categorization may be seen in the work of our contributors. In assembling this volume, we invited contributors who would explore performance studies theory and practice from disparate viewpoints. We wanted to bring top scholars together to address those issues that seemed the most stimulating for performance studies and teaching. We did not ask that the contributors ally themselves with a particular definition of performance; rather, we encouraged each writer to explore her or his own vision. While the collection includes a wide group of scholars, it cannot represent all of performance studies.

The book's focus on teaching performance studies indicates our purpose to examine ways in which performance studies informs the teaching of scholars with heterogeneous backgrounds and institutional affiliations and to expand the conversation about pedagogy across disciplines. Many of the essays are grounded in the specific fields of study of their authors. They address concerns identified with a range of perspectives (e.g., African American studies, anthropology, education, English, interdisciplinary studies, speech communication, theatre, gay and lesbian studies, and theology). As Freire points out, academic departments need to engage in a

> quest for an interdisciplinary understanding of teaching, instead of merely a disciplinary one. . . . to work in this way is an attempt to overcome the compartmentalization of views to which we subject reality, and in which, not infrequently, we become lost. (193)

The interdisciplinary nature of the pedagogies represented in this volume points toward the diversity and breadth of the field. Of course, there is need for additional work, especially from writers outside the United States. Our objective is not to reify the disciplinary identifications of our writers but to expand the dialogue within the United States and abroad.

Part one is entitled "Positioning Performance Studies." Reflecting some of the primary disciplinary and theoretical imprints of performance studies, each author contributes a distinct thread to the narrative of the field's development. In chapter 1, Joseph Roach addresses the field from a theatre/literary studies perspective. In chapter 2, Elyse Lamm Pineau discusses critical performative pedagogy. Richard F. Ward's theological schoolteaching frames his discussion of performance as human communication in chapter 3. Craig Gingrich-Philbrook's work in chapter 4 demonstrates the influence of gender studies and queer theory. William O. Beeman addresses the field from an anthropological perspective in chapter 5. And Michelle Kisliuk's essay (chapter 6) evidences the international impulses of performance studies.

Joseph Roach positions performance studies by tracing its historical emergence and by mapping its growth in departments of theatre and communication. He develops a model for teaching performance studies, in concert with theatre and cultural studies, that includes a wide variety of genres, such as Mardi Gras, jazz funerals, and tourist performances. The work of Mikhail Bakhtin, Victor Turner, Erving Goffman, and Bertolt Brecht serves as an important theoretical grounding for Roach's discussion of the cultural performances of New Orleans. (Bakhtin has proven an important theorist for other performance scholars as well; see chapter 12 by Arthur J. Sabatini in this volume). Roach locates his study in "teaching a performance studies course as a cultural studies elective in a department of English literature." From this context, Roach builds an argument about the "suppleness" of performance theory in contrast with the "inelasticity of the three [neoclassical] unities." Roach contends that *performance* is a key term mediating between theatre studies' attraction to "high culture" and the "predominant focus in cultural studies on popular culture and media." Roach offers a theoretical grounding for performance studies framed by theatre and cultural studies, a historical and institutional context for performance studies, and a brief application of performance studies methods to the fieldwork of studying the public performance of culture in New Orleans.

We also position performance studies pedagogy in this book by noting the widespread emergence of body-centered research. This research reflects important impulses in performance studies pedagogy revolving around concepts of liberatory education, specifically education toward greater social justice, especially as informed by the critical pedagogies of Freire, Giroux, and McLaren. While a number of chapters here respond to those impulses, Elyse Lamm Pineau's work elaborates the interconnectedness of performance studies and critical pedagogy by offering a "typology for how performance praxis can be linked to educational critique and school reform." Building on her earlier work ("Teaching Is Performance"), Pineau's new typology consists of viewing bodies in the classroom through three lenses: first, the ideological body, "connoting all the social factors that might influence physical modes of experience and expression"; then, as the ethnographic body, proposing further research/observation and "critical analysis of the social codes articulated by those bodies," research then made available through "imagistically vivid prose that moves beyond description to evocation"; and finally, the performing body, advocating a pedagogy that moves from performance as demonstration of skills learned to performance as "a critical methodology that can be fully integrated throughout the learning process." Pineau's exploration of critical performative pedagogy proposes ways to understand how bodies are schooled and ways performance can address the body politics inherent in that schooling.

Richard F. Ward discusses the comparatively recent introduction of performance studies to the centuries-old field of theological studies. As a new, and often misunderstood, participant in this enterprise, performance's purpose is contested within the current disciplinary structure of academia. In a parallel path with educating leaders for management and administration of spiritual communities ("a clerical paradigm"), Ward focuses on the process of performance as a means for spiritual growth, as a pathway for knowing God and "naming God," as a practice "where 'faith' is constituted, configured, and displayed." He explores the connections between orality and homiletic performance and the Christian doctrine of incarnation, an "event of embodiment" of the *Word* that informs pedagogy in the theological school. Ward then discusses the "incarnational aesthetic" in this performance pedagogy and the negotiation between an antitheatrical prejudice in theological communities and the concept of the *holy actor* (the preacher as a "dramatic" actor in a holy ritual). Finally, Ward argues that an emphasis on developing a renewed *habitus* of "naming God" means that, for his theological pedagogy, embodiment is "doing theology."

Ward's discussion of the Word and his conception of incarnation resonate with Craig Gingrich-Philbrook's exploration of the tension between the written and the oral in his students' work. In teaching queer performance as a "mode of inquiry" (rather than an "object of inquiry"), Gingrich-Philbrook situates queer performance, like all "performance praxes struggling to bring subjugated knowledges across that well-regulated border," as "archivable." We see queer studies as centrally important in performance studies in part because of its fundamental interest in issues of representation, presentation, and identity. The performance studies pedagogy Gingrich-Philbrook elucidates is taken from four positions he reads from Pelias and VanOosting's "A Paradigm for Performance Studies": Performance studies is concerned with aesthetic communication; it contests the canon; it requires performance as its method; and it requires writing. Gingrich-Philbrook discusses how these principles are elaborated through interactions with his students. During this process of elaboration, he and his students confront the political responsibility of the control of the *archive* with performances that are viewed as both "*acts of* and *acts upon*" that archive. The *double bind* of an archive that constrains creativity even as it provides models for us to emulate while actively creating performances is of particular interest to Gingrich-Philbrook's argument.

William O. Beeman positions performance studies within his work as an anthropologist. He argues that "performance is an inherently human activity" and discloses his methodology for teaching students to answer important larger questions about the functioning of the performance event in specific social/cultural frameworks. Beeman wants to help his students "understand the basic human questions that the investigation of performance raises," and he wants to teach them the skills needed for ethnographic observation; he wants them to analyze their observations in performance terms and to understand the broad implications of performance in human life, "including the ways that performance transforms and is transformed by everyday life." Beeman establishes a series of objectives for teaching performance anthropology; he methodically surveys his process, listing components of his assignments and describing the basic skills his students need (e.g., training to conduct ethnographic fieldwork) to understand performance as a transformational force socially and personally in the lives of his students. Beeman maintains that "One of the great lessons most students learn is a personal one: They come to terms with their own performance abilities in a powerful way."

Weaving together experiences of her *fieldlife* with the BaAka of the Central African Republic and her teaching and writing in the United States, Michelle Kisliuk addresses "strategies for bridging contexts of research and teaching and questioning boundaries between 'here' and 'there.'" "Theorizing about performance processes, activist pedagogy, and the reconfiguration of socioesthetic experience," Kisliuk blends field notes with class notes, personal history with critique, and demonstrates the "undeniable melding of worlds" that can occur both when ethnographers work and write from the field and when they transport elements of another performance culture, in this case traditional African music and dance, to the American college classroom. Her evocative writing alludes to the triune educative possibilities of performance studies: cognitive, through examination of the implications of this melding; somatic, through student embodiment of African performance practices; and spiritual, through induction of a few eager students into *Elamba*, with its "ancestral sorcery." Kisliuk discusses her use of two concepts, *the fixed/mixed dialectic* and *the object(ive) subjectively conceived*, that help to move students from dualistic thinking to multiplex thinking, an activist pedagogy that examines a "dialectical concept of cultural processes." Her essay argues that research is "personal history, a history for which we are politically and aesthetically responsible."

Although pedagogies of embodiment and a diffuse interest with epistemology are both signatures of performance studies theory and practice (and consequently inform the essays in part one), the essays collected in part two, "Embodiment and Epistemology," specifically elaborate dynamic orbits of each of these spheres and of their interaction. The first five essays elaborate specific techniques of embodiment, each to a specific end, and the final essay focuses specifically on epistemology. In chapter 7, Judith Hamera has students examine their relationships with their own performing bodies, while in chapter 8,

Nathan Stucky has them reproduce and inhabit the vocal patterns of another person. In chapter 9, Phillip B. Zarrilli focuses on students' performance of emotion, while in chapter 10, Michael S. Bowman and Ruth Laurion Bowman ask their students to perform their own social, historical selves. In chapter 11, Joni L. Jones addresses the performance of racial and ethnic others, and in chapter 12, Arthur J. Sabatini discusses the epistemology of performance as a dialogic project.

For more than a decade, Judith Hamera has gathered autobiographies of her students, discovering in the process that they seldom consider their engagements with formal training in recitals, exhibitions, and games when they think about their performance training. With her training in dance and her interest in ethnography, however, it is this disciplining of the body that captures Hamera's attention. How does the classroom constrain the body? Hamera examines what sorts of knowledge are reclaimed by activated student bodies and explores the *dualist axis*, "this split between bodily experience and conceptual life," in a pedagogical way that makes that axis and its physical and phenomenological consequences both "vivid and visible."

Hamera's discussion of the possibility of "linking the conceptual and the corporeal in and through reperformance" resonates with Nathan Stucky's interest in what bodies know when they work through behaviors once performed by another. Stucky describes *everyday life performance* (ELP) as a process in which "the student actor virtually shares the breath of another person." Locating *natural performance* in everyday theatrical events such as greeting rituals and conversation, Stucky interrogates this particular kind of mimesis, ELP, as epistemology that works "to reveal the intricacies and nuances of human interaction." While Stucky has written elsewhere of the theoretical underpinnings and implications of natural performance and ELP, here he traces and fleshes out the steps he and his students take to reproduce everyday conversations of others as exactly as possible: tape-recording a naturally occurring interaction, transcribing it carefully using methods developed by conversation analysts, and then learning to perform it by "replicating the intricate detail" (pauses, coughs, laughs, hesitations) and the interpersonal intricacy of the prototype. This particular kind of performance pedagogy calls upon students not to act *as if* but to act *as* another. Students attempt to replicate behaviors originating in other bodies and find themselves interrogating that other body and its social construction through their reenactment. The responses of Stucky's students demonstrate that the epistemological significance of this *deep embodiment* is at once personal and social.

Like Hamera and Stucky, Phillip B. Zarrilli is interested in bodies in the act of performance. Zarrilli's contribution manifests the intercultural impulse of much performance studies practice. His actor-centered discussion of Western traditions of the performance of emotion and of the performance of emotion in India's *kathakali* dance-drama demonstrates the bodily enactment of intercultural borrowing and translation. Zarrilli argues that "each time an actor performs, he or she implicitly enacts a 'theory' of acting," but that, for the actor, such theories remain "at the periphery of consciousness," if at all. Zarrilli critiques Western theoretical formulations of acting for reflecting a body-mind dualism that cannot account adequately for the process of acting, especially the nature of emotion. At issue here for performance studies are questions of culture, embodiment, and psychophysiological acting technique.

In a chapter that addresses the consequences and uses of theory in performance, Michael S. Bowman and Ruth Laurion Bowman describe *mystory*, a kind of personal experience narrative, or "autoperformance," that asks students to engage critical and creative issues simultaneously through writing and performing. Bowman and Bowman chart a way to navigate the Scylla and Charybdis of theory and practice. By building on Gregory Ulmer's concept of *textshop*, they offer a way to bring contemporary theory and performance practice together, drawing on the example of performance art. Much like learning in a "hard" science laboratory, where students reproduce experiments until they achieve a level that then permits them to advance to exploring the unknown, the mystory gives students the practical tools they need to experiment. Since the performance of personal experience narratives raises new questions for teachers regarding how to evaluate a person's life, Bowman and Bowman describe a classroom autoperformance project that shifts the focus of student work away from personal self-disclosure toward intertextual experimentation with models of autobiographical writing and performance. While their primary example is drawn from an intermediate-level performance studies classroom, Bowman and Bowman note the adaptability of their approach for introductory classes to graduate seminars as well as for "professional development workshops with groups of nonstudents." The latter group suggests a "market value" for performance studies knowledge that addresses issues raised in the chapters by Linda M. Park-Fuller, Cynthia Wimmer, and Eric Dishman.

Joni L. Jones situates her classroom as "a liminal space capable of disrupting the social order," "a laboratory for the exploration of race and ethnicity," and "a borderland in which [students] must challenge the construction of the self along with the construction of the other." Jones uses in-class performances of fictional people and scenes from African diasporic literature to challenge students to put issues of archetypes and stereotypes, identity construction, and the continuation of oppression "inside of themselves as they embody the characters."

Providing and discussing several journal assignments and exercises that lead students into explorations of self and other, Jones discusses

stereotyping as a way of organizing material, "a way of controlling an other," that converts people "into stable and predictable objects." In performance, stereotypes become a "sort of shorthand" used to communicate. Rather than suppress the tendency to know people/characters as stereotypes, Jones allows these suppositions "to live" in her course in order that they be worked through to a point of developing other resources to take students through the stereotype, resources partly discovered during students' participation in ELP and improvisation to balance "the power relationship between the self and the other." Hers is not a pedagogy designed to teach students to perform, however. Jones says that "at its best, [this embodiment of the other] is human training."

With periodic humorous thrusts, Arthur J. Sabatini weaves a discussion of the performance of pedagogy, Bakhtinian theory, epistemology, comedy, and trust in the classroom experience. Sabatini considers Bakhtin's work to be "a comprehensive theory of performance at the core of which is a philosophical epistemology." Informed by Bakhtin's lexicon and his concepts of *authorship, co-participation, co-experience,* and *utterance,* Sabatini develops and discusses three "axioms that are basic for an epistemology of performance": that "distinct systems of reference and meaning" comprise our understandings of genres, and "epistemologically, performance genres represent modalities of social organization"; "that exegesis and analysis proceed from representations of performances as texts"; and "that knowledge requires a theory of signification and communication." He then moves to address trust as a dialogic category in terms of performance and epistemological issues and comedy as a subversive genre whose disruption of predictable systems of meaning creates a space for alternative responses. Describing a pedagogical posture that is open-ended, dialogic, and even comedic, Sabatini's pedagogy is "consciously oriented toward accentuating [the] *polyphony* of voices" in his classroom and developing "students' awareness of their own subject positions and relationships."

The essays in part three, "Negotiating Borders," highlight the cross-disciplinary future of performance studies. These essays expand the body of work known as performance studies and demonstrate a deliberate commerce between fields and classrooms. In chapter 13, Linda M. Park-Fuller dislodges naturalized reliance on the geographical metaphor of borders. In chapter 14, Cynthia Wimmer blurs the idea of a discrete border around ivory-tower knowledge by bringing employment possibilities into the classroom, while Eric Dishman (in chapter 15) crosses the border from classroom to corporation with his performance studies training. In chapter 16, Bruce McConachie brings tech-

niques developed under an oppressive political regime across na-
tional/ideological borders into the American college classroom; and in
chapter 17, John Emigh brings us back into the academy, but an academy where "hard" science and the humanities profitably and inti-
mately intermingle.

Linda M. Park-Fuller's chapter positions performance studies
metaphorically as theatrical improvisation, which she describes as
ever tentative, ongoing, and resistant to judgment. Park-Fuller begins
by offering a teaching philosophy polished in ever transforming and
evolving experiences in the theatre classroom and in directing and
writing for the stage. She is concerned with "marketplace" questions
students may ask. Her response to these concerns (e.g., "Of what use is
the knowledge and training I will acquire?" "Can this learning help me
to make a living?") develops in a five-step approach that probes deeply
by locating the rich theoretical themes under the pragmatics of teaching. She offers a response derived from performance itself, an improvisational approach to theorizing pedagogy, in which the teacher's relation to the student is viewed as a metaphor of emergent possibility.

Negotiating the territory in both academia and organizational cultures, Cynthia Wimmer explores these employment sectors as sites of
multiple performances. Wimmer's agenda is to demonstrate the market value of performance studies training in consulting to business,
government, and nonprofit organizations, a demonstration reminiscent of what Edwards describes as nineteenth-century elocution's pas-
sionate belief in the practicality of performance knowledge. In this
way, Wimmer's chapter, like Park-Fuller's, participates in a conversation that raises specific questions about the economics of performance
studies training. Wimmer identifies performance as a central idea in
management literature and organizational climates; and she describes
ways that performance studies practitioners can enter the worlds of
business, government, and nonprofit organizations. She demonstrates
that proficiency in particular performance studies techniques, perspectives, and analyses are not only marketable but also "have the potential to affect ethical and humanistic changes" in organizational cultures. Wimmer reminds us that such cultures are comprised of
individual human beings; within these cultures, there are opportunities for performance-trained scholars to study and contribute their
specific expertise.

Based on three years of fieldwork in Silicon Valley, Eric Dishman
has developed a theoretical conjuncture and methodological bricolage
that he calls *informance design*. Dishman particularizes this concept
and describes his implementation of a pedagogy of embodiment in a
synergistic performance that reveals to designers their ideological and
authorial power and responsibility to a technologized future culture.
Illuminating how dialogism is a performance theory which encom-

passes a philosophy of social and individual responsibility, Dishman argues that the practice of theatre generates specific knowledge that holds out the hope for moving beyond a techno-commercialized world, to a more empowering democratic, and contingent view of what the futures can be. Dishman uses his special ethnographic performance to teach computer designers ways to examine the sociocultural norms of design, including the gendered thinking that prompts particular assumptions.

To train students to empower others through the "practice and [analysis of] interactive political theatre," Bruce McConachie has taken up the challenge of offering a course for college credit that is based on Boal's original three forms of theatre. In his chapter, McConachie evaluates this performance pedagogy's potential for political action in the context of an "elite" institution whose students experience "the immense gap between Boal's Marxist assumptions about oppression and [their own] lack of experience of oppressive situations." McConachie's students experienced units on *image theatre*, where trust exercises "generated student solidarity" and where Campbell's wheel exercise helped to "elaborate a shared language of the body"; *invisible theatre*, where they left "the warm cocoon of classroom relationships" to perform elsewhere on campus and faced the ethical questions of "experiment[ing] on people without their consent"; and *forum theatre*, where they struggled with the concept of oppression and finally "recognized a massive but hidden form of oppression and identified with one of its victims." Through these exercises, McConachie demonstrates that even "privileged" students can come to recognize "that the binary of oppressor/oppressed does fit many situations in the real world today—especially situations centering on conflicts over race, class, and gender that involve them in the wider contradictions of our society."

With his theoretical and pedagogical dialogue combining neuroscience and performance studies, John Emigh's work exemplifies the interdisciplinary momentum and the power that such unique compounds create. Emigh provides an innovative epistemic framework for how we think about theatre and theatricality, as well as performance and performativity. For Emigh, neuroscience shares with performance interests in the manipulation of attention and arousal, with perception and deception and with "the construction of meaning through symbolic representation." Emigh's view of performance is historically broad, stretching from shamanic traditions to postmodern artistry. In the process, he raises significant questions: What is the nature of performance at a biological level? How is culture constructed within the neural networks of individual brains? What is the survival value of performance for the human species?

Each of this book's three parts, "Positioning Performance Studies,"

"Embodiment and Epistemology," and "Negotiating Borders," suggests the scope of performance studies theory, practice, and pedagogy. The contributors to this volume provide their sense of the excitement and dynamism, the elasticity and tentativeness, and the sheer enjoyment of teaching performance studies. Together with the other contributors, we, as editors of this volume, have set a flexible agenda to create a foundation that can be shaken, to leave gaps that others can fill, and to guide those who would join us in teaching performance studies.

WORKS CITED

Albright, Ann Cooper. "Dancing Across Difference: Experience and Identity in the Classroom." *Women and Performance: A Journal of Feminist Theory* 6 (1993): 41–54.

Alexander, Bryant Keith. "Performing Culture in the Classroom: An Instructional (Auto)Ethnography. *Text and Performance Quarterly* 19 (1999): 307–31.

Bacon, Wallace A. "The Dangerous Shores—One Last Time." *Text and Performance Quarterly* 16 (1996): 356–58.

Bell, Elizabeth. "Performance Studies as Women's Work: Historical Sights/Sites/Citations from the Margin." *Text and Performance Quarterly* 13 (1993): 350–74.

Buckingham, David, ed. *Teaching Popular Culture: Beyond Radical Pedagogy.* Bristol: UCL, 1998.

Carlson, Marvin. *Performance: A Critical Introduction.* New York: Routledge, 1996.

Case, Sue-Ellen, and Janelle Reinelt, eds. *The Performance of Power: Theatrical Discourse and Politics.* Iowa City: U of Iowa, 1991.

Chazan, Barry. *Contemporary Approaches to Moral Education.* New York: Teachers College, 1985.

Conquergood, Dwight. Introductory Note. Performance Studies Formations/Connections/Contestations/Coalitions Conf. Evanston, Ill. Mar. 1996.

———."Poetics, Play, Process and Power: The Performance Turn in Anthropology." *Text and Performance Quarterly* 9 (1989): 82–88.

———. Response to Wendt. *Text and Performance Quarterly* 10 (1990): 256–59.

Dailey, Sheron J., ed. *The Future of Performance Studies: Visions and Revisions.* Annandale: National Communication Assoc., 1998.

———. Response to Wendt. *Text and Performance Quarterly* 10 (1990): 256–61.

Denzin, Norman. *Interpretive Ethnography: Ethnographic Practices for the 21st Century.* Thousand Oaks: Sage, 1997.

Diamond, Elin, ed. *Performance and Cultural Politics.* New York: Routledge, 1996.

Dolan, Jill. "Geographies of Learning: Theatre Studies, Performance, and the 'Performative.'" *Theatre Journal* 45 (1993): 417–41.

———. Response to Worthen. *Drama Review* 39.1 (1995): 28–35.

Edwards, Paul. "Unstoried: Teaching Literature in the Age of Performance
Studies." *Theatre Annual: A Journal of Performance Studies* 52 (1999): 1–147.

Ellsworth, Elizabeth. *Teaching Positions: Difference, Pedagogy, and the Power of
Address.* New York: Teachers College, 1997.

Fine, Elizabeth C., and Jean Haskell Speer, eds. *Performance, Culture, and Identity.* Westport: Praeger, 1992.

Forbes, Scott H. "Values in Holistic Education." *Putnam Pit* 28 June 1996. 17
Jan. 2002 <http://putnampit.com/holistic.html>.

Franko, Mark, and Annette Richards, eds. *Acting on the Past: Historical Performance Across the Disciplines.* Hanover: Wesleyan UP, 2000.

Freire, Paulo. *Pedagogy of Hope: Reliving "Pedagogy of the Oppressed."* New York:
Continuum, 1995.

Fuoss, Kirk. *Striking Performances/Performing Strikes.* Jackson: U Mississippi P,
1993.

Giroux, Henry A. "Is There a Place for Cultural Studies in Colleges of Education?" Giroux and Shannon 231–70.

Giroux, Henry A., and Patrick Shannon, eds. *Education and Cultural Studies:
Toward a Performative Practice.* New York: Routledge, 1997.

Girton, Bethany. "The Future of Performance Studies in the High School
Classroom." Dailey, *Future* 156–57.

Goffman, Erving. *The Presentation of Self in Everyday Life.* New York: Doubleday, 1959.

Gray, Paul H. Response to Wendt. *Text and Performance Quarterly* 10 (1990):
262–63.

Harrison-Pepper, Sally. *Drawing a Circle in the Square: Street Performing in New
York's Washington Square Park.* Jackson: U of Mississippi P, 1990.

Hart, Lynda, and Peggy Phelan, eds. *Acting Out: Feminist Performances.* Ann
Arbor: U of Michigan P, 1993.

Holistic Education Network of Tasmania Home Page. 28 Oct. 1999. 18 Jan.
2002 <http://www.neat.tas.edu.au/HENT>.

hooks, bell. *Teaching to Transgress: Education as the Practice of Freedom.* New
York: Routledge, 1994.

HopKins, Mary Frances. "The Performance Turn—and Toss." *Quarterly Journal of Speech* 81 (1995): 228–36.

Howard, Diane. *Autobiographical Writing and Performing: An Introductory, Contemporary Guide to Process.* New York: McGraw, 2000.

Jackson, Shannon. "Professing Performance: Disciplinary Genealogies."
Drama Review 45.1 (2001): 84–95.

Kistenberg, Cindy. *AIDS, Social Change, and Theatre: Performance as Protest.*
New York: Garland, 1995.

Knight, Lester N. "Holistic Teaching/Learning." Online posting 28 Oct. 1999.
18 Jan. 2002 <http://www.coe.utk.edu/units/holistic.html>.

Langellier, Kristin M. "Personal Narrative, Performance, Performativity: Two
or Three Things I Know for Sure." *Text and Performance Quarterly* 19
(1999): 125–44.

Lee, Josephine. "Disciplining Theater and Drama in the English Department: Some Reflections on 'Performance' and Institutional History." *Text and Performance Quarterly* 19 (1999): 145–58.

Madison, D. Soyini. "Performing Theory/Embodied Writing." *Text and Performance Quarterly* 19 (1999): 107–24.

McLaren, Peter. *Critical Pedagogy and Predatory Culture: Oppositional Politics in a Postmodern Era.* London: Routledge, 1995.

———. "Liberatory Politics and Higher Education." McLaren, *Revolutionary Multiculturalism* 42–75.

———, ed. *Revolutionary Multiculturalism: Pedagogies of Dissent for the New Millennium.* Boulder: Westview, 1997.

———. *Schooling as a Ritual Performance: Towards a Political Economy of Educational Symbols and Gestures.* 2nd ed. London: Routledge, 1993.

McLaren, Peter, and Henry A. Giroux. "Writing from the Margins: Geographies of Identity, Pedagogy, and Power." McLaren, *Revolutionary Multiculturalism* 16–41.

Noddings, Nel. *Philosophy of Education.* Boulder: Westview, 1998.

Parker, Andrew, and Eve Kosofsky Sedgwick, eds. *Performativity and Performance.* New York: Routledge, 1995.

Pelias, Ronald J. *Performance Studies: The Interpretation of Aesthetic Texts.* New York: St. Martin's, 1992.

———. *Writing Performance: Poeticizing the Researcher's Body.* Carbondale: Southern Illinois UP, 1999.

Pelias, Ronald, and Lynn C. Miller, eds. *The Green Window: Proceedings from the Giant City Conference on Performative Writing.* Carbondale: Southern Illinois University, 2001.

Pelias, Ronald, and James VanOosting. "A Paradigm for Performance Studies." *Quarterly Journal of Speech* 73 (1987): 219–31.

Phelan, Peggy. *Unmarked: The Politics of Performance.* New York: Routledge, 1993.

Pineau, Elyse Lamm. "Performance Studies Across the Curriculum: Problems, Possibilities, and Projections." Dailey, *Future* 128–35.

———. "Teaching Is Performance: Reconceptualizing a Problematic Metaphor." *American Educational Research Journal* 31.1 (1994): 3–25.

Pollock, Della, ed. *Exceptional Spaces: Essays in Performance History.* Chapel Hill: U of North Carolina P, 1998.

Reinelt, Janelle G., and Joseph R. Roach, eds. *Critical Theory and Performance.* Ann Arbor: U of Michigan P, 1992.

Roach, Joseph. Response to Worthen. *Drama Review* 39.1 (1995): 35–36.

Rorty, Richard. *Philosophy and the Mirror of Nature.* Princeton: Princeton UP, 1979.

Schechner, Richard. General Introduction to the Performance Studies Series. *The Anthropology of Performance.* By Victor Turner. New York: PAJ, 1987. N.pag.

————. "Magnitudes of Performance." Schechner and Appel 19–49.

————. "A New Paradigm for Theatre in the Academy." *Drama Review* 36.4 (1992): 7–10.

————. *Performance Studies: An Introduction.* New York: Routledge, 2002.

————. Response to Worthen. *Drama Review* 39.1 (1995): 36–38.

Schechner, Richard, and Willa Appel, eds. *By Means of Performance: Intercultural Studies of Theatre and Ritual.* Cambridge: Cambridge UP, 1990.

Schneider, Raymond. Response to Wendt. *Text and Performance Quarterly* 10 (1990): 264–65.

Shields, Ronald E. "Disciplinary Narratives for Change: The Emergence of Performance Studies within ATHE and SCA." *Journal of American College Administrators* 3 (1994): 185–91.

Stern, Carol Simpson. Response to Wendt. *Text and Performance Quarterly* 10 (1990): 265–67.

Stern, Carol Simpson, and Bruce Henderson. *Performance: Texts and Contexts.* White Plains: Longman, 1993.

Strine, Mary S., Beverly Whitaker Long, and Mary Frances HopKins. "Research in Interpretation and Performance Studies: Trends, Issues, Priorities." *Speech Communication: Essays to Commemorate the 75th Anniversary of The Speech Communication Association.* Ed. Gerald M. Phillips and Julia T. Wood. Carbondale: Southern Illinois UP, 1990. 181–204.

Turner, Victor. *The Anthropology of Performance.* New York: PAJ, 1987.

VanOosting, James, and Ronald Pelias. Response to Wendt. *Text and Performance Quarterly* 10 (1990): 267–68.

Wendt, Ted A. "The Displacement of the Aesthetic: Problems of Performance Studies." *Text and Performance Quarterly* 10 (1990): 248–56.

Winn, James Anderson. *The Pale of Words: Reflections on the Humanities and Performance.* New Haven: Yale UP, 1998.

Worthen, William B. "Disciplines of the Text/Sites of Performance." *Drama Review* 39.1 (1995): 13–28.

————. "Drama, Performativity, and Performance." *PMLA* 113.5 (1998): 1093–107.

Yordon, Judy. *Experimental Theatre: Creating and Staging Texts.* Prospect Heights: Waveland, 1997.

Zarrilli, Phillip. Response to Worthen. *Drama Review* 39.1 (1995): 38–41.

Part One
Positioning
Perform-
ance
Studies

Theatre Studies/Cultural Studies/ Performance Studies

1
Joseph
Roach

The Three Unities

No opera should neglect the customary explanation of the three most important points in every drama: the time, the place, and the action, indicating that
the time is *from 8* PM until midnight, *the place* such and such a theatre, *the action* the bankrupting of the impresario.

—BENEDETTO MARCELLO, *Il teatro alla moda*

Students of the drama will remember "the three unities" as Aristotelian, neoclassical limitations on the scope of what plays can properly represent. Strictly interpreted, the unities restricted *time* to one
day, *place* to one location, and *action* to one plot. Satirically reinter-
preted by Benedetto Marcello in his send-up of the baroque opera, "the
unities" represent something else: Rather than merely circumscribing
the aesthetic limits on drama, they ironically emphasize the material
considerations of performance. In teaching a performance studies
course as a cultural studies elective in a department of English literature, I use an approach that, like Marcello's, centers on the materially
embodied experience of time, place, and action. What follows is a description of that approach in the context of my understanding of the
development of the field of performance studies itself.

Today, the dynamism and prolific variety of research on the "essentially contested term" *performance* is remarked by all those who attempt to summarize its trends (Carlson 10–75). The interdisciplinary,
even antidisciplinary study of performance draws on theoretical and
practical research in communication (including linguistics and ethno-
linguistics), the social sciences (sociology, anthropology, and ethnography), and the performing arts (theatre, dance, and performance art).
It has recently connected with powerful theoretical approaches to gender and sexuality, including psychoanalysis, as well as with concepts of
"high performance" from business and technology. If *performance* is a
fundamentally contested term, then it is also an extraordinarily opportunistic one, skating rings around other, more rigid concepts as
they take their spills on the slippery surfaces of postmodern culture. I
propose to explore the contrast between the apparent inelasticity of
the three unities and the suppleness of performance theory. In that
way, I hope to underscore the indebtedness of performance studies to
theatre and drama as well as the boldness of its move beyond them.

The decisiveness of the transition from theatre and drama to performance studies may be measured by perusing the issues of the *Tulane*

Drama Review, beginning in 1967, as it made the move to New York University and eventually became *The Drama Review: The Journal of Performance Studies*. Although criticism of Euro-American bourgeois theatre and drama continued—and still continues—to receive its due, over the years *TDR* has steadily devoted more of its pages to events in which the material facts of the performance outside of traditional theatrical venues predominate: "Happenings" in the 1960s and 1970s; paratheatrical interventions in political crises; ethnographic performances from an increasingly globalized network of practitioners. *TDR* editor Richard Schechner's collaboration with anthropologists, especially Victor Turner, exemplified the interdisciplinary claims of performance studies as the field that mediated between the arts and human sciences.

During the same years, there was another significant institutional development in the move beyond theatre and drama, not to discard them but to expand their conceptual frame of reference. The Department of Oral Interpretation at Northwestern University, the founding department of the School of Speech a century ago, changed its name to the Department of Performance Studies and broadened what had been its traditional emphasis on canonical literature; soon thereafter, the Department of Theatre at Northwestern widened the scope of its doctoral research by establishing an interdisciplinary program. Institutional innovations in performance studies elsewhere could certainly be cited—for instance, the development of performance studies programs in schools of communication at the University of Texas, Louisiana State University, and the University of North Carolina-Chapel Hill—but the special influence of the departments at New York University and Northwestern was evident in the 1980s and 1990s, especially in the organization of the first three national conferences in the field. Recently, the Centre for Performance Research at the University of Wales, Aberystwyth, has staged a series of conferences and launched *Performance Research: A Journal of Performing Arts*. The majority of the contributing and corresponding editors of this new journal have affiliations as dramaturges, theatre critics, or performance practitioners. This follows a pattern similar to the work of Eugenio Barba, founding director of the Odin Teatret in 1964 and the International School of Theatre Anthropology in 1979. Barba puts the question that launched many a career in performance studies: "Where can performers find out how to construct the material bases of their art?" (Barba and Savarese 8).

The claim that I want to make after reviewing this history is a simple one. Academic fields are evaluated largely by the original research methods that they develop and the results that they achieve. Performance studies is the most prominent research tradition to have been developed by the academic study of theatre and drama in the

United States, and arguably, this is true for its more recent emergence in the United Kingdom as well, though here the earlier formation of cultural studies was also instrumental. The rubric of theatre studies/ cultural studies/performance studies in my title is not meant so much to suggest contention (or harmony, for that matter) as it is to trace a genealogy of intellectual descent from drama to performance, with *performance* as the mediating term between the predilection in theatre studies for high-culture forms and the predominant focus in cultural studies on popular culture and media. The role of theatre practice in this process has been crucial. Many if not most of those who identify themselves with performance studies have begun by posing Barba's question to themselves and their colleagues. In other words, they have experienced firsthand the materiality of "the three unities" as directors, actors, dancers, choreographers, performance artists, or oral interpreters. They have scheduled the events. They have hired the halls. They have, now and then, bankrupted the impresarios.

With due attention to considerations of time, place, and action, practitioners have also enlarged the sphere of performance beyond the theatre to frame a great variety of other genres. Although no two performance theorists would come up with exactly the same list, the category of material events to which they attend includes carnivals, funerals, demonstrations, gender impersonations, medical procedures, guided tours, speech acts, and the practices of everyday life, such as eating dinner or walking in the city. Drawing particularly on the theoretical writings of Mikhail Bakhtin, Victor Turner, and Bertolt Brecht, the overall scheme of such a prolific material dramaturgy may be represented by the following diagram:

TIME	PLACE	ACTION
past/future	inside/outside	habitual/critical
Bakhtin	Turner	Brecht
CHRONOTOPE	LIMINALITY	DEFAMILIARIZATION

In each case, the third term—*chronotope* (literally, "time-space"), *liminality* (from *limen*, or "threshold"), and *defamiliarization* ("making the familiar strange and the strange familiar")—dynamically unsettles the binary opposition above it. In each case, its meaning overlaps with those of the other two terms, an elision that may be demonstrated by the contingency of three questions that students of performance studies ought to be ready to pose of any event: "When is it?" "Where is it?" "What's happening?" In drama, the answers to those questions reside safely within the fiction of the play, and they may be answered by reading; in performance, they rudely spill out into the streets, and they must be answered by participation. This participation includes the critical observation of the three unities.

Time (Chronotope)

36

Joseph
Roach

First, there is the supreme fiction, time. Bakhtin advanced the term *chronotope* to explain how time is created and manipulated in the novel. His theory also illuminates the construction of time in performance. This construction depends on the tensions between the clocked time one measures as having *spent* ("from 8 PM until midnight," as Marcello says) and the elastic experience of time one *gains* before, during, and after one is present in the place of performance. Here, the mind can entertain past and future events as convergent. For Bakhtin, the fiction of time is mutually constitutive with space—the question "What time is it?" inseparable from another, "Where are we?" Citing Einstein's theory of relativity in *The Dialogic Imagination*, Bakhtin explains the relationship of interdependence of the two:

> Time, as it were, thickens, takes on flesh, becomes artistically visible; likewise, space becomes charged and responsive to the movements of time, plot, and history. This intersection of axes and fusion of indicators characterizes the chronotope. (84)

My way of explaining the chronotope derives from observing and participating in the performances most readily available to me over the past seven years in New Orleans, though my understanding of the techniques of fictionalizing time come from directing many plays.

In a performance-saturated city of memory—and New Orleans is certainly that, though not alone as that—chronotopes proliferate. There, the present can be seen as a point of struggle between conflicting versions of the past and opposed visions of the future.

At Tulane, I offered performance studies in the spring semester and used the multilayered festivities of Mardi Gras as a text for the course, supplemented by a preliminary reading of Bakhtin's *Rabelais and His World* and a postcarnival look at Peter Stallybrass and Allon White's *The Politics and Poetics of Transgression*. Debating their experience of Bakhtin's "carnivalesque," with its "grotesque body" and "world upside down," against Stallybrass and White's more critical view of the liberating potential of such festivities, students could juxtapose their participation in the revels with a deepening sense of the history of Mardi Gras. That history, they discover, is performed in the present by contemporary parades, masquerades, and street parties that make claims on both the past and the future. The festive holiday compresses within its ambit "privileged moments" for retrospection and anticipation. The idea that carnival is "time out of time" is true to the extent that the everyday artifice of time is inverted: It is not that revelers are "watching the clock"; the clock is watching them.

A chronotopic performance puts flesh on memory, on dreams, on fears. In New Orleans, the predominantly white carnival "krewes," for instance, constantly recycle imagery from their own past Mardi Gras floats and costumes. They sometimes quote, wittingly or unwittingly, racist images from the days of Reconstruction and Southern Redemption, when some of the krewes served as secret societies devoted to ensuring the future of white supremacy. An ironic countermemory and an alternative future are performed by the "Krewe of Zulu," an African American parading organization that spoofs racist stereotypes by blacking up, wearing grass skirts, and passing out decorated coconuts. Each parade, following its historic route along the venerable avenues of the city, is a chronotope on wheels. Layers of the deeply troubled and conflicted past become visible as they are festively performed in the present. Like geologists standing before a freshly exposed cut in a hillside, performance studies students doing fieldwork at Mardi Gras can look back through the layers of time to earlier historical strata. The shocking meaning of the chronotope, however, is that ancient strata have been there all along, impinging upon the present, making the place the way it is now and threatening to keep it that way. The future towards which the parade wants to head looks like the past from which it emerged. Fossils come to life. The night parades of the predominantly white krewes are lit by "flambeaux," African American torchbearers, who shuffle along under the weight of tanks of fuel oil, carrying steel racks with jets that discharge open flame inches above their heads and shoulders. Balancing precariously, they bend over and scrape up coins thrown on the street as gratuities by spectators who are themselves begging for beads tossed to them by masked krewe members riding the floats and the horses. As restorations of antebellum behavior, assigning the revelers to roles as planter aristocracy, field slaves, and servile white trash, the night parades of Mardi Gras are hard to equal and impossible to excel. In such performances, as Bakhtin theorized for the novel, time "takes on flesh," while "space becomes charged and responsive to the movements" of history. In other words, the performance of time—manipulating fictions of past and future—turns space into a place.

37
*Theatre
Studies/
Cultural
Studies/
Performance
Studies*

Place (Liminality)

Victor Turner's *Anthropology of Performance* (1987) and its antecedents in Arnold van Gennep's *The Rites of Passage* (1908) enabled my students to develop a concept of place that is defined by liminality. The liminal zone is the place between the inside and the outside. It is almost always marked by performance. Van Gennep noted, for example, that the ancient triumphal arch served as a boundary marker, a literal and symbolic threshold, between the interior of the Roman imperium and the "barbaric" world outside. The victorious legions had to pass through the arch in order to purify themselves. Such a ritual journey has three parts—going outside, coming back inside, and passing across the margin "betwixt and between." Acknowledging his indebtedness to *The Rites of Passage*, Turner writes:

> A *limen*, as the great French ethnologist and folklorist Arnold van Gennep has pointed out, is a "threshold," and he uses the term to denote the central of three phases in what he called "rites of passage." He looked at a wide variety of ritual forms, taken from most regions and many periods of history, and found in them a tripartite processual form. Rituals *separated* specified members of a group from everyday life, *placed them in a limbo* that was not any place they were in before and not yet any place they would be in, then *returned* them, changed in some way, to mundane life. (25)

A limbo is actually a very lively place to be in.

In addition to encouraging students to talk about their liminal experiences at family weddings, I have tried to capitalize on the local tradition of jazz funerals. We can make do with videotapes of recent funerals, but the physical experience of actually following the "Second Line" of mourners/revelers cannot be satisfactorily represented in two dimensions. It is admittedly somewhat ghoulish to leave an opening in the syllabus, waiting for a member of the community to pass away so that a week of classes may be devoted to his or her final performance, but in New Orleans, funerals "with music" are important public events, to which everyone is invited. The three stages of the "tripartite processual form" are strongly marked. After a service and "final viewing" in the funeral home, the casket is carried out to the hearse. As the band strikes up a slow dirge, the procession moves forward toward the burial place. At a spot along the route that must be chosen by the "marshal," the parade stops, and the casket is removed from the hearse and lifted up. If the deceased was particularly venerated, the casket will be raised and lowered four times. This is called—in a phrase that brilliantly illustrates the Van Gennepian phase of separation—"cutting the body loose." At this point in the ceremony, there is a pause—a moment of intense liminality. It is truly a *place* that must be reached, a threshold that must be crossed. Then, usually after the family members have driven away with the body (but not necessarily so), the band strikes up a raucous jazz tune, typically one with dirty lyrics, and everyone marches and dances to the new beat. The final phase of the funeral reincorporates the memory of the deceased back into the community, which is itself reborn as it raises a "joyful noise" in chorus. It can affirm itself as a community by this rite because its "inside" and "outside" have been tangibly located by the "passing" of one of its own; not only located, but no matter how habitual, made to seem new.

Action (Defamiliarization)

The translation of the word *Verfremdungseffekt* as "alienation effect" does Bertolt Brecht's theory of theatre a disservice. Who really wants to be alienated? "Making strange" or "making new, even amazing" gets closer to the core of the idea. "Defamiliarization," though it does not roll off the tongue, is probably the best English substitute, with its reversible sense of making the familiar strange and, at the same time, the strange familiar. Brecht's own account is always worth quoting yet another time:

> The achievement of the A-effect constitutes something utterly ordinary, recurrent; it is just a widely practised way of drawing one's attention to a thing, and it can be seen in education as also in business conferences of one sort or another. The A-effect consists in turning the object of which one is to be made aware, to which one's attention is drawn, from something ordinary, familiar, immediately accessible, into something peculiar, striking, and unexpected. What is obvious is in a certain sense made incomprehensible, but this only in order it may then be made all the easier to comprehend. Before familiarity can turn into awareness the familiar must be stripped of its inconspicuousness; we must give up assuming that the object in question needs no explanation. (143–44)

Defamiliarization is the enemy of habit — or of habitual ways of seeing things. It interrupts habit by insisting on the strangeness of familiar things and then demanding an explanation of their newly discovered unfamiliarity. I relate it to action because, if everything is working as it should in a performance, defamiliarization is what happens as a result.

Tourist performance provides the case studies I use so that students can experience defamiliarization. We read Erving Goffman's *The Presentation of Self in Everyday Life*, especially the chapter titled "Regions and Region Behavior," and Dean MacCannell's *The Tourist: A New Theory of the Leisure Class*, especially the Goffmanesque chapter titled "Staged Authenticity." I require that everyone take a guided tour of a place with which they are already at least somewhat familiar. We warm up by taking the tour for prospective students at Tulane or by watching the promotional video that the office of admissions shows as a recruitment device. It is relatively easy to provoke critical responses to this tour, as the students can quickly discern the "front region" performances from the "back." Then they are off on their own, individually or in small groups, to the French Quarter, the River Road plantations, the swamps, or wherever their interests and ambitions take them. The most effective spur to critical thinking is the defamiliarizing experience of seeing the city or region in which one lives while in the company of tourists. It is inherently defamiliarizing—and perhaps even alienating—to be a native (student) tourist among tourist tourists. The familiar is "stripped of its inconspicuousness," as Brecht puts it. That is particularly so because everybody hates tourists and hates being seen as a tourist. Scorn and self-loathing, not pity and fear, predicate the action and intensify a critical attitude.

This brief survey of the three unities of performance studies underscores the obvious fact that theory and practice should be fitted to the opportunities of the locale. But it further suggests that theatre and drama have resilient strength because their theories and practices are portable across boundaries that local cultural performances cannot (or at least do not often) cross. Aristotle said that tragedies can have the same impact when they are read as when they are performed. As for Mardi Gras, it is not a moveable feast.

WORKS CITED

Bakhtin, Mikhail. *The Dialogic Imagination*. Ed. Michael Holquist. Trans. Caryl Emerson and Michael Holquist. Austin: U of Texas P, 1981.

———. *Rabelais and His World*. Trans. Helene Iswolsky. Cambridge: MIT, 1968.

Barba, Eugenio, and Nicola Savarese. *A Dictionary of Theatre Anthropology: The Secret Art of the Performer*. Ed. Richard Gough. Trans. Richard Fowler. New York: Routledge, 1991.

Brecht, Bertolt. *Brecht on Theatre*. Trans. John Willet. New York: Hill, 1964.

Carlson, Marvin. *Performance: A Critical Introduction*. New York: Routledge, 1996.

Goffman, Erving. *The Presentation of Self in Everyday Life*. Garden City: Doubleday, 1959.

MacCannell, Dean. *The Tourist: A New Theory of the Leisure Class*. 1976. Rev. ed. London: Macmillan, 1989.

Stallybrass, Peter, and Allon White. *The Politics and Poetics of Transgression*. London: Methuen, 1986.

Turner, Victor. *The Anthropology of Performance*. New York: PAJ, 1987.

Van Gennep, Arnold. *The Rites of Passage*. 1908. Chicago: U of Chicago P, 1960.

Critical Performative Pedagogy

Fleshing Out the Politics

of Liberatory Education

2

Elyse
Lamm
Pineau

When Peter McLaren's *Schooling as a Ritual Performance* was first published in 1986, it caught the mainstream education community largely unprepared. At the time, there were few precedents for examining the performative dimensions of schooling, and terms such as *enfleshment*, *embodiment*, and *ritual* held little currency. When the third edition of *Schooling* was released in 1999, however, the ground of educational philosophy had shifted radically. Within the literature loosely labeled as critical pedagogy, an increasing number of educators were turning toward performance as a means to understand and reform the institutions that discipline our minds and bodies. In their introduction to *Education and Cultural Studies*, Giroux and Shannon note the heuristic potential of performance as both method and metaphor for critical educational research.

> The concept of the performative provides an articulating principle that signals the importance of translating theory into practice while reclaiming cultural texts as an important site in which theory is used to "think" politics in the face of a pedagogy of representation that has implications for how to strategize and engage broader public issues. (2)

Critical educators explore how sociopolitical relations are simultaneously reflected in, and constituted through, educational practice at the macro level of public policy as well as the micro level of classroom interaction. The turn toward performativity in general, and critical analysis of the performing bodies of teachers and students in particular, has opened an interdisciplinary dialogue that is as politically efficacious as it is theoretically provocative.

This essay offers a typology for how performance praxis can be linked to educational critique and school reform. It does so by mapping the cross-disciplinary terrain between performance/theatre studies and critical pedagogy. The purpose of the essay is to offer critically minded and/or performance-based educators with some heuristic

guidelines for generating research questions, developing methodologies, and enhancing classroom practice that marshals the performing body for political change. The essay is structured around two agendas: to identify representative scholarship in education that takes
"schooling the body" as its conceptual point of entry, and to bring into
focus an emergent research trend that I have called *critical performative
pedagogy*.

To elaborate these points, I identify three interconnected means of
thematizing the body that collectively document how performance
currently is shaping pedagogical praxis that can be articulated as follows. Theorizing *the ideological body* provides a generative conceptual
metaphor for critiquing how schools reproduce gender, ethnic, and
economic injustice by schooling bodies. It follows that detailed analysis of *the ethnographic body* offers a systematic, microanalytic method
for identifying and theorizing the conventions through which students'
and teachers' roles are constructed and contested. Finally, research that
focuses on *the performing body* yields a repertoire of strategies for curriculum design and classroom instruction that can encourage students'
active and critical participation within and beyond the classroom. After briefly synthesizing the tenets of critical pedagogy out of which
these approaches to the body have emerged, I shall explore, more con-
cretely, how research on the ideological, the ethnographic, and the performing bodies can facilitate a liberatory agenda. In conclusion, I return to the notion of critical performative pedagogy as it is being
developed and practiced within my own and others' classrooms.

Convictions and Commitments in Critical Pedagogy

An overview of critical pedagogy is a presumptuous task. Over the last
two decades, critical approaches to education have evolved into a provocative but tangled interdisciplinary maze of specialized vocabularies
and diverse social agendas. For my purposes, critical pedagogy is best
understood as a network of convictions and commitments that draw a
"language of critique" from the Marxist social theories of the Frank-
furt School and a corresponding "language of possibility" from John
Dewey's charge that schools should be public arenas that prepare citizens for active participation in a democratic society. The democratiza-
tion of education has been articulated most cogently, of course, in the
work of Paulo Freire, the legendary educator-activist whose *Pedagogy
of the Oppressed* laid the conceptual and methodological groundwork
for much contemporary critical pedagogy. Freire's legacy is twofold:
(a) his critique dismantles the "banking system" of instruction through
which passive students are indoctrinated into social mores as well as
socioeconomic positions, thus disabling the development of critical
consciousness and political action, and (b) his method of critical col-

laboration between teachers and learners explores pragmatic solutions to everyday oppressions even while it facilitates a metalevel critique of the process of education itself. This dialectical emphasis on critique and possibility, the pragmatic and the epistemological, the abstract and the embodied, continues to characterize critical theory and practice in education.

In the broadest terms, critical educators view education as a form of cultural politics and so commit themselves to teaching and learning in the service of social justice. As Giroux has argued: "schools are more than instructional sites; they are cultural sites that are actively involved in the selective ordering and legitimization of specific forms of language, reasoning, sociality, daily experience and style" (qtd. in McLaren, *Schooling* xxiv). This covert curriculum functions systemically to preclude ways of thinking, speaking, and being in the world that do not reflect or reinforce the values of the culture of power.

Critical educators solidify their convictions into concrete commitments in the public as well as the educational sphere. Within the classroom, this commitment to action might mean developing inclusive curricula, encouraging critical thinking, decentering teacher authority, facilitating interactive and peer-oriented learning, and ensuring that all students have equal access to instructional resources. In the realm of public policy, critical educators are likely to point out the cultural bias that underlies standardized tests and curricula, to support affirmative action in hiring and admissions, and to oppose property taxes as the sole basis for funding school districts. While critical educators do not always agree on the appropriate form of activism nor even the most salient forms of oppression (i.e., ethnicity, class, gender, etc.), they share a common vision of a more egalitarian society in which all members have the opportunity and skills necessary for full participation, and where public policy is motivated by a deep sense of social responsibility. Ultimately, critical pedagogy is about empowerment.

In summary, critical educators believe that intervention is needed (the language of critique), that renewal is possible (the language of possibility), and that our privileged position as educators makes us personally responsible for enacting both at every level of our professional lives (the commitment to action). We may ask, then, by what themes will a focus on the performing body contribute to this emancipatory project?

The Ideological Body

It has become a common trope in contemporary theory to argue that the physical body is a site of cultural inscription. We understand that there is no unmediated or ahistorical body that can stand outside itself, literally outside its own skin, and therefore outside its sociocultural situation. From the moment of birth, cultural associations regarding ethnicity, class, gender, sexual orientation, able-bodiedness, and so on are imprinted into our very musculature. In palpable ways, these social norms shape our posture, measure out our movements, inflect our voices, and pattern the ways we touch, experience, and interact with the bodies of others. Scholars within communication, gender studies, performance and theatre, phenomenology, ethnography, and cultural studies, to name just a few contributing disciplines, all have developed persuasive arguments that knowledge is grounded in embodiment and that ideology exacts a toll upon living flesh.

What precisely do I mean by "the body," specifically the "ideological body," and how can we research its presence and function in the classroom? I want to distinguish for the moment between *body* as a literal term denoting one's physical being and *body* as a metaphor connoting all the social factors that might influence physical modes of experience and expression. Any substantive discussion of the body must speak to the *relationship* between physical behaviors and cultural norms, and it must do so, moreover, in a way that is neither theoretically reductive nor so abstracted from daily practice that it is functionally meaningless for classroom teachers. I propose the phrase "the ideological body" for three reasons. First, I want to define the focus of research as the relationship between physical bodies and the cultural baggage they carry, acknowledging that this relationship is neither simple nor direct. Second, I want to suggest research procedures that begin by gathering concrete data about how particular bodies present themselves in the classroom and then reflect upon how these behaviors indicate cultural attitudes regarding a body's ethnic, gender, or class identifications. Finally, I want to caution against the kind of abstract theorizing that does not advance, in any concrete way, a teacher's ability to understand or interact with the bodies encountered everyday in her or his classroom. The conjoined term *ideological body* places dialectical emphasis on what a body *does* in the classroom and what *meanings* we might ascribe to those actions.

McLaren has proposed the terms *enfleshment* and *refleshment* to describe the dialectical interplay between oppression and resistance ("Schooling"). Enfleshment connotes the process through which a body acquires certain habits over an extended period of time. These habits become sedimented such that they appear to ourselves and to others as if they were natural rather than culturally constructed. Refleshment, on the other hand, invokes a body's innate ability to learn alternative behaviors. Habits can be broken; what was learned can be unlearned, and new ways of being can be developed that are more enabling than the old habits. The discipline of performance, argues dance theorist/practitioner Ann Cooper Albright, provides practical methods for breaking through, breaking down, and rebuilding the body's naturalized habits. "If, as a feminist, I realize that bodies are deeply constructed by cultural attitudes and economic conditions," she argues, "as a dancer, I am aware that bodies can also be physically retrained and consciously re-theorized" (45). We all have experienced this kind of physical reconfiguration to some degree in our own lives, or perhaps we have observed it in the lives of others struggling to retrain their bodies following a debilitating illness or disability. Through deliberate, arduous, and consistent effort, bodies can acquire a new way of being. It is precisely this capacity for bodies to learn to act in ways other than they do that undergirds critical theory and drives critical practice.

There is another danger, however, in thinking about schools simply as mirrors of society without accounting for the unique contextual factors that influence individual classrooms. Every classroom is permeated by specific institutional, disciplinary, and pedagogical norms that work within, and sometimes against, the social context. According to Grossberg: "what we have here is not the equation of education and culture, an equation which would erase the specificity of schooling altogether, but a space which extends from the pedagogy of culture to the culture of pedagogy" (11). We might ask, then, what physical constraints are specific to educational culture, and what additional burdens does the body bear when it steps inside the classroom?

I think we can agree that bodies in the classroom are overwhelmingly inscribed as *absence*. Steeped in the tradition of Cartesian dualism, students and teachers effectively have been schooled to "forget" their bodies when they enter the classroom in order that they might give themselves more fully to the life of the mind. So endemic is this antisomatic prejudice, argues bell hooks, that seriously questioning how the body is schooled is, in itself, an act of subversion tantamount to academic heresy (113). Schooling systematically domesticates our bodies; it incarcerates them in rows of wooden desks, robs them of spontaneity through rigid demarcations of time and space, and in fact devotes a great deal of energy to hiding the fact that we have bodies at all. "What did one do with the body in the classroom?" hooks wondered in her first year of teaching when she found herself trapped at the front of her classroom, needing desperately to go to the bathroom. "Trying to remember the bodies of my professors," she continues, "I find myself unable to recall them. I hear voices, remember fragmented details, but very few whole bodies" (113). I, too, have suffered the embarrassing impropriety of a body that refuses to disappear despite my best efforts to erase it. Returning to the classroom five weeks after my son was born (in itself, a form of bodily oppression), I found myself in a large lecture hall making the familiar argument that communication is an embodied process, when to my horror, the fleeting thought of my infant son triggered lactation. Determined to maintain my instructional composure—to enact the mind/body separation I had been taught was both necessary and possible—I continued to *talk* about embodiment while surreptitiously drawing my jacket closed to hide the widening stains that were quite literally marking my body as a specifically gendered (and indirectly sexual) being.

The discomforting irony of that moment remains uniquely instructive to me. Even the act of relating this incident in a scholarly essay arouses the fear that my confession is at best, theoretically suspect, and at worst, grossly socially inappropriate. Yet, I have come to believe that habitually ignoring my own and my students' bodies is not a benign or prudish oversight, some innocuous standard of classroom decorum. I have found, increasingly, that it undermines my ability to engage myself and my students in meaningful ways, to provide immediate examples of the performative principles that I teach, and to genuinely confront issues of prejudice and exclusion that have become such an important dimension of my course content. Too often, I find myself at a loss when confronted with student bodies that do not conform or that express themselves in ways that are culturally unfamiliar or socially distasteful to me. As teachers increasingly face culturally diverse classrooms, I believe that we must be prepared for a broader spectrum of student behavior. This is not to suggest that all behaviors are acceptable or even constructive, for it is reductive to equate inclusiveness with anarchy, and it is irresponsible not to set guidelines for student interaction. It is to argue, however, that when I invite my students to discuss their experiences of prejudice, I must be prepared for a full-bodied response to that invitation. Young people do not live in a disembodied or dispassionate world, so how can I presume to teach effectively or with any relevance if I do not similarly engage their bodies?

Research on the ideological body begins with the acknowledgment that we enter our classrooms as embodied persons and that our bodies are differentially marked by cultural norms. It demands that we confront ideology in concrete rather than abstract terms by attending to the particularized ways in which individual bodies experience and express their position within a classroom culture. This means developing methodologies that enable us to take the body at "face value," in the deepest sense of that term. So, what does it mean to conduct body-sensitive research in the classroom? How would a researcher position her or his own body within the culture, and what might one discover from that vantage point?

The Ethnographic Body

I propose methods of detailed observation of physical bodies in action within particular classrooms and critical analysis of the social codes articulated by those bodies. The qualitative case study enjoys a long tradition in educational and instructional communication research. Since the mid-1970s, researchers have sought to balance empirical studies that correlate teaching behaviors and student learning with detailed participant-observation studies of naturally occurring behavior in particular field settings (Magoon; Wilson). In *The Enlightened Eye*, Elliot Eisner offers a cogent methodological synthesis. His six qualitative touchstones are: (1) field-specific methodologies that include, but are not limited to, participant-observer ethnographies; (2) an attitude of critical reflexivity that tries to account for the researcher's subjective experience of events; (3) interpretive analysis that "penetrates the surface" of observable behaviors; (4) focused attention to detail within the unique particulars of the field environment; (5) narrative reporting that situates the writer/researcher while enabling readers to "experience the heat" of the research situation; and (6) validation of the study through coherence, consensus, and instrumental utility (34–39). For the performance ethnographer, these basic principles are deepened by full bodily immersion in the field site and consideration of how all members of the research situation—teachers, students, and researchers—experience classroom life.

Performative ethnography is a special form of qualitative field study that "takes as both its subject matter and method the experiencing body situated in time, place, and history" (Conquergood 187). Performance ethnographers replace distanced observation with active participation in the host community, arguing that sensuous engagement and kinesthetic empathy between researchers and subjects can best illuminate the experiential complexities of human interaction, the texture of a living moment. By cultivating a deep, multisensory awareness of how persons appear to inhabit, experience, and negotiate their shared space, performance ethnographers are able to attend to the embodied particularities of the research situation. A body-centered, performance ethnography can provide empirical, microanalytic data about how sociosymbolic forces are kinesthetically experienced, kinetically represented, and communicatively negotiated.

At the most basic level, a performance-sensitive ethnography of schooling can restore the nonverbal and paralinguistic dimensions of classroom interaction that often are occluded in more traditional instructional research. Rather than producing disembodied, coded transcriptions of teacher-student talk, the performance ethnographer would strive to capture the nuances of inflection, rhythm, pause, and emphasis that characterize human speech in context. Moving beyond the arrangement of desks or immediacy behaviors, the researcher would look to how particular bodies inhabit and negotiate their place within the classroom culture through posture, poses, gestures, and degrees of muscular tension. More significantly, such studies could identify recurring patterns of behavior that signify the ritualized traditions through which instruction unfolds and which often obscures the political agendas and assumptions that undergird it.

McLaren's *Schooling as a Ritual Performance* is a prototypical example of a body-centered instructional ethnography that theorizes sociopolitical relations in terms of how they are embodied in classroom rituals. Based on extended fieldwork in an urban, multiethnic Catholic school, McLaren's microanalysis of student behaviors is organized, in part, around four bodily states—home, school, sanctity, and streetcorner—through which he observed students moving in the course of a typical school day. McLaren characterizes each state by a set of distinct bodily energies, habits, and displays. For example, the exuberant, agonistic, rebellious, often blatantly sexual embodiment of students' "streetcorner state" juxtaposes sharply with the "school state's" regulation of those bodies into straight, silent rows, or the ritual "sanctity state" enforced during chapel services. McLaren places particular emphasis on how the ethnic and class distinctions between the teaching clergy and their working-class students became apparent in both talk and behavior. He perceived direct connections between the ways teachers talked about their students—"culturally deprived, naturally divested of an innate access to intelligence, obstreperous, not yet adequately socialized, and given to deception, carnal appetites and unrestrained libidinal expressions" (210)—and the ways their bodies interacted with one another in the classroom. "By observing the cramped, defensive posturing of the students and the brusque, authoritative gestures of the teachers, it was possible to see how the relationships of power were grafted onto the medium of living flesh and marrow" (89). Throughout his richly textured account, McLaren draws attention to the ways in which competing ideologies were played out, and played upon, each student body.

A performance-centered ethnography of schooling reconfigures the relationship between researchers and subjects into one of reciprocal vulnerability and dialogue. The research relationship is an interpersonal one, Conquergood reminds us; the shared space and time of fieldwork "situates ethnographers within the delicately negotiated 'facework' that is part of the intricate and nuanced dramaturgy of everyday life" (187). Jean Clandinin's innovative work with narrative in teacher education exemplifies the interpersonal nature of this kind of research. Her method of "collaboration-through-conversation" brings together students, teachers, researchers, administrators, and community members as co-participants on research teams in which "the concern for confidentiality needs to be situated within an ethic of care" as "all participants are trying to find ways to live out and tell their stories" (Clandinin et al. 209–10). As we move toward deeper understanding of ethnographic informants as embodied persons rather than sources of research data, the interpersonal complexities of co-presence, conversation, and collaboration become the necessary currency of our methods.

Finally, performance ethnographies of schooling encourage new strategies for sharing research. At the annual Pedagogy and Theatre of the Oppressed conference, for example, performance is the cultural norm for presenting scholarship. Typical sessions include solo and group performances, dramatic workshops, reenactments of field site experiences, group discussion facilitated by improvisational role-plays, and scripted conversations between research participants. Such strategies bring our research alive in immediate, human, and provocative ways that simply cannot be captured through more traditional forms of academic presentation.

To the extent that academic culture insists upon print publication, however, our scholarly reports can rise to the occasion with imagistically vivid prose that moves beyond description to evocation. A poetically crafted narrative can enable a reader to feel into the research situation, to participate kinesthetically as well as intellectually, to "experience the heat," as Eisner describes it, of the learning situation. The special issue of *Communication Education* entitled "When Teaching 'Works': Stories of Communication in Education" (Rosenfeld) gathered together a series of "docu-stories" that bring to life an instance of successful learning by engaging all the techniques one normally associates with literary fiction: personal voice, symbol and metaphor, descriptive imagery, dramatic dialogue, and narrative commentary. The results are multilayered mise-en-scènes that stunningly capture the thrill of learning in a particular moment, within a particular community. Similarly, Alexander's experimental work in instructional auto-ethnography dramatically situates his researching body within the classrooms he studies through the use of poetic/performative writing. In "Performing Culture in the Classroom," Alexander articulates his ongoing interpretation of student behaviors within and against his own educational biography, weaving moments of narrative, dramatic scene, and theoretical reflection together in a complex and splendidly rendered bricolage of form. These are the kinds of writing to which we should aspire if we wish to create an imagined, shared space in which the human bodies of researchers, subjects, and readers can touch and be touched by one another.

The Performing Body

Teachers who routinely engage their own and their students' bodies in the classroom have always recognized that teaching and learning are fundamentally somatic processes. It is notable that the move from theory to practice is being spearheaded by performance and theatre educators for whom "enfleshment" is more than a theoretical abstraction; it is the disciplinary heart of our pedagogies. Each time that a student explores her or his presentation of self through an autobiographical monologue, or struggles to assume the voice and body of a dramatic character, or whirls through space in an interpretive dance, these educators find further evidence that when students engage their physical bodies they "come to know" things in a uniquely personal and heuristic manner.

In instructional contexts, performance generally is used in two basic ways, as demonstration and as methodology, each of which asks students to use their bodies differently. Performance as demonstration arises from the logic that intellectual comprehension has little practical value if students cannot apply what they claim to understand. Performance, in these instances, functions as a cumulative product of instruction in which students display their bodies for the consideration, assessment, or entertainment of others. The body is used primarily as evidence of what students have learned, a way for teachers to measure understanding of a concept or mastery of a skill. Education has a long tradition of using performance as demonstration; public speeches, oral presentations, and performances of literature are all valuable ways to incorporate performance as the applied capstone to a unit of study. Indeed, a defining feature of Western education is the insistence that students demonstrate what they know in the presence of others.

But the pedagogy that I am advocating embraces performance as a critical methodology that can be fully integrated throughout the learning process. The shift from the "body-on-display" to the "body as a medium for learning" requires clarification. In disciplinary terms, performance methodology means the rigorous, systematic, exploration-through-enactment of real and imagined experience in which learning occurs through sensory awareness and kinesthetic engagement (Pineau). In more colloquial terms, performance methodology means learning by doing and might include any experiential approach that asks students to struggle bodily with course content. In addition, performance methodology emphasizes process over product by requiring students to use their bodies systematically over a period of time, rather than simply at the end of a unit. For a ready example of the difference between demonstrative and methodological uses of performance, consider the difference between observing a round of completed performances and leading students through a series of incremental workshops in which they are free to explore and experiment with various dimensions of characterization.

But the distinction between demonstration and method involves more than when and why a teacher asks students to perform. Performance methodology describes a deliberate act, a self-conscious act, an act that requires performers to think about how and why their bodies are behaving in the ways that they are. Performance demands acute physical awareness; an underlying goal of any performative exercise is the refinement of one's kinetic and kinesthetic senses. As performance heightens our attention to our bodies, it provides a way for breaking down and breaking through the habits we take for granted. Finally, performance enables an imaginative leap into other kinds of bodies, other ways of being in the world, and in doing so, it opens up concrete and embodied possibilities for resistance, reform, and renewal. The following examples illustrate the connection between critical performative pedagogy and cultural transformation.

I teach a course in the performance of gender in which undergraduate and graduate students explore everyday as well as staged performances of gender and sexual identity. Students had read Iris Marion Young's *Throwing Like a Girl,* in which she argues that people experience their bodies in gender-specific ways and, further, that patriarchy eroticizes the female body by transforming it into a object of desire for men, while delimiting women's sense of their own physical capacity. In a student-designed workshop based on Young's essay "Breasted Experience," class members donned various sizes of "breasts" (bras filled with sacks of rice) while doing such everyday physical activities as running, lying down, hugging someone, and engaging in conversation. After each activity, students recorded their physical sensations as well as how those around them responded to the presence (or enlargement) of their breasted bodies. Predictably, male students were shocked to discover the sheer physical discomfort of running or lying on their stomachs. They reported changes in their posture, a reluctance to cross their arms for fear of accentuating breast size, and the unfamiliar intimacy of crushing their breasts against another man's chest when hugging. One man was so enraged by a classmate's fixation on his breasts during an interview that he offered an impassioned (and, I believe, heartfelt) apology to all the women he had ever "complimented" by ogling. Several female students, on the other hand, discovered a new relationship to their bodies by virtue of having to attend to the infinitesimal ways they habitually compensated for, or capitalized on, the fact of their breasts. By performing their gender reflectively—critically—students began to come to terms with what breasts "mean" in a patriarchal society. Whereas the Young text offered a way to think about gendered bodies, the performance method taught students about how they "do" gender in immediate, concrete, and visceral ways.

Few scholar/practitioners have been as direct or incisive in articulating the political potential of performance methodology as feminist educator and dancer Ann Cooper Albright. In "Dancing Across Difference," Albright cogently demonstrates how identity politics get negotiated through physical bodies and, further, how a body-centered pedagogy can open possibilities for a reconstructed world. Albright's primary method is Contact Improvisation, a modern dance technique in which two dancers support one another's weight while allowing the point of contact to revolve around their bodies as they jointly move through space. Her rationale for this technique is worth quoting at length.

> Because it locates its practice in the moving body, Contact can deconstruct the notion of a singular, stable identity without destroying the presence of that material reality, the physical body, which insistently foregrounds the importance of gender, race, class, and body image. . . . Contact Improvisation incorporates experiences of self and other, marginality and centrality, dependence and autonomy, difference and sameness, in a way that actually complicates those very categories. It provides a space of improvisation—a space for experimentation—in which individuals can physically negotiate the minefield of identity politics, without losing contact with one another. (53)

As an applied metaphor of human relations, Albright argues, Contact works as "a kind of existential dance" in which bodies willingly bear the weight of one another and the "shifting of positions allow for a certain reorganization of social relationships" (46). This dialectic emphasis on the literal and the metaphoric body, the discipline-specific and the heuristic objectives, the classroom and the world, is the hallmark of a critical pedagogy grounded in the performing body.

For some time, I have been struggling to articulate my own commitment to critical pedagogy with my conviction that performance provides a theoretical lens and a pedagogical method for achieving social change. Several factors have brought me to this point. I want to be an idealistic teacher, in the richest sense of that term. I believe that my research and teaching needs to be motivated by a gnawing disturbance at the inequities that plague our society, funded by compassion for those who stand outside the circle of power and privilege, cognizant of my own complicity in perpetuating that circle, and driven by a committed vision that our world can be other than it is. As a performance studies teacher, moreover, I have the opportunity to observe every day what happens when my students' bodies become actively engaged in learning. They have taught me that "the ideological body" is not academic jargon but a tangible expression of the political forces in our lives. They challenge me to pay close attention to how their bodies inhabit my classroom and to stop assuming that simply by gathering them into the same space I have somehow leveled the political playing field. Most importantly, they continue to prove to me that an active body *learns* in ways that are eminently more personal, applicable, critical, and long-lasting than any other teaching method I have tried. On the basis of these experiences, then, let me offer my own agenda for critical performative pedagogy.

(1) Acknowledge that inequities in power and privilege have a physical impact on our bodies and consequently must be struggled against bodily, through physical action and activism. Critical performative pedagogy puts bodies into action in the classroom because it believes this is the surest way to help those bodies become active in the social sphere. To paraphrase Ernest Boyer, it uses the classroom as "a staging ground for self and social renewal" by requiring students and teachers to rehearse more equitable and impassioned ways of being and behaving.

(2) Develop research that accounts for how particular bodies present themselves in the classroom and provide detailed and evocative accounts of what one *sees* and *experiences* in the course of a study. Use all the techniques of a good storyteller in bringing one's research to life for a reader, in "fleshing out" the characters in ways that make them human, complex, and compelling.

(3) Think about what it means to teach performatively across disciplines and at all levels of curriculum design and implementation. What might one do, for example, in a large lecture class that disallows student "performance" in the traditional sense of moving through space? What would a course look like—and more importantly, feel like—if the syllabus were designed according to the model of collaborative group rehearsal? Can performance methodology be integrated across the curriculum in the ways that writing has come to be implemented? An important test of critical performative pedagogy will be to apply it as fruitfully to courses in the hard sciences as to those in the performing arts.

I am well aware that in advocating such a pedagogy, I am opening the door to a seemingly chaotic classroom in which everything I ask students to do can be "contested" and where politics are always at the forefront of the agenda. I cannot apologize for that, because I am convinced that political agendas so permeate education that bringing them to the foreground is the only way to deal with them in a critical and constructive manner. I also know that I run the risk of broadening the definition of performance beyond recognition, to the point that simply "being" in a classroom might be considered a performance of sorts. I am willing to take those risks, however, because I am convinced that only through means of performance—however broadly one wishes to define it—can liberating pedagogies be developed that will enable students to construct meanings that are lived in the body, felt in the bones, and situated within the larger body politic.

WORKS CITED

Albright, Ann Cooper. "Dancing Across Difference: Experience and Identity in the Classroom." *Women and Performance* 6 (1993): 41–54.

Alexander, Bryant K. "Performing Culture in the Classroom: An Instructional (Auto)Ethnography." *Text and Performance Quarterly* 19 (1999): 307–31.

Boyer, Ernest. Keynote Address. Western States Communication Conf. San Jose. Feb. 1994.

Clandinin, Jean, A. Davies, P. Hogan, and B. Kennard, eds. *Learning to Teach, Teaching to Learn: Narratives of Collaboration in Teacher Education.* New York: Teachers College, 1993.

Conquergood, Dwight. "Rethinking Ethnography: Towards a Critical Cultural Politics." *Communication Monographs* 58 (1991): 179–94.

Dewey, John. *Democracy and Education.* 1916. New York: Macmillan, 1966.

Eisner, Eliot. *The Enlightened Eye: Qualitative Inquiry and the Enhancement of Educational Practice.* New York: Macmillan, 1991.

Freire, Paulo. *Pedagogy of the Oppressed.* Trans. Myra B. Ramos. Rev. ed. New York: Continuum, 1993.

Giroux, Henry, and Peter McLaren, eds. *Between Borders: Pedagogy and the Politics of Cultural Studies.* New York: Routledge, 1994.

Giroux, Henry, and Patrick Shannon, eds. *Education and Cultural Studies: Toward a Performative Practice.* New York: Routledge, 1997.

Grossberg, Lawrence. Introduction. "Bringin' It All Back Home—Pedagogy and Cultural Studies." Giroux and McLaren 1–25.

hooks, bell. "Eros, Eroticism, and the Pedagogical Process." Giroux and McLaren 113–18.

Magoon, A. J. "Constructivist Approaches in Educational Research." *Review of Educational Research* 47 (1977): 651–94.

McLaren, Peter. *Schooling as a Ritual Performance: Towards a Political Economy of Educational Symbols and Gestures.* Rev. ed. New York: Routledge, 1999.

———. "Schooling the Postmodern Body: Critical Pedagogy and the Politics of Enfleshment." *Postmodernism, Feminism, and Cultural Politics: Redrawing Educational Boundaries.* Ed Henry Giroux. New York: State U of New York P, 1991. 144–73.

Pineau, Elyse Lamm. "Re-Casting Rehearsal: Making a Case for Production as Research." *Journal of the Illinois Speech and Theatre Association* 46 (1995): 43–52.

Rosenfeld, Lawrence, ed. "When Teaching 'Works': Stories of Communication in Education." *Communication Education* 42.4 (1993).

Wilson, S. "The Use of Ethnographic Techniques in Education Research." *Review of Educational Research* 47 (1977): 245–65.

Speaking of God

Performance Pedagogy

in the Theological School

3

Richard F. Ward

> As we face the crises of knowledge, power and values, knowledge of God and world requires a new aesthetic funding, a way of knowledge that is productive of new forms of survival and flourishing. To do this, aesthetics plays an important role in the language of theology.
>
> —REBECCA CHOPP, *Saving Work*

I attended a reunion dinner of my college class not too long ago, and as the round of introductions proceeded, one of my friends took his turn. "Divinity!" he announced as the subject for graduate study. And what, pray tell, was his vocational plan? "Why, I plan to become . . . divine!" he coolly replied. Guffaws broke out all around the table as he sat down. When the word *divinity* is turned loose in polite conversation among educators, it creates awkwardness and uncertainty. Lest we get too cavalier about the importance of divinity as a subject for inquiry, however, we should heed what William Dean says in "The Irony of Atheism in America." If the question of "God" is not taken up at all, then it will be "left to fester in the darkness of inattention or answered in ways dangerous to this republic's openness and its people's freedom" (1).

I write as a practitioner of performance studies whose professional life sits at the convergence of two streams: the project of "naming God," and an interest in "performance" in art and culture. I have enacted this vocation within the setting of three theological schools. Most of the students I teach are planning careers in ministries with social agencies or in positions of leadership within Protestant, Christian churches. I myself am ordained by one such church body to teach in a theological school but also to practice within the wider Christian communion the very things that I teach: preaching, storytelling, oral interpretation, and study of biblical literature.

Theological Education as a Contested Enterprise

Theological education itself is an intensely contested enterprise in the three university-related schools where I have exercised my vocation.[1] An ethos pervades where commitment to "God," "church," "canon," and "creed" are often suspect, and where the question persists whether the theological or divinity school should even be located within the university. Theological education takes place in what Stephen Carter has called a "culture of disbelief" where "those who believe in God are encouraged to keep it a secret, and often a shameful one at that" (4). What Della Pollock has said about performative writing is particularly apt for describing the situation. Performance studies conducted within the parameters of the theological school is like the enterprise of theological education these days, "nervous"; that is, "it anxiously crosses various stories, theories, texts, intertexts and spheres of practice, unable to settle into a clear, linear course, neither willing nor able to stop moving, restless, transient and transitive, traversing spatial and temporal borders" (90–91).

In order to "name God" in theological education, one must be prepared to migrate between "spheres of practice" and agree to "remain restless" in the spaces between many fields of inquiry. The climate within the theological school is restless as students, teachers, and administrators struggle with what theological education means. What is theological education for? What purposes and publics does it serve? What does a graduate of a theological school know, and what does that graduate do with what is known? And (more to the point of this essay) what does "performance studies" find to do in a divinity school?

The ecclesia (the organized communities of faith) is a primary constituency for theological education and presses the theological school to develop a curriculum suitable for training its clergy. Since leadership in religious communities requires that a candidate for ministry perform effectively in a social and communal role, it takes on a "practical" dimension. One function of theological education is to equip students with the skills necessary for "effective" performance in their social and ecclesial roles as "minister."

One pair of theological educators has developed a typology for interpreting the purpose and goals of theological education. They suggest that the sociocultural type that dominates training for religious leadership is that of "manager." The reason the manager is the model is that churches have followed the "general pattern of bureaucratization" and "have focused on routinized problem solving in the organization of maintenance of their institutions" (Hough and Cobb 78). Communities of faith expect that the theological school will be the place where the ministerial student will be adequately equipped for leading communities through performances of their primary commitments while running an efficient organization. Edward Farley suggests that this managerial ethos of "professionalism" has indeed become the unifying end of theological education; it is a pedagogy shaped by a "clerical paradigm" (87–88).

Another primary constituency for the theological school is the university. *Theology* literally means "God-talk." Since "God-talk" is suspect within the university, theology must justify itself as an "academic" enterprise and perform in the university as "a disciplined, reasoned in-

quiry and reflection on ultimate meaning and value" (Copeland 283).
Divinity students, for example, must learn how to derive ideas and images from an extended, critical reflection upon "sacred" texts and traditions. The subject for this reflection is both the student's own enactment of his or her professional identity as minister and also the communities' own performances of commitment and belief. "Practical" theologians explicate the personal and social significance of these enactments to inform future practice.

Theological education has organized itself into discrete subdisciplines[2] to negotiate the tension between its two competing primary constituencies. We might imagine this as a binary relationship between theory and praxis. A student is expected to know how to freely transgress spheres framed as "theoretical" and those framed as "practical," first to achieve unified and coherent structures of knowledge and then to translate the arcana of divinity into forms of speech, rites, and rituals that communities will recognize and frame as sacred.

Those of us whose pedagogy is informed both by theology and performance theory and whose professional lives have developed in relation to Protestant theological schools have focused on a wide range of practices where "faith" is constituted, configured, and displayed. The ways that God is named in the performance of worship and the manner in which sacred texts are orally rendered and interpreted through the act of preaching are central to our concern.

The Pinch of an Ill-Fitting Space:
The Predicament of the Speech Teacher in the Theological School
The study of human communication has had, for the most part, great difficulty legitimizing itself alongside other disciplines of inquiry in the theological school. This is an all-too-familiar narrative. As in other university departments, communication studies in general (and performance studies in particular) struggles to define itself to its colleagues and to identify a theoretical core of conviction, method, and perspective. The space allotted in this essay will allow me to make only two historical reference points: Charles Woolbert writes that in the formative years of the discipline in the late nineteenth century, young scholars returning to America from Germany with fresh doctorates in biblical criticism, church history, or theology had only a remote interest in a discipline such as communication that "had no standing at Heidelberg and Jena and Gottingen" (9). The rapid ascent of telecommunications put other kinds of pressures on the pedagogical constructs and structures of theological education. Since the theological school is a culture highly shaped by literacy and print, it has consistently had difficulty dealing with "urgent problems of oral performance" (Ong 26).

Communication enjoys status as a generative term in many parts of the university but continues to be a problematic term in the theological school. In 1991, Peter Hawkins prepared a report on communication education within the theological school for the faculty of Yale University Divinity School. Some seminal contemporary theologians (e.g., Edward Schillebeekx, Bernard Lonergan, David Tracy, Paul Ricoeur, and Jacques Ellul) have taken up questions of communication to give form, direction, and purpose to their own work. Nevertheless, Hawkins found that communication remained narrowly construed as a discrete subdiscipline in the theological curriculum. He was surprised to learn that in the theological schools the overwhelming emphasis was on skill acquisition and refinement, rather than on any serious consideration of the relationship of communication and the Christian tradition. Hawkins cited an earlier survey of one hundred ninety-eight theological schools conducted by Jurgen Hilke in 1985 that concluded, "'Communication' is not considered important enough to warrant exclusive attention in theological education" ("Communication" 10).[3]

An additional burden upon the legacy of instruction that performance studies practitioners inherit is the "anti-theatrical prejudice" that Jonas Barish writes about. "Performance," like "art" and "rhetoric," is too often used to demean or devalue expressive speech. At best, such terms describe artifices or novelties that "add force to a particular message" (Childers, *Performing* 38). The following is a scene where this theme played itself out. During an animated discussion about a course listed in the catalogue entitled "The Oral Performance of Scripture and Sermon," a colleague turned to me and said, "You don't think of preaching as a performance, do you?" Apparently, in my colleague's way of thinking, talk about "authentic" preaching or even questions of "truth" were tainted by performance categories. In spite of the best efforts of rhetoricians, communication scholars, and even some theologians and homileticians, *performance* is still primarily associated with theatrical imagery and used pejoratively. *Dramatic*, for example, lingers in the homiletical vocabulary to describe preaching that is suspect. It refers to an expressive and highly animated style, but one that is perilously close to being emotionally "excessive."

Narrow definitions of communication and performance and the dominance of a "clerical paradigm" place particular constraints on the one teaching public speaking, preaching, and other "oral" arts in the theological school. Within this framework, our discipline tends to secure its place and justify its presence by emphasizing skill building. Performance pedagogy in the theological school can easily become trivialized as a means of "helping people develop an agile professionalism in leading worship, reading the scriptures, preaching, and administering the sacraments" (Bartow, "Doing" 284). The speech teacher, communications scholar, and certainly the performance studies practitioner have very little room to flourish in a curriculum shaped by a clerical paradigm; they have little to lose and a lot to gain by seeking alliances with others who are seeking new meanings and directions for theological education.

From "Professionalism" to "Embodiment":
New Directions in Theological Education

Many other theological educators are growing increasingly uneasy with the clerical paradigm and are restless for change. Performance studies practitioners and other colleagues in the theological school have expanded upon "practice" as an organizing construct. Rebecca Chopp speaks for many others when she says "Education is not simply about correct ideas or handing down tradition or training, it is also about human change, transformation and growth" (13). Chopp is among those who look to the actual practices that constitute theological education as sites for inciting change, transformation, and growth, not simply as instruments for either transmitting what one knows or for illustrating theory. For her, practice not only encompasses pedagogical strategies but also how pedagogy is integrated with governance, development, advisement, and administration. From within these varying sets of practices, the student hopes to name "God" and "understand God more truly" (Kelsey 165).

The shift from "professionalism" to "understanding God more truly" has created a new political climate in the theological school. Every field of knowledge and inquiry is holding its own disciplinary boundaries up for renewed scrutiny. Our experience in the evolving discipline of performance studies teaches us to be opportunistic during such times of conceptual ferment and to be alert for chances to "shape new forms of survival and flourishing," not only for disciplinary survival but for the students we serve (Chopp 12).

Other educators are apprehensive of these paradigmatic and pedagogical shifts. Thomas Oden, for example, fears that "classical Christian faith might not survive" any more pushing toward "process." Oden thinks that he is hearing the death throes of a "once vital ethos of liberal learning" in those schools that are risking this turn and laments the passing of "the institutional establishments of old-line bureaucratic ecumenism" (20).

The turn toward praxis changes the kind of place the theological school is. Rather than simply being a site where one acquires the equipment needed to perform a social role, the curriculum of the theological school orients the soul towards the project of "naming God" for self, faith community, and society. The push is away from professionalism, or "a matter of mastering specific skills or acquiring specialized knowledge for which others have no use" (Lovin 127); it is rather towards naming God and bringing about personal and social liberation and transformation. This stance repositions theological education to become "saving work, sets of practices that offer a material vision and an embodied wisdom for a new form of Christianity in our day and age" (Chopp 76).

Performance Pedagogy: Doing Theology in a New Key

Performance studies pushes against the constraints of the ill-fitting clerical paradigm, positioning itself with a widening epistemic as a vital resource for doing "saving work" in the theological school. It has a rich and durable legacy of creating, evaluating, and doing performances within church and culture and even within the theological school itself. It bears eloquent witness to the efficacy of embodiment as a way of knowing. Practitioners of performance studies (some of whom trace their legacy to elocutionists, expressionists, interpreters, or teachers of speech) have emphasized the importance of the body for doing theology.

One theological theme that consistently animates performance pedagogy is *incarnation,* or "word-made-flesh." *Word* still remains in the theological vocabulary as a constitutive and creative construct. Some of us understand ourselves to be "in service to the words—and the Word—the people of God would hear" (Bartow, *God's Human Speech* 2). One of the sources for (what Alla Bozarth Campbell called) the "incarnational aesthetic" in performance pedagogy in the theological school is the Gospel According to St. John 1.1–3:

> In the beginning was the Word, and the Word was with God, and the Word was God. The Word was in the beginning with God. All things were made through the Word, and without the Word not anything made that was made. And the Word became flesh and dwelt among us, full of grace and truth; we have beheld the Word's glory, glory as of the only Child from God the Father and Mother. (*Inclusive Language* 35)

The Word's definitive quality as the event of embodiment informs pedagogy in the theological school and animates a student's engagement of a set of practices that we frame as performances: the public reading of texts; traditions of liturgical enactments, personal narratives, and rituals; and communal performances of rites, festivals, prayers, and protests. Speech, gesture, and movement make visible some characteristics of the Word, while others remain hidden and ineffable. Preachers attempt to locate (by faith and reason) the Word in their experience and interpret it by enfleshing it through speech, gesture, action. At the same time, the Word remains radically Other.

Performance studies' regard for embodiment has grounded reflection on the Word in actual practices of speech and enactment and nourished our own lines of inquiry within the context of a theological school. Though the "Word" is now contested as an efficacious metaphor in performance theory, theology and performance studies still share a regard for the "body" as a "highly-informed source of experiential knowledge" (Warren 257). Bjorn Krondorfer notes how much "body language" has punctuated theological reflection over the last two decades and wonders what sites we will visit in our own teaching to explore such questions as "Is the body merely a cultural construct, or is it a residue of one's authentic self?" (27). The preaching classroom, for instance, is a place where the body is believed to be a site for knowing and naming God in relation to the Self. Charles Rice believes that the preaching event is an "embodiment" of Word and Presence. Don Wardlaw invites students to strive for "embodied delivery" when they preach (Wardlaw et al.). Jana Childers believes with Charles Bartow that "preaching is a theological enterprise embodied at any given time in a human voice, body, and person" (Foreword xiii).

Embodiment is a construct that helps to tell us what preaching means. The preacher enters the pulpit as a cultural performer who sustains his or her cultural identity through an infinite array of embodiments, inscriptions, or enactments that include that of preacher. The criteria for effective preaching is, of course, widely variable and negotiated within the congregational cultures themselves for themselves. Certainly, one aspect of effective preaching is the quality of the preacher's engagement with the Other. The preacher's body becomes a site where he or she embodies (through the form and event of preaching) an engagement between self and Other, inscribed, expressed, and formulated as a sermon.

The preacher also enters the pulpit as an aesthetic performer. Preaching requires the performance of invention, inscription, and intention. As a result of his or her sustained engagement with "the aesthetic communication of others" (Pelias 47), specifically as one "addressed" by the speakers, the preacher finds in sacred texts and theological traditions, but also from speakers from everyday life, a Presence he or she names as God. From this engagement, the preacher invents a language act, shapes it into a rhetorical form that the community recognizes as a sermon, and enacts it in a time and space especially designated for its utterance. Performance theorist and theatre director Richard Schechner provides an image appropriate for this process. A sermon in preparation is not unlike "an unproduced play" in that it is "a shard of an as yet unassembled whole" (120). I have said elsewhere that preaching is a context-specific act in which the "shard" of language that is called a sermon achieves its entelechy in the body and voice of the preacher. It is also an event when the personal, individual consciousness of the preacher is enfleshed, authorized, and legitimated in the community of which he or she is a part (Ward 4). We might also call the preacher a "holy actor," two words that when conjoined are likely to raise some eyebrows!

Towards a New Poetics and Pedagogy:
The Preacher as a Holy Actor

Acting in the homiletician's vocabulary usually refers to a constellation of that which is "theatrical" about preaching. The "actor" is a stand-in for all cultural performers who realize intentionality, attitude, and perspective in literary texts through voice, gesture, movement, and/or impersonation.

When one teaches preaching and draws an analogy between the art of the preacher and that of the actor, one is certain to draw objections. Acting connotes the use of flashy, stylistic devices that only help "embalm the sermon and put it on view" (W. J. Beeners, qtd. in Bartow, "Doing" 19). Acting can also be used more constructively to describe a particular kind of preaching where the preacher impersonates a fictive speaker and addresses the audience in the form of a monologue. The assumption is that by speaking "as if" the preacher were from the world of the biblical text as one of the characters within that world, the preacher-as-actor can involve the listener in the psychological drama unfolding in a biblical character's interiority. Since biblical narrators hardly ever disclose this interior landscape, a preacher's dramatic monologue aims to close the distance between text and listener by adding dimension to biblical characterization and by giving language to a character's thought, motive, belief, and sense of self.

For example, in one monologue, a speaker portrays a biblical character identified simply as a "Good Samaritan" in the Gospel of Luke 10.25–37. The monologue begins, "I was on my annual trip to Jerusalem and Jericho to sell my pottery wares. I always dreaded those visits for such a spirit of hatred existed between Samaritans and Jews. Yet it was necessary for my business for me to make the trip every year to Judea" (Blevins and Bailey 63). The strategy for this kind of preaching is to create a relationship between the fictive speaker and the listener, thus awarding the listener status as an insider (and perhaps even confidante) to the drama unfolding between the biblical world and the listener's own. The assumption is that preaching in the form of a dramatic monologue makes the listener more competent to hear messages drawn from the dramatized world of the biblical text.

Some homileticians quickly devalue this kind of preaching as "pulpit theater" and discount the monologist as a mere stand-in for the real preacher. David Buttrick warns that the drama monologue in the pulpit edges out the "mystery of God-with-us," displacing it with "psy-

chologies of faith" (334). Elizabeth Achtemeier dismisses this homiletical form as an "experimental" genre that "abandons the biblical message altogether and becomes nothing more than artistic or symbolic
performance, open to a wide variety of meanings." Dramatic monologues are not, she declares, "adequate substitutes for the proclamation
of the biblical Word" (29). Despite their critics, preachers who adopt
this kind of strategy for preaching stand on firm traditional ground.
Quintilian turned the orators' attention to actors by claiming that impersonation might enable them to "display inner thoughts of adver-
saries, introduce conversations, bring down gods from heaven, raise
the dead, or give voice to entire cities and peoples" (391). Jana Childers
stands within this tradition when she links the art of the preacher to
that of the actor.

> Preachers are concerned, as are actors, with the truthful interpre-
> tation of texts. This interpretative process is . . . a generative and
> incarnational activity. Something new is born out of the coming
> together of text and interpreter, something in which the integrity
> of each is still preserved. (*Performing* 100)

Childers shows us that we can get even more work out of the word
drama in understanding preaching. The processes of preparing sermons might also be thought of as "dramatic" and the preacher as an
"actor" in the process of constructing meaning. Preachers put words
(and worlds) together in (and from) different contexts in and for the
performance of their sermons. Yet, a stress upon the role of language in
imaginatively constructing worlds of perception exposes the limits of
language to explain what is "real," "truthful," and "believable" in sermon performance. Does "truth" lie beyond the reach of the preacher's
vocabulary? Or can the preacher, through a "strategy of grace, tell the
story of transcendent experience in a period when people commonly
lack the words to express it?" (Hawkins, email). This is the suspense
that makes the processes of homiletical preparation dramatic.

Preachers as actors in their own dramas of preparation and embodiment learn to be "two-faced," that is, they learn to look at theater and
ritual at the same time. Two-faced actors that enter worship spaces and
step into pulpits play a significant role in homiletics' realization of a
"new" poetics. *Congruence* is a god-term in contemporary homiletical
theory. It refers to a qualitative relationship between what the preacher
says is true and how the preacher says it. Theology is voiced and bod-
ied forth in the sermon as lived experience. It is both a "doing" and a
"showing," an enfleshing enactment that makes a preacher radically
present in the worshipping community. The preacher-as-actor is present first as an equation of congruity; action is suited to the words and
the words to the action (Shakespeare, *Hamlet* 3.2.20). Preachers who

imagine themselves as actors in their own dramas of sermon preparation and performance will work toward congruity by embodying the truth of their experience and interpretation through voice, body, and display in the moment of utterance. As actors, they are "doers of the Word, and not hearers only" (James 1.22, KJV).

The drama that a preacher stages in sermon preparation and performance is not an end in itself. "A sermon belongs to ritual and shares in its ambiguities" (Driver 88). What is dramatic about religious, liturgical performances is the pull of this (an order of worship) against that (the structures of everyday life) in ways that open up "holes in the fabric of things, through which life-giving power flows into the world" (Lathrop 214). As a "doer of the Word," the preacher "acts" with an eye toward "fullness," that is, the completion of the act of preaching. Performance is first an act that makes the sermon. Performing it as a liturgical act, however, is an action that breaks it. Preaching is the creation of a finite form (sermon) that is brought into the assembly in order to be broken by a Presence who is named as God and who is radically other than festival, ceremony, or even ritual performance.

The preacher as an actor in a holy ritual seeks the emptiness of "holes" that liturgical performance aims to open up. The pull toward this (the enactment of the sermon) against that (the creation of empty spaces in liturgical structures) is a necessary dynamic in a new, performance-centered poetics of preaching. Without the theatricality of the performed speaker's drama, we have liturgy performed poorly. Without an awareness of its location in ritual performance, we veer toward "entertainment with too little efficacy" (Schechner 120). Actors from Peter Brook's "holy" theater ask questions relevant for preaching, such as "Can the invisible be made visible through the performer's presence?" (52). The central paradox animating liturgical performance is that it uses ordinary things (bread, wine, books, cloth, fire, and water) to speak of the Holy. The preacher becomes radically present in the assembly as a "holy" actor when he or she stages the drama of the sermon as an "ordinary" thing. The enacted sermon is an aesthetic object that finds completion in performance but that is also being brought into the liturgical frame in order to be broken by a "language of actions, a language of sounds" (Brook 49). It is in this breaking that a Divine Presence acts and is therefore known and recognized in the holy theater of liturgical performance.

Those of us who have experienced the emergent and expansionist, interdisciplinary impulses in performance-centered studies in human communication have often felt the pinch of an ill-fitting space in the theological school. As long as a clerical paradigm dominates, there is very little room for performance studies to flourish. Conversations with other colleagues in theological education about who we are and what we teach have a history of awkwardness and confusion.

The shift from professionalism to a new theological concern with naming God in our learning practices opens up a new future for performance studies in theological education. We meet in the highly charged spaces between disciplines to share an emergent regard for the body. The Word lends coherence and unity to performance pedagogical practice within the theological school but no longer enjoys status as an uncontested link between performance theory and theology. The body, however, is named by both as a site for practicing transforming knowledge. It is there, on that conceptual dancing ground, that performance studies can press its claim for legitimacy as a partner in theological education. There, it can reclaim its rich legacy of pedagogical practices in the theological school and help fashion a new poetics for the public enactment and expression of Faith.

NOTES

1. I have taught at the Candler School of Theology at Emory University and the Divinity School at Yale University and am presently at the Iliff School of Theology in Denver.

2. The subdisciplines are normally identified as Bible, church history, theology, and the practice of ministry.

3. A notable exception among the "elite" theological schools of the Northeast is Princeton Theological Seminary. Education in a variety of speech arts has been an established part of theological education at Princeton for 134 years. For a history of speech instruction at Princeton, see Bartow, "In Service."

WORKS CITED

Achtemeier, Elizabeth. "The Artful Dialogue." *Interpretation* 35 (Jan. 1981): 18–31.

Barish, Jonas. *The Anti-Theatrical Prejudice.* Berkeley: U of California P, 1981.

Bartow, Charles L. "Doing the Word: A Performatory View of the Preacher's Task in Hermeneutics and Proclamation." *Papers of the Annual Meeting of the Academy of Homiletics.* Madison: Academy of Homiletics, 1988. 19–44.

———. *God's Human Speech: A Practical Theology of Proclamation.* Grand Rapids: Eerdmans, 1997.

———. "In Service to the Servants of the Word: Teaching Speech at Princeton Seminary." *Princeton Seminary Bulletin* 13.3 (1992): 274–86.

Blevins, James L., and Raymond Bailey. *Dramatic Monologues: Making the Bible Live.* Nashville: Broadman, 1990.

Brook, Peter. *The Empty Space.* New York: Atheneum, 1984.

Buttrick, David. *Homiletic: Moves and Structures.* Philadelphia: Fortress, 1987.

Campbell, Alla Bozarth. *The Word's Body: An Incarnational Aesthetic of Interpretation.* Tuscaloosa: U of Alabama P, 1979.

Carter, Stephen L. *The Culture of Disbelief: How American Law and Politics Trivialize Religious Devotion.* New York: Basic, 1993.

Childers, Jana. Foreword. *God's Human Speech: A Practical Theology of Proclamation.* By Charles L. Bartow. Grand Rapids: Eerdmans, 1997.

———. *Performing the Word: Preaching as Theatre.* Nashville: Abingdon, 1999.

Chopp, Rebecca. *Saving Work: Feminist Practices of Theological Education.* Louisville: Westminster, 1995.

Copeland, M. Shawn. *Dictionary of Feminist Theologies.* Ed. Letty Russell and J. Shannon Clarkson. Louisville: Westminster, 1996.

Dean, William. "The Irony of Atheism in America." Working paper. Iliff School of Theology Faculty Colloquium. Denver. 6 Sept. 1999.

Driver, Tom Faw. *The Magic of Ritual: Our Need for Liberating Rites that Transform Our Lives and Our Communities.* San Francisco: Harper, 1991.

Farley, Edward. *Theologia: The Fragmentation and Unity of Theological Education.* Philadelphia: Fortress, 1983.

Hawkins, Peter S. "Communication Study at Yale Divinity School: A Proposal." Unpublished report, 1987.

———. Email to the author. 17 Sept. 1995.

Hough, Joseph C., Jr., and John B. Cobb, Jr. *Christian Identity and Theological Education.* Chico: Scholars, 1985.

An Inclusive Language Lectionary: Readings for Year B, Revised. Atlanta: Cooperative Assoc., 1987.

Kelsey, David H. *To Understand God Truly: What's Theological about a Theological School.* Louisville: Westminster, 1992.

Krondorfer, Bjorn. "Bodily Knowing, Ritual Embodiment, and Experimental Drama: From Regression to Transgression." *Journal of Ritual Studies* 6 (1992): 27–38.

Lathrop, Gordon W. *Holy Things: A Liturgical Theology.* Minneapolis: Fortress, 1993.

Lovin, Robin W. "The Real Task of Practical Theology." *Christian Century* 109.5 (1992): 125–28.

Oden, Thomas. *Requiem: A Lament in Three Movements.* Nashville: Abingdon, 1995.

Ong, Walter, S.J. *The Presence of the Word: Some Prolegomena Cultural and Religious History.* New Haven: Yale UP, 1967.

Pelias, Ronald J. *Performance Studies: The Interpretation of Aesthetic Texts.* New York: St. Martin's, 1992.

Pollock, Della. "Performing Writing." *The Ends of Performance.* Ed. Peggy Phelan and Jill Lane. New York: New York UP, 1998.

Quintilian. *Institutio Oratoria.* Trans. H. E. Butler. Loeb Classical Lib. Cambridge: Harvard UP, 1963.

Rice, Charles L. *The Embodied Word: Preaching as Art and Liturgy.* Minneapolis:
Fortress, 1992.

Schechner, Richard. *Performance Theory.* New York: Routledge, 1988.

Ward, Richard F. "Performance Turns in Homiletics: Wrong Way or Right
On?" *Journal of Communication and Religion* 17.1 (1994): 1–11.

Wardlaw, Don M., Fred Baumer, Donald F. Chatfield, Joan Delaplane, O.P.,
O. C. Edwards, Jr., James A. Forbes, Jr., Edwina Hunter, Thomas H.
Troeger. *Learning Preaching: Understanding and Participating in the Pro-
cess.* Lincoln: Lincoln Coll. and Seminary P, 1989.

Warren, John T. "The Body Politic: Performance, Pedagogy, and the Power of
Enfleshment." *Text and Performance Quarterly* 19.3 (1999): 257–65.

Woolbert, Charles. "The Teaching of Speech as an Academic Discipline."
Quarterly Journal of Speech Education 9 (1923): 1–18.

The Queer Performance That Will Have Been

Student-Teachers in the Archive

4

Craig
Gingrich-
Philbrook

I would say that teaching queer performance is not like teaching something instrumental—like how to use a wood plane—except that I have seen my grandfather use a wood plane, have watched him work both to make something of, and reveal something—some potential—in, the wood. Like me, working in the theatre, he worked in the garage, shaping furniture, *his* performances, with someone in mind. For example, when I was twelve, he made me the desk I revise on now, writing these words, going back over them, shaving away, planing them down to an unforeseeable future I nonetheless try to reveal. He made the desk to reveal an academic potential for me, an option he did not have. I took the wood plane away with me after his death. I had never thought to want it before, invisible while he used it, but I treasure it now that his carpentry has—for him—reached closure but—for me—remains open, suggestive, instructive, reinterpretable, inexhaustibly meaningful.

Like my grandfather's carpentry, the queer performance I teach to students (and they to me) one day "will have been." What we make, what we reveal, passes. We strive to use the phrase *queer performance* to talk about texts and to talk about talk-about-texts; we try to recognize this dialogue as an ongoing process that makes and reveals ideologies, preferences, and embodiments. As interlaced acts of language, our queer performances are always *acts of* and *acts upon* [1] the archive we encounter, making and remaking it together.

In this essay, I situate our work with each other as we perform the roles of audience, performer, student, and teacher. First, I explicate the performance studies paradigm that most influences my contributions to our work. Second, I review the heuristic, but underutilized, communication theory that describes performance as creative double bind; this will situate (queer) performance [2] as a problematic we live through. Third, I turn to the particular double bind of encountering the archive of queer performance and its models, without fully consigning our subjectivity to them.

These three themes, versions of one another, offer testaments in dif-

ferent languages to the open, ephemeral qualities of queer performance. Together, these testaments suggest a perspective on queer performance as a *mode of inquiry* requiring ongoing metamethodological
reflection-in-participation, rather than as an *object of inquiry* that requires an essentializing definition. They also situate (queer) performance as an orientation toward the "future anterior," that is, the future, the performance, that will have been.

A Performance Studies Paradigm

I bring my perspective on performance studies to my students; while I
appreciate and, indeed, greedily consume and disseminate the work of
such theorists as Richard Schechner, Peggy Phelan, Philip Auslander,
and Herbert Blau, my initial exposure to performance studies came
from what was then perceived as another tradition: the transformation, in the discipline of speech communication, of oral interpretation
into performance studies. In particular, I credit an essay by two men,
Ronald J. Pelias and James VanOosting, who later became my teachers,
with inaugurating my subjectivity as a "performance studies practitioner." In this section, I explicate four positions I read in that essay
and then give specific examples from classes I have taught that deal in
whole or in part with queer performance.

The Concern with Aesthetic Communication

Pelias and VanOosting credit Paul Campbell with first using the paired
term *communication aesthetics* to "break the yoke of positivism which
he saw as dominating the speech communication field" (220). Campbell, highlighting the aesthetics of communication by emphasizing its
dramatic nature, wished to consider "the dimension of language in
which we create and re-create ourselves in relation to the 'real' world
around us and in which we use those imaginative or artistic events
(originated by others or by ourselves) to become new beings or *personae*" (Campbell 9).

This re-creative power of language characterizes performance as,
according to Richard Bauman, reflexive in at least two senses: *formally*
as "a cultural means of objectifying and laying open to scrutiny culture
itself" (47), and *sociopsychologically* as "an especially potent and heightened means of taking the role of the other and of looking back at oneself from that perspective, in a process . . . constitutive of the self" (48).

In my classes, then, we search for those performative acts of and
upon language that create and re-create "queer." We do look at conspicuously aesthetic performances (e.g., Fuoss; Hughes; Hughes and
Román; T. Miller, *My Queer Body;* Pomo Afro Homos; Split Britches;
Taylor, "Is There"). But we also look at performances from everyday
life to reveal the aesthetic communication that re-creates "queer" at

several levels, including: particular forms of conversational exchange, such as snapping (Johnson); formation and maintenance of communities in public spaces, such as pubs (Corey, "Performing") and theater/cafes (Solomon); managing racial identity as a factor in the reception of one's public performance of queerness (Chung et al.); and threats that haunt (allegedly) heterosexual rituals of masculine initiation (Gingrich-Philbrook).

Contesting the Canon

Since its inception, the paradigm has called into question the performable/unperformable distinction that established oral interpretation of literature as a discipline concerned primarily with the exclusionary conception of the aesthetic that supports canon formation. This distinction relays the representable/unrepresentable distinction Craig Owens identified early in the theorizing of postmodern aesthetic praxis:

> It is precisely at the legislative frontier between what can be represented and what cannot that the postmodernist operation is being staged—not in order to transcend representation, but in order to expose that system of power that authorizes certain representations while blocking, prohibiting or invalidating others. (59)

Queer performance has a stake in this operation and this exposure of power: a stake shared, however differently, with feminist performance, postcolonial performance, and other performance praxes struggling to bring subjugated knowledges across that well-regulated border. For Pelias and VanOosting, performance studies must contest the assumption that the aesthetic ever achieves "purity" and insist upon retaining it in its open form. They argue that,

> Performance studies calls into question the privilege of academic authority by including all members of a speech community as potential artists, all utterances as potentially aesthetic, all events as potentially theatrical, and all audiences as potentially active participants who can authorize artistic experience. By rejecting canonical security and exclusionary conventions, performance studies practitioners eschew artistic imperialism in favor of aesthetic communalism. These claims, then, yield an ideology that is radically democratic and counterelitist. (221)

Thus, the everyday queer performances—which would previously be judged unaesthetic—that the students and I relate in our conspicuous queer performances for the class become aesthetic by re-creating "queer." They become "archivable." In their presentation, they provide what José Muñoz identifies as the critical evidence, the "ephemera," queer performances leave behind. This evidence includes:

> alternate modes of textuality and narrativity like memory and performance; . . . All of those things that remain after a performance, a kind of evidence of what has transpired. . . . It does not rest on epistemological foundations but is instead interested in following traces, glimmers, residues, and specks of things. . . . ephemera is a mode of proofing and producing arguments often worked by minoritarian culture and criticism makers. (10)

In class, we resist the academic impulse that would deploy performance studies to authorize the study of queer performance as a prelude to canon formation within this genre. We do so by attending to competing evaluations of the efficacy of particular performances. For example, alongside the text of Tim Miller's *My Queer Body* and his countercritique—with David Román—of the critique of "preaching to the converted," we read responses to the performance by Peggy Phelan and by Fredrick Corey ("Gay Life"). These authors provide competing perspectives on Miller's performance. They re-create *queer performance* as a highly contested term, dependent upon the uses to which audiences, critics, and the performers themselves put it.

The Performance Requirement

Pelias and VanOosting make the claim that performance studies takes participation as its working procedure. Its mode of inquiry demands physical, sensuous involvement in a performance event. The methodology depends upon personal responsiveness, somatic engagement, and cognitive analysis (221–22). A *performance*, in this paradigm, is something other than a *routine;* by claiming the paradigm's status as a mode of inquiry, we consent to an uncertain outcome, placing our bodies on the line.

This *out*come comes *out* through*out* the performance as a revelatory process conducted before an audience and structured, epistemologically, like a closet. Eve Sedgwick has described the closet as both a *viewpoint* (a position to view the world from) and a *spectacle* (something viewed from a different, although proximate, position) (222–23). To come out does not trade one view for the other altogether; coming out produces an oscillation between viewpoints, cultivates an awareness of the interdependence in which they reflexively re-create one another. Likewise, the disclosures of performance, those reflexively communicated aesthetic and epistemological moments, do not presume a point at which we have traded our uncertainty for knowledge. Put another way, performance as a mode of inquiry, unlike statistical experiments based on mathematical formulas, defies linearity and privileges no one epistemological moment as the equal sign marking the temporal point in an equation at which a (queer) performer should have achieved knowledge.

To explore this position in the paradigm, I ask students to construct conspicuous performances (such as might occur on a stage, and which they will perform in class) re-creating performance in everyday life. They write three texts explicitly designed to demonstrate (queer) performance knowledge as an ongoing, embodied process, rather than a linear achievement from a distant perspective. Writing from several perspectives, many tell us what they have learned about queerness from the viewpoint of the closet and the ongoing epistemology of coming out of it.

Most of the students, however, write using the spectacle of the closet and the ongoing epistemology of (1) watching others struggle in it and at its doors and (2) realizing their own part in maintaining that closet. These students tell me, the out class members, and each other that they are straight. I ask them only to choose or to generate "out" texts to perform, defining "out" as acknowledging a stake in the re-creation of queer. The out students and I take the straight-identified students' participation in class as evidence of a desire to explore queerness *through* performance from any epistemological position. Some of these students, of course, *do* choose or generate texts that, linguistically at least, come from the viewpoint of the closet.

This approach to assignments allows us to disclose queerness as a cultural resource we have a shared stake in understanding. Those of us who do identify as queer struggle to give up our perceived ownership of "queer" and recognize instead the folly of insisting upon such a heroic conception of our subjectivity and ability to control discourse.

The straight-identified students struggle to recognize their stake in homosexuality as the constitutive outside that enables them to articulate their heterosexuality, a recognition sponsored by their readings of Judith Butler. Some of them go further and critique the inside/outside binary implied by Butler. Such a student uses (queer) performance to articulate experiences of aesthetic communication in relationships with queers. These queer friends, siblings, family members, teachers, and so on provide more than armature for the student's heterosexual identity. These students reveal their construction of that identity, not over and against the queer relationship partner(s) but in dialogue with that person or those persons, a dialogue that transforms the student's own notions of her or his communicative possibilities. Both groups of students distinguish between sex acts and sexuality as a primary message system in human communication. In performance before the class, we seize our power to act as archives for one another's experience, insisting upon our mutual right to the aesthetic, the reflexive power of performance outside the canon.

The Writing Requirement

In addition to contesting the canon's privilege to authorize some texts for performance and not others by requiring performance itself, Pelias and VanOosting note that the new paradigm calls for "new pedagogical procedures" (219) and a "new critical vocabulary that is sensitive to the interactive and proactive audiences" of contemporary performance (227). I begin my search for new pedagogical procedures by trying to bring students into the search for that critical vocabulary; I ask them to write—a lot. I ask them to produce a series of documents, differently structured and from different positions, at different times in their performance processes. I do this to contest their perception of the performance as an isolated set of moments on stage, to help them recognize those moments as the surfacing, perhaps, of a larger project.

First, I ask them to write a performance prospectus, identifying and exploring a problematic they've felt/discovered in our readings and discussions, in a video we've seen or a script we've read, in another's performance, and/or in their everyday lives. The fundamental task of their performance prospectus is to articulate the changing discursive environment in which the performance will occur.

Second, they produce the text of their performance, as script or protocol of actions. We discuss a variety of textual strategies for them to choose from (Park-Fuller and Pelias): relatively traditional oral interpretation performances of prose fiction or poetry (Gray and VanOosting; Pelias); their own critical intervention on an extant literary text (Allison and Mitchell; Bowman and Kistenberg; Split Britches); ethnographic performance of personal narrative collected by them or anthologized (Langellier; Peterson and Langellier, "Politics"; Stucky); more conspicuously performative, personal narrative/autobiographical performance art (Dillard; Hughes; L. Miller; Miller and Román; Taylor, "On Being"); image-based performance art where speaking is inessential, though welcome (Apple; Hamera; Steinman); and so on.

The final assignment has several parts, and they prepare most of it after the performance, though I encourage them to keep a notebook about their rehearsal experience in order to complete it. First, they must take one moment in the performance that underwent the most change from conception to performance and trace it through several stages of rehearsal (playing, testing, choosing, repeating, and presenting) to show how and why it evolved and what assumptions/insights sponsored the changes (Pelias). Second, I ask them to make a record of the performance in the manner of Jerri Allyn's documentation in "A

Waitress Moment." Allyn records, for each performance, thoughts about the piece's relation to art in general and her everyday life, favorite remarks from audience members, and other heuristic topoi. Third, I ask them to reflect on the round of performances as a whole, to tell us what the performances revealed about queer performance, communication theory, and possibilities for performance they want to explore in their future assignments. They present summaries of these final papers to the class.[3] By stressing these four principles, I show the students my paradigmatic preferences. I show myself under the enduring power of pedagogy. Each decision I make reveals my own past, my connection to a tradition. As I scan that tradition for fissures and gaps, for places it forgets, I show the students my own (loving) resistance to it, side by side with my quest to keep it alive by incorporating new information, much of it learned from them. I am indebted, as we all are, to students whose performances provide citable examples that enliven our talk with subsequent classes. These students extend and refresh, over time, the archive of (queer) performance as we deploy it. But this archive brings with it considerable peril; to understand this more fully, we must recognize (queer) performance as double bind.

Queer Performance as Creative Double Bind

Because I practice performance studies in a communication theory environment, I recognize in the problem of the archive the makings of a creative double bind. As explored by Eric Peterson and Kristin Langellier,

> double bind theory elucidates problems of context and choice in human communication as questions about distinction and classification. . . . This discontinuity is often breached such that double bind—choice between equally valued and equally insufficient messages—exists. ("Creative" 243)

The double bind depends upon inherited, situational bifurcations expressed in paired terms that articulate a contest of the best ways to value and explain a key phenomenon for the community in which the double bind occurs. For example, in performance generally, the pair *technique/spontaneity* represents one such contest, in this case, over the performer's primary responsibility. In queer theory, the pair *essentialism/construction* represents a contest over the primary explanation for queer identity. In aesthetics generally, the pair *form/content* has also sponsored its share of contests over where artists should concentrate their activity and evaluations of that activity. Likewise, the pair *original/derivative* haunts the evaluation of work that must both be recognizable by and transform the archive.

Double binds often seem enduring, even timeless. The contests these pairs represent, particularly as they accumulate in one's working vocabulary, are not dry logic problems. They mark embodied struggles to orient activity in time; to go back into the studio or rehearsal hall; to return to the essay the teacher has asked one to write about the last round of performances; to explain—or at least disclose—one's desire on stage. Deconstruction can show us how these terms rely on one another, but it does not tell us what comes next. Double bind becomes creative when we realize that "one must choose and yet cannot choose one alternative without the other" (Peterson and Langellier, "Creative" 245).

Students of queer performance find themselves in a situation with a set of constraints and traditions, many of which present themselves as paired terms that sponsor double bind. I ask them to represent themselves, "queer," and performance. I ask them to take some of their life on stage and recognize that, while they do so, they are not "out of life," speaking from an extraexistential point. I ask them to welcome the instability of what they will produce in this context and to acknowledge the power of the double bind whereby "in the process of performing, new and unforeseen possibilities for communication are elaborated" (Peterson and Langellier, "Creative" 249). To do these things, they must recognize that, to paraphrase Anthony Wilden, every performance is simultaneously a report about performance and a command to perform.

Queer Performance as Archive

The possibilities for performance studies students to elaborate seem "new" or "unforeseen" in relation to an archive of expectations. Queer performance occurs in the shadow of such an archive. In this section, I describe the creative double bind offered by the archive and its shadow, reinforced by the pedagogical activity of providing models. By establishing a double bind where assumed oppositions are named, elaborating the double bind in the elucidation of its limits, and exceeding the double bind through the transformation of boundaries in performance (Peterson and Langellier, "Creative" 249–50), I pay particular attention to how, especially with queer performance, the provision of models interpellates students.

Establishing the Double Bind

Queer performance occurs in the shadow of an archive because it occurs in the shadow of expectations generated by encounters with models and other discourse. The archive makes and reveals an assemblage of rumors, recollections, reviews, readings, and other responses. Like other *performers*, those who engage in queer performance "assume a responsibility to an audience and to tradition as they understand it" (Dell Hymes, qtd. in Carlson 15). This assumption requires an embodiment—as when I, in response to a police officer, "assume the position"—and an attendant subject position. To take a class in queer performance is to hear the authoritative call to assume its subject positions.

Scholars have transcribed the commands embedded in this call in many ways. In the preface to *Queer Theatre*, Stefan Brecht offers his three-paragraph manifesto of a definition, linking queer theatre to "derisive low comedy and burlesque" while upholding "the aesthetic ideal, aspiring to invest itself . . . with beauty" (9). Brecht claims a lot of ground for queer theatre, as if asking, "Is there something queer at the very heart of performance, in its constituent double binds?" By connecting *pattern* and *transgression,* Ian Lucas identifies queer performance as occupying the very double bind between potentially binary terms the performer must take up together (23).

Indeed, this necessity to take up the terms, not into a final synthesis but into an imperfect gesture, an actual performance, in order to participate in the re-creation of "queer," signals an ethical moment over and against the impulse to concede the futility of queer performance in the face of the instability of the term *queer*. Jill Dolan articulates this tension beautifully:

> If queer means anything at all, especially as an adjective for the-
> atre, it means multiplicity. . . . And that's good. Yet at the same
> time, the insistent anti-hegemonic pose of "queer" can also be a
> ruse for not taking responsibility for the vagaries of a movement,
> a style, a life. I'd like to retain the sense that queerness has no
> leader, no authority, really, but insert my own sense of responsi-
> bility into what I see as my community. (2)

Peterson and Langellier maintain that, by establishing, elaborating, and exceeding double binds, performers "open up the theory and practice" of performance, "as well as its response-ability" ("Creative" 252). By identifying responsibility with an ability (and willingness) to respond to situational constraints, they use this re-creation of the word to mark the productive power of performance, and Dolan's insight links that power to queer performance.

Students, confronted with any of these definitions, would not have achieved any certainty about what queer performance "is." Next, they may demand a review of the archive. At this moment, we encounter that which is most taken for granted in (performance) pedagogy: that students need models, and that the instructor must provide them. Providing a model requires the instructor, as a privileged audience member for the discourse of a genre, to select models, examples, for (the un-modelable) class; the students then repeat this gesture when they select a model among the provided models to write about, emulate, resist, discuss as class leader, or in other ways respond to. These models can only function metonymically and will only reveal the partiality of their selection upon close scrutiny.

But even this linguistic structure, "they choose a model to _____," presumes a distinction between the student and the model—as if the students and the models we choose for them are mutually exclusive, meeting for the first time in our midst. This position errs in three ways. Queer performances,

> are *about* something, *by* someone, and *for* someone. Communicative praxis thus displays a referential moment (about a world of human concerns and social practices), a moment of self-implicature (by a speaker, author, or actor), and a rhetorical moment (directedness to the other). (Schrag viii)

Students and models are, then, always implicated in one another in at least two of the three elements: They share a world of concerns *about* which the model performs something *for* the student, sutured into the model's assumptions and address. Additionally, given their partial responsibility for the model, in the sense that they must "read" it in order to participate in its production as a text, students are also implicated in the third term; the model is always, in an important sense, constructed *by* the student. In this way, students assume responsibility for a tradition—in one point of view—constructed by them, gradually, of available materials, much in the way a snail assumes a shell.

In their nakedness, they may become *en mal d'archive*, "in need of the archive," to such an extent that they seem, if not ill, then at least burdened by a desire to fill the void of their uncertainty. Derrida explains this condition:

> It is to run after the archive, even if there's too much of it, right where something in it anarchives itself. It is to have a compulsive, repetitive, and nostalgic desire for the archive, an irrepressible desire to return to the origin, a homesickness, a nostalgia for the return to the most archaic place of absolute commencement. (91)

I read this description and think of myself as a younger man, "discovering" queer performance and drowning in the library, thinking I could touch bottom. I see it in some of my best students, hungry for examples of everything but their own work.

Elaborating the Double Bind

To elaborate the double bind of the archive, we need to move from a focus on what models and students are as separate entities to a focus on "modeling" and "studying" as functional relations, gestalts we may reverse. I try to help students locate their implication in the queer performances I provide them in their suffering desire for more examples. I try to help them, queer or straight identified, to recognize their response-ability, their ability to perform an aesthetic response that recreates their implication in these texts.

This operation is delicate. Peterson and Langellier tell us that students will often attempt to escape the double bind at this point ("Creative" 250). Students may sacrifice their own re-creative powers by acceding to what they take to be the archive's authority. By retreating from the-model-themselves (in the sense of avoiding their implication in it and their response-ability to it as communicative praxis), these students also, ironically, embrace the-model-not-themselves (in the sense of its assumed distinctiveness). Here, the situation of queer performance becomes particularly dire. I try very hard not to advocate a particular response to a model but to provide students with a surplus of responses. This is the touchiest moment of performance pedagogy and the very kernel of experience I have spun this essay around.

Too often, we enable, or perhaps even demand, these escape attempts by assuming the position of the gatekeeper to a discourse. By doing so, we compel a subjectivity in our students. If, for example, I take the position that I know what queer performance is and describe the term as the name for a praxis that preceded that name, I sponsor the view that academe "discovers" communicative praxes, linguistically intervenes, and then operates in lieu of the original communicators to measure the achievement of "wannabes" by comparing their fidelity to the model. This process is analogous, for example, to the subjectivation made possible by the Catholic Church, which intervened upon a particular communicative praxis, a "crucifixion," named it "the death of god," and then developed procedures to judge those who want to prove themselves faithful by comparing them to, say, saints, as it compels subjectivity.[4]

Acquainting students with their relation to the archive—their stake in it—demonstrates two etymological features identified by Derrida. From the Greek *arkhe*, an archive marks a commencement (inauguration) and a commandment (a juridico-discursive formalization of demands and expectations). When, in a unit or course on queer performance, we show, say, a Tim Miller video, having previously asked students to read the script, they "take up" the piece on their way to an assignment. They put two and two together before we can warn them about the instability of four and *begin* their understanding of queer performance by searching for the desire of the authority.

This structure of the simultaneity of commencement and command mirrors, or perhaps simply is, the structure of the performative, constituting (i.e., "commencing") a subject that it names and, by so doing, introducing that subject into a nomological field of culturally constructed privileges, duties, and constraints that allow, compel, and prohibit—without entirely preventing—certain behaviors (i.e., "commands"). Additionally, like—or perhaps *as*—the performative (the insufficiency of which requires its citational repetition), the archive's commencements and commandments must recur but will always do so insufficiently. Hence, the students who attempt to opt out by responding only to authority (commandment) can never foreclose the next, ever-commencing encounter with the archive. Students cannot discharge their relationship with the archive because, as the collected theorizing about their relationship to "queer," the archive marks a protracted mode of sociality that demands re-creation.

From this protracted sociality stems the ambiguity of the archive, which provides us with identification that authorizes recognizable, valued, competent, social, and conspicuously aesthetic performance. Yet, this same archive may also attempt, in a driven, methodical, relentless way, to colonize the reaches of our creative capacity in the name of its own traditions/knowledges, transforming us thereby into the agents of its reproduction, however much we mutate it as we go, insufficient to the task of that reproduction.

Exceeding the Double Bind

What remains is for the student to exceed the double bind by creating performances that draw "strength from the ambiguity of double bind by moving against over-worn paths" (Peterson and Langellier, "Creative" 250) of their own performance habits unimplicated in response to the model or the performance choices of the model unimplicated in that response. To paraphrase Peterson and Langellier, in queer performance, the student cannot distinguish between the authority of the model and her or his own authority as an aesthetic communicator; the student is carried away, played before the distinction into model and communicator. They become embedded, situated, and played out in such a performance.

By recognizing the power of performance to become the site at which the archive of queer forgets and re-creates itself, students recognize their political responsibility. As Derrida acknowledges, "there is no political power without control of the archive, if not of memory" (4). Performance studies pedagogy cannot promise students absolute control over the archive. It can, however, ask them to acknowledge the political power of aesthetics, of suspicion toward the canonical, of embodiment, and of theoretical exploration; it can ask them to embrace the creative power of the double bind in order to establish, elaborate, and exceed the distinction between themselves and the models they choose from that archive. By doing so, performance studies pedagogy provides them with their share of that power as they face the front between the representable and unrepresentable in order to re-create the possible; making something of (and revealing something in) the worldly, queer performance that will have been.

NOTES

1. See de Certeau (33) for an account of this distinction.
2. When I use the typed expression "(queer) performance," I am elaborating a dynamic that could be attributed to most performance rather than one I view as pertaining specifically to queer performance.
3. This description of assignments represents an approximate model. I am indebted to Kristin Langellier for her recommendation to ask for a reflection on an entire round of performances.
4. See Badiou for an extensive treatment of this example.

WORKS CITED

Allison, John M., Jr., and Karen S. Mitchell. "*Textual Power* and the Pragmatics of Assessing and Evaluating 'Powerful' Performances." *Communication Education* 43 (1994): 205–21.

Allyn, Jerri. "A Waitress Moment." *Reimaging America: The Arts of Social Change.* Ed. Mark O'Brien and Craig Little. Philadelphia: New Society, 1990. 255–63.

Apple, Jacki. "Performance Art Is Dead: Long Live Performance Art." *High Performance* 66 (1994): 54–59.

Auslander, Philip. *Presence and Resistance: Postmodernism and Cultural Politics in Contemporary American Performance.* Ann Arbor: U of Michigan P, 1992.

Badiou, Alain. "On a Finally Objectless Subject." Trans. Bruce Fink. *Who Comes After the Subject?* Ed. Eduardo Cadava, Peter Connor, and Jean-Luc Nancy. New York: Routledge, 1991. 24–32.

Bauman, Richard. "Performance." *Folklore, Cultural Performances, and Popular Entertainments: A Communications-Centered Handbook.* Ed. Richard Bauman. New York: Oxford UP, 1992. 41–49.

Blau, Herbert. *The Audience.* Baltimore: Johns Hopkins UP, 1990.

Bowman, Michael S., and Cindy J. Kistenberg. "'Textual Power' and the Subject of Oral Interpretation: An Alternate Approach to Performing Literature." *Communication Education* 41 (1992): 287–99.

Brecht, Stefan. *Queer Theatre*. 1978. New York: Methuen, 1986.

Butler, Judith. *Bodies That Matter: On the Discursive Limits of "Sex."* New York: Routledge, 1993.

Campbell, Paul. "Communication Aesthetics." *Today's Speech* 19 (1971): 7–18.

Carlson, Marvin. *Performance: A Critical Introduction.* New York: Routledge, 1996.

Chung, Cristy, et al. "In Our Own Way: A Roundtable Discussion." *Asian American Sexualities: Dimensions of the Gay and Lesbian Experience.* Ed. Russel Leong. New York: Routledge, 1996. 91–99.

Corey, Fredrick. "Gay Life/Queer Art." *The Last Sex: Feminism and Outlaw Bodies.* Ed. Arthur Kroker and Marilouise Kroker. New York: St. Martin's. 121–32.

———. "Performing Sexualities in an Irish Pub." *Text and Performance Quarterly* 16 (1996): 146–60.

de Certeau, Michel. *The Practice of Everyday Life.* Trans. Steven Rendall. Berkeley: U of California P, 1984.

Derrida, Jacques. *Archive Fever: A Freudian Impression.* Trans. Eric Prenowitz. Chicago: U of Chicago P, 1996.

Dillard, Scott. *"Breathing Darrell:* Solo Performance as a Contribution to a Useful Queer Mythology." *Text and Performance Quarterly* 20 (2000): 74–83.

Dolan, Jill. "Building a Theatrical Vernacular: Responsibility, Community, Ambivalence, and Queer Theatre." *Modern Drama* 39 (1996): 1–15.

Fuoss, Kirk. "A Portrait of the Adolescent as a Young Gay: The Politics of Male Homosexuality in Young Adult Fiction." *Queer Words, Queer Images: Communication and the Construction of Homosexuality.* Ed. Jeffrey Ringer. New York: New York UP, 1994. 159–74.

Gingrich-Philbrook, Craig. "'Good Vibration' or Domination? Stylized Repetition in Mythopoetic Performance of Masculinity." *Text and Performance Quarterly* 14 (1994): 21–45.

Gray, Paul H., and James VanOosting. *Performance in Life and Literature.* Boston: Allyn, 1996.

Hamera, Judith. "Postmodern Performance, Postmodern Criticism." *Literature in Performance* 7.1 (1986): 13–20.

Hughes, Holly. *Clit Notes: A Sapphic Sampler.* New York: Grove, 1996.

Hughes, Holly, and David Román, eds. *O Solo Homo: The New Queer Performance.* New York: Grove, 1998.

Johnson, Patrick. "SNAP! Culture: A Different Kind of 'Reading.'" *Text and Performance Quarterly* 15 (1995): 122–42.

Langellier, Kristin. "Personal Narratives: Perspectives on Theory and Research." *Text and Performance Quarterly* 9 (1989): 243–76.

Lucas, Ian. *Impertinent Decorum: Gay Therical Manoeuvres.* London: Cassell, 1994.

Miller, Lynn C. "'Polymorphous Perversity' in Women's Performance Art:
The Case of Holly Hughes." *Text and Performance Quarterly* 15 (1995):
44–59.

Miller, Tim. *My Queer Body. Sharing the Delirium: Second Generation AIDS Plays
and Performances.* Ed. Therese Jones. Portsmouth: Heinemann, 1994.
309–36.

Miller, Tim, and David Román. "Preaching to the Converted." *Theatre Journal*
47 (1995): 169–88.

Muñoz, José Esteban. "Ephemera as Evidence: Introductory Notes to Queer
Acts." *Women and Performance* 16 (1996): 5–16.

Owens, Craig. "The Discourse of Others: Feminists and Postmodernism."
The Anti-Aesthetic: Essays on Postmodern Culture. Ed. Hal Foster. Port
Townsend: Bay, 1983. 57–82.

Park-Fuller, Linda M., and Ronald J. Pelias. "Charting Alternative Performance and Evaluative Practices." *Communication Education* 44 (1995):
126–39.

Pelias, Ronald J. *Performance Studies: The Interpretation of Aesthetic Texts.* New
York: St. Martin's, 1992.

Pelias, Ronald. J., and James VanOosting. "A Paradigm for Performance Studies." *Quarterly Journal of Speech* 73 (1987): 219–31.

Peterson, Eric, and Kristin Langellier. "Creative Double Bind in Oral Interpretation." *Western Journal of Speech Communication* 46 (1982): 242–52.

———. "The Politics of Personal Narrative Methodology." *Text and Performance Quarterly* 17 (1997): 135–52.

Phelan, Peggy. "Tim Miller's *My Queer Body:* An Anatomy in Six Sections."
Theater 24.2 (1993): 30–34.

Pomo Afro Homos. *Dark Fruit. Staging Gay Lives: An Anthology of Contemporary
Gay Theater.* Ed. John M. Clum. Boulder: Westview, 1996. 319–43.

Schechner, Richard. *Between Theater and Anthropology.* Philadelphia: U of
Pennsylvania P, 1985.

Schrag, Calvin O. *Communicative Praxis and the Space of Subjectivity.* Bloomington: Indiana UP, 1986.

Sedgwick, Eve Kosofsky. *Epistemology of the Closet.* Berkeley: U of California P,
1990.

Solomon, Alissa. "The Wow Cafe." *A Sourcebook of Feminist Theatre and Performance.* Ed. Carol Martin. New York: Routledge, 1996. 42–51.

Split Britches. *Split Britches: Lesbian Practice/Feminist Performance.* Ed. Sue-
Ellen Case. New York: Routledge, 1996.

Steinman, Louise. *The Knowing Body: Elements of Contemporary Performance
and Dance.* Boston: Shambhala, 1986.

Stucky, Nathan. "Performing Oral History: Storytelling and Pedagogy." *Communication Education* 44.1 (1995): 1–14.

Taylor, Jacqueline. "Is There a Lesbian in This Text? Sarton, Performance, and Multicultural Pedagogy." *Text and Performance Quarterly* 15 (1995): 282–300.

———. "On Being an Exemplary Lesbian: My Life as a Role Model." *Text and Performance Quarterly* 20 (2000): 58–73.

Wilden, Anthony. *System and Structure: Essays in Communication and Exchange.* 2nd ed. London: Tavistock, 1980.

Performance Theory in an Anthropology Program

5
William O.
Beeman

If man is a sapient animal, a toolmaking animal, a self-making animal, a symbol-using animal, he is, no less, a performing animal, *Homo performans*, not in the sense, perhaps that a circus animal may be a performing animal, but in the sense that a man is a self-performing animal—his performances are, in a way, reflexive, in performing he reveals himself to himself.

This can be in two ways: the actor may come to know himself better through acting or enactment; or one set of human beings may come to know themselves better through observing and/or participating in performances generated and presented by another set of human beings.

—VICTOR TURNER, *The Anthropology of Performance*

Teaching performance theory in an anthropology program requires relating the act and practice of performance to the broad questions posed by the field of anthropology. In the most general sense, these questions lead to a comparative analysis of human similarities and differences in all times and over all geographical locations. Such an analysis also involves the four theoretical subfields of anthropology: archaeology, biological anthropology, linguistic anthropology, and sociocultural anthropology.

With this broad set of concerns in mind, in my teaching I help bring students to an understanding of performance as an inherently human activity. It is presented as having origins in prehistoric behavior and having functional value in the evolution of human cognitive functions. Performance is seen as an essential aspect of human communicative capacity that cannot be completely understood without a full appreciation of the roles of language and other semiotic behavior in human life. In cultural terms, performance is seen as pervading virtually all institutions of public expressive behavior.

In general, there are four pedagogical goals in my instruction of performance theory. First, I want to help students understand the basic human questions that the investigation of performance raises. Second, I want to provide them with observational and analytic skills that will help them to conduct ethnographic observation of performance activity. Third, I want them to be able to analyze the activities that they observe and read about in terms of performance-specific criteria. Finally, I want to help them to understand the "big picture"—the meaning of performance activity for broad patterns of human life, including the ways that performance transforms and is transformed by everyday life. My discussion below is organized to address these pedagogical goals.

Basic Human Questions

86
William O.
Beeman
Anthropological approaches to performance go beyond description. I try to help students to begin to think in terms of explanation. Questions such as the following are posed early in the course and direct much of the reading, discussion, and research undertaken by students.

- Why are activities involving display and evaluation/appreciation so essential and endemic to the human condition?
- Why do such activities convey meaning in such a powerful fashion?
- What special tools for behavior and communication are found in performance mode, and what do they do?

Central to helping students develop their understanding is to show them how performance is not so much a cultural institution as a set of clear accomplishments. In particular, successful performance represents the accomplishment of cultural representation resulting in transformations in society. These transformations can be very small or cataclysmic, but no one is left unaffected by performance behavior.

I start with some conventional observations about "performance" and move to a gradual discussion of "performative behavior," which I consider to be a separate concept and the main subject of instruction. My characterization of the concept of performance is influenced by the work of Richard Schechner.

First, I begin with a discussion of performance as mimetic behavior (in the conventional Aristotelian sense) and how it is imitative of an "action." "Tragedy is the imitation of an action that is serious, complete and of a certain magnitude" (Aristotle, qtd. in Schechner 37).

Second, performance is presented as "cooked" in the Lévi-Straussian sense, meaning that it is action that is transformed through culture into a conventionally understandable symbolic product. Helping students come to a clear understanding of this aspect of performance brings them to an understanding of the difficulty anthropologists face in making direct perceptions of reality. "Making art is the process of transforming raw experience into palatable forms. This transformation is a mimesis, a representation" (Schechner 38).

Third, I show performance as one of the most basic ways to study human behavior and that regularities in performance derive from human interaction. This observation has been made by Clifford Geertz and many others. It has a long pedigree dating back to Durkheim and Simmel.

Fourth, I aim to help students see performance behavior as socially cocreated, with continual evaluative feedback. They are brought to realize that evaluation of auditors/spectators/consumers (the audience) is crucial for the continuance of the communication.

Fifth, students are shown that performance is intentional. It aims to be transformational, or "effective" (Beeman, *Language* 6–10 and "An-thropology" 379). It has the qualities of the speech act as treated by Austin, Searle, Halliday, and others, in that, if successful, it does cul-tural work in the world. It strives to affect human affairs, leaving the individuals involved in the performative act in a changed state. This approach is in contrast to many anthropological approaches to culture that view cultural products as passive derivatives of the cultural dy-namics of a given society.

Sixth, I help students to see that the effects of performance only take place in a rich context, taking account of all environmental fac-tors. Therefore, performance is always "emergent." "The emergent quality of performance resides in the interplay between communica-tive resources, individual competence, and the goals of the partici-pants, within the context of particular situations" (Bauman 38).

Finally, students are shown that there is always an element of skill in performance, whether it be in speaking, narration, acting, song, dance, or the synthetic structures such as the numerous music-theatre forms throughout the world. This reflects the problem on the part of all humans engaging in performative behavior of determining what can best convey the complexity of the particular human condition they wish to represent in "concrete" representative form. For this reason, performance behavior can always be judged as relatively successful or unsuccessful, depending on the particular individual and the particu-lar event. Performance can fail through lack of skill on the part of the performer, lack of receptivity on the part of an "audience," or because some unforeseen event intervenes. Of course, the play fails when the actors are ineffective at conveying the text or their characters, but not all depends on the personal skills of the performer. The political speech fails when the electricity in the town is knocked out by a storm. The rock concert fails when the audience gets into a brawl.

In summary, by helping students to understand performance be-havior, I hope to bring them to focus on a display, a mimetic represen-tation of views of human interaction, human situations, human condi-tions, and human structurings.

The Ethnography of Performance:
Discovering Objects and Settings

The study of anthropology involves experiential learning. Research by professionals is most commonly carried out through the practice of participant-observation in an ethnographic field setting. It is most ef-fective to give students some experience of this kind of experiential learning. Therefore, my teaching of performance theory balances the-oretical material with practical experience in both participating in, and observing the process of, performing.

My classes typically consist of students from the performing arts who have no experience in social science research and students from the social sciences and humanities who have little or no performing experience. It is a challenge to bring these students into dialogue with each other. This is partly accomplished through reading and seminar discussion of a wide variety of theoretical works in performance theory. To acquaint everyone with the process of ethnographic participant-observation, I devise a series of short field exercises. These consist of observing and reporting mundane everyday experiences that are nevertheless highly performative, such as the eating of a meal in the company of others or carrying out greeting rituals. Students proceed from this introduction to the principal exercises for the course.

The "participant" aspect of instruction is accomplished by having everyone perform. The course finishes with a "cabaret" in which every member must perform for five minutes. This aspect of instruction also involves observation. Every student must observe his or her own preparation for the cabaret and the preparation of one other class member (or group of class members). These observations are written in performance diaries that students maintain throughout the course and turn in at the end of the course. In addition, each student prepares a research paper for the course centering on the observation of a performance event seen throughout its preparation, incorporating the theoretical materials read for the course. This research paper must go beyond mere description and attempt to answer an important larger question about the functioning of the performance event in a larger sociocultural framework.

In the past, student research for the course has consisted of studies of theatrical presentations, dance troupes, political speeches, and musical events, as well as performative aspects of everyday life. One of the most interesting papers in recent years was a study of a high school student preparing for her high school prom, studied as a performative event. The researcher went shopping with the student, interviewed her family, kept a record of her interactions with her date and her friends, and attended the prom. Another paper investigated my own classroom teaching style—a very enlightening study for me. Still another was an early study of the "mosh pit"[1] and the performative dimensions of being an audience member at rock concerts.

In general, the broad approach taken in this class has given it applicability and breadth beyond the usual clientele for performance studies courses. It is a course that students regularly seek out as part of their graduate and advanced undergraduate training. At this time, when performance studies is just gaining a foothold in the university curriculum, I find this broad approach not only pedagogically satisfying but also politically useful. Paradoxically, its construction is itself a conscious performance strategy.

The schema outlined above provides a wide palate for the investigation of performance behavior. Some of the more common forms in human life that students study include:

- Face-to-face interaction
- Verbal play
- Rhetoric and public use of speech
- Storytelling and allied arts
- Acting/theatrical performance

Another group of activities could be labeled semiperformative. Such activities involve the use of performance behavior, and they require the presence of an "audience" to witness their execution, but the activity is not directly communicative or is not directly affected by positive or negative evaluation. These include:

- Spectator sports
- Didactic communication
- Rehearsal for performance
- Ceremony and ritual

Finally, we can contrast the above categories of activity with human endeavors that embody few, or minimal, performative skills. Although they are culturally patterned, these are largely activities that have minimal communicative or cultural transformational intent and do not require observers for their execution. These events can quickly turn into performative events, if the individuals engaging in them want to convey a sense of the activity to others. These include:

- Unobserved work activities
- Solitary activities, such as reading, eating in private, hiking alone, driving a car

Observing Performance Skills and Their Development

Seeing how performers learn performance skills is an essential aspect of learning to study performance. Individuals who want to achieve success in performance behavior need to recognize their own abilities—knowing what they are good at and have an easy facility for. Skills can always be developed. The process of honing any performance skill involves three dimensions:

Analytic. Performers must assess the task and what they need to accomplish to achieve successful representation.
Technical. Performers must develop the necessary motor skills to actually carry out the performative activity.
Interpretive. Performers must develop a method of making the performative activity uniquely their own—an embodiment of their own skill.

To these ends, the rehearsal process is crucial. Schechner's description of performance as "twice behaved" is an essential statement of the fact that all performative activity is repeated activity.

Strategies of performance are varied, but the following skills are commonly sought to make performance more effective.

> *Timing.* The ability to display symbolic elements precisely at a time when they will most effectively convey an intended meaning.
>
> *Charisma.* The ability to engage and hold the attention of an audience. This can be a shared function, as in a conversation in which individuals take turns at narration.
>
> *Focus and concentration.* The ability to concentrate fully on the task of accomplishing a representation. This provides engagement for individuals being affected by the performance.
>
> *Freshness and spontaneity.* The ability to display symbolic materials in novel and unexpected ways. This is a means of capturing the attention of an audience.

Performers have a set of universal difficulties that hamper the effectiveness of their performance. Among these are:

> *Pushing.* Showing obvious effort in the representation of symbolic materials can be read by others and distracts them from seeing the message of the performance.
>
> *Losing concentration.* When the performer is not totally engaged with the task of performing, this also provides a distraction for the audience.
>
> *Underpreparation.* Lack of adequate preparation and rehearsal makes it impossible to present material in a smooth and spontaneous way.
>
> *Overpreparation.* Too much rehearsal or preparation dehumanizes the performance and makes it less believable.
>
> *Miscalculation of context.* The performer may misread the audience and present something that they already know and will be bored with or that is so esoteric that they cannot comprehend it.

Other possibilities include presenting offensive material or material that is insulting to persons of importance.

Every performer must perfect a certain basic set of skills. The techniques used to implement these skills vary from society to society and place to place, but the skills are human abilities. These skills vary depending on the specific performative action being undertaken. Among them are:

> *The ability to communicate clearly.* Skilled performative behavior, depending on the genre and type of performance, involves the use of a wide range of communicative tools. Among them are clean, purposeful

actions, words, physical objects in the world, music, and symbolic movement.

The ability to focus other people's attention. This is known as stage presence. Like Coleridge's ancient mariner and stage magicians, persons adept at performance skills can get people to pay attention to what they want them to see.

The ability to contextualize actions and words by "setting up" the performance for participants and observers. The process of using the elements of communication to constrain and define the contexts for one's own interpretation is a basic performative skill. This can be done verbally (storytelling) or through "production" techniques using costumes, sets, props, lighting, and other players.

The ability to enter "flow." The psychologist Mihalyi Csikszentmihalyi has worked for some years studying the concept of "flow," the experience of loss of sense of the physical body or of conscious control of one's own actions when one becomes totally engaged in a given activity.

The ability to enter into framed behavior. The concept of the cognitive "frame" in human behavior is now well established. Nevertheless, it is important to mention it here. Framing is a cognitive contextualization device whereby all rules for behavior, symbols, and their interpretation are bounded by a particular activity with its own overall structure. Play is a quintessential example of framed behavior. Individuals engaged in play suspend the rules of everyday life when play is deemed to have begun. They then regulate their behavior according to a set of rules that operate only as long as the play frame is in force.

The ability to work in ensemble with other performers. The ability to perform in consort with others is an ability that is essential to any performative activity. In face-to-face interaction, it must be possible to maintain contact with others and to bring an interaction through its various stages of development, from opening to closing. In ritual, it is necessary to be able to coordinate activities with others so that the ritual process can continue from beginning to end in an uninterrupted stream. In stage performance, it is essential for performers to be totally engaged with other performers and with the performing space or the performance will fail.

The ability to work in ensemble with an audience. This latter point is most subtle. Most often we think of performer-audience interaction as if it were action and reaction, whereas it is in reality an ensemble event with no clear boundaries demarcating the originator of the stimulus from the performance product.

The ability to acquire and execute set performance routines. With some inspection, the range of these routines can be seen to be quite extensive. Some examples include:

- a stage play
- a stand-up comedy monologue
- a night-club torch song
- a political stump speech
- a sales pitch
- a standard marital argument
- a pick-up line in a bar

Students come to see the development of these basic skill sets by working on a specific performance for presentation to the class at the end of a semester, keeping a performance diary, observing another person preparing his or her own performance, and keeping a careful diary of what the other person is doing. These "field notes" are preparatory to the final term paper in the course, in which students use a large repertoire of observational performance skills to trace the course, and analyze the dynamics, of a particular performance.

Analyzing Performance

The observational exercises, prepared performances, and term papers used in course work are designed to lead students to see that performance is structured and regular—indeed, that it must be to achieve any effect. Students are often surprised to see that even a simple greeting routine has structure, or on a more complex level, that a television drama is usually organized into a simple three-act form. Only by observing raw data themselves can students fully appreciate the highly organized nature of any performance form.

Once they are able to see the overall pattern of any given performance form, students are then able to see how the individual performative elements are arranged within the pattern to provide overall effectiveness for the form. A simple example is the pattern of volume contrast in a good public speech. When students have a grasp of the overall structure of the speech, they can then see how elements such as volume serve performatively to make the message of the speech effective.

Once they are able to see the organized nature of performance, students find it particularly interesting to discuss the reasons why performance is positively or negatively valued. I help students to see that in order for performance activity to be positively valued, it must accomplish a successful representation of symbolic reality. It must also fulfill a series of additional criteria. It must be spontaneous, true, skillful, and effective.

Seeing a successful performative representation of symbolic reality requires an observer to be able to see how that performance correctly embodies a culturally recognizable form and displays it so that it can be recognized and reacted to by observers. The number and range of culturally recognizable forms are infinite and ever expanding, since members of a society can continually create new ones, provided they can constrain events in such a way that these new forms become recognizable. Among possible forms that performers can represent are emotional states (anger, sincerity), values (human rights, basic decency, etiquette, pity, kindness), culturally recognizable arguments (contradiction, congruity, paradox, authority, common knowledge, scientific method), cultural archetypes (martyr, hero), actual or legendary figures (Christ, Rama, Mohammed).

Usually, the repertoire for representation is drawn from a stock of cultural material that is readily accessible to members of the public. The performer must then invoke the correct form, draw attention to that which is to be represented, and attempt the representation.

The requirement that the representation be spontaneous refers to the need for evaluators to see that the representation is being presented directly, without the need to account for the mediation of the act of presentation. This is difficult to achieve, but when performance falls short of spontaneity, it is less effective, because it is seen as less "pure." Sincerity and truth in performance are related to the relative perception of mediation. Negatively valued performance is, by contrast, nonfluid or stilted, self-conscious, inept or unskillful, and therefore ineffective.

The audience shows positive evaluation by symbolically encouraging continuance of the performance, requesting repetition of the performance, and rewarding the performer. It shows negative evaluation by symbolically discouraging the continuance of the performance through withdrawal of attention, through lack of enthusiasm, through overt disapproval, by failing to request repetition of the performance, and by failing to reward (or by actually punishing) the performer. The performer learns to recognize the symbols of positive and negative evaluation.

In the research exercises carried out in class, students come to see how performance can be successful or unsuccessful even in very small and limited situations, such as in greetings or in retail interactions, using these criteria. This helps them to be able to evaluate more complex forms of performance and to see the skills that are needed in any performative situation.

Understanding the Big Picture

Merely understanding how a particular performance works is not adequate for the anthropological study of performance. Students must eventually be directed to the large human questions mentioned at the beginning of this discussion that the study of performance can answer.

In helping students develop a "big picture" approach to performance, the work of Victor Turner is very helpful. His interest in performance centers on concerns with universal institutions. His work therefore plays a large role in my performance theory courses. Turner helps students to unify in their minds the institutions of drama, ritual, and liminal behavior. Additionally, Turner's work demonstrates connections with the universal processes of social dramas, ritual processes, and the social construction of meaning.

Regarding the ways in which societies construct meaning in life, Turner writes:

> any society which hopes to be imperishable must whittle out for itself a piece of space and a while of time, in which it can look honestly at itself . . . the supreme honesty of the creative artist who, in his presentations on the stage, in the book, on canvas, in marble, in music, or in towers and houses, reserves to himself the privilege of seeing straight what all cultures build crooked. (*Anthropology* 122)

Turner's concerns reflect those of Milton Singer, whose *When a Great Tradition Modernizes* is often cited as the starting point for most anthropological studies of performance phenomena. Indeed, Singer identified the object of study as "cultural performances." They included what:

> we in the west usually call by that name—for example, plays, concerts, and lectures. But they include also prayers, ritual readings and recitations, rites and ceremonies, festivals and all those things which we usually classify under religion and ritual rather than with the cultural and artistic. (71)

Cultural performances are composed of "cultural media" consisting of "modes of communication" that include not only spoken language but also nonlinguistic media such as song, dance, acting (and acting out), graphic arts, and plastic arts. All of these phenomena combine and contribute to creating an event for public expression and display that accomplishes representation in everyday life.

Performative events have other qualities that relate to their basically social nature. First, they are not so much reflective as reflexive[2]—they have concrete effects on the societies in which they occur. Some of the principal functions they serve are cultural prophylaxis, cultural regeneration, and cultural reinforcement.

There is also the point, as noted by Turner, that "mainstream society generates its opposite" (*Anthropology* 24). That opposite picture is then presented in performance frames to indicate both the possibility of change and the importance of the basic structure of society.

Performance is subjunctive. Turner has used the notion of *liminality* extensively in his discussions of ritual and performance. Liminal (from *limen*, Latin for "threshold") states are states of cultural functioning in which normal social order is suspended or reversed. Liminal states dissolve all factual and commonsense systems into their components and "play" with them in ways never found in nature or in custom, at least at the level of direct perception (*Anthropology* 25).

Most of my students come to the study of performance because they are specifically interested in drama and theater. Drama, as my students conventionally understand it, is seen as a set of literary compositions that tell a story, usually of human conflict, by means of dialogue and action performed by actors and presented to an audience. The anthropological perspective helps them see that the nature and degree of involvement and participation of audience and performer, the kinds of themes presented in drama, and the range of events in which drama occurs vary widely from culture to culture. Helping students to expand their definition and see drama in a larger cultural context is a challenge, particularly because so many of them are involved in dramatic training and performance and tend to see their narrower understanding of drama as an all-encompassing environment.

In having students study performance ethnographically, I hope to help them realize that drama can be an effective way to scrutinize the quotidian world. Here, too, Turner's work is an essential element through his analysis of *social drama*—public events that have a ritual or semiritual character and that involve performative actions. These social dramas are often seen as political in nature. They are outlined extensively in Turner's publications, particularly *Dramas, Fields, and Metaphors*, and *The Anthropology of Performance*.

Seeing What Performance Can Do

The bottom line for my instruction is to bring students to the realization that performance is the means—perhaps the principal means—through which people come to understand their world, reinforce their view of it, and transform it on both the small scale and the large scale. It can be employed for conservative and for revolutionary uses. As a conservative force, it reinforces the truth of the world and enacts and verifies social order. It does this by example, as in dramatic presentations showing the workings of good and evil as culturally defined. It also does it by contrast, showing the world as it looks in an inverted state through paradox, contradiction, comedy, and confrontation.

As a transformational force, performance behavior has the power to restructure social order through the persuasive power of rhetoric and through the power of redefinition of both audience and context. It has the power to transform social structure in several ways. First and foremost, performance skills can be used to redefine the role of the performer himself or herself. Richard Bauman, commenting on the autobiography of Dick Gregory, notes that "through performance, Gregory is able to take control of the situation creating a social structure with himself at the center" (44).

Studies of performance skills are, for general anthropological understanding of human societies, extremely valuable. Performance is generally highly valued in society. Successful performers are usually rewarded. One needs only look at the role of successful examples (e.g., former president Ronald Reagan, West African praise singers, rock and opera stars, and shamans and healers of all cultures) to see this dynamic at work. Performers also have the power to sway public opinion regarding other individuals. Invective, praise, public recognition, and vilification are important tools for reordering the social universe. When students see this clearly, their ability to analyze and understand ongoing social and political events in their own lives becomes greatly enhanced.

What Students Gain

An anthropological approach to teaching performance with a serious ethnographic component is ideal for a broad constituency of students. Students from the performing arts regularly come to see the interconnection of performance activity with "real life," and students from the social sciences and humanities gain an appreciation of the power of performance to transform society and culture.

One of the great lessons most students learn is a personal one: They come to terms with their own performance abilities in a powerful way. Students in the performing arts are able to examine what they do as performers in ways that help them become more effective. Students with little performance experience are surprised at what they can do themselves and at how sharp their observational skills become with regard to other performers and performances.

The lesson is particularly effective. Much of anthropology has taken the lead presented in literary studies and has treated culture as a "text" to be read and analyzed. The study of performance in human life shows that culture is dynamic and mutable and that much of the unexpected changes that take place in cultural life are the result of effective performative activity on the part of strong members of the society. In this way, the study of performance not only helps students, it helps strengthen a view of culture in which individuals have an essential role.

NOTES

1. This term is already fading from consciousness, so I note here for readers in the future that the *mosh pit* is a closely packed group of audience

members at a rock concert who support with their hands other fans who, in the heat of the concert, throw themselves off the stage into the crowd below as part of the activity of attending the concert.

2. This formulation is taken from Turner, who credits it as follows: "As Barbara Babcock has written: 'many cultural forms are not so much reflective as reflexive'" (*Anthropology* 24).

WORKS CITED

Bauman, Richard. *Verbal Art as Performance.* Rowley: Newbury, 1977.

Beeman, William O. "The Anthropology of Theater and Spectacle." *Annual Review of Anthropology* 22 (1993): 369–93.

———. *Language, Status, and Power in Iran.* Bloomington: Indiana UP, 1986.

Csikszentmihalyi, Mihalyi. *Beyond Boredom and Anxiety: The Experience of Play in Work and Games.* San Francisco: Jossey, 1975.

Schechner, Richard. *Performance Theory:* New York: Routledge, 1988.

Singer, Milton. *When a Great Tradition Modernizes.* New York: Praeger, 1972.

Turner, Victor. *The Anthropology of Performance.* New York: PAJ, 1986.

———. *Dramas, Fields, and Metaphors.* Ithaca: Cornell UP, 1974.

The Poetics and Politics of Practice

Experience, Embodiment, and the

Engagement of Scholarship

6

Michelle
Kisliuk

We are in the midst of a postcolonial shift, a developing zeitgeist, not only in arts and scholarship but in the politics of everyday life. What I want to get at in this essay is how that shift bears on what any of us do as scholars and artists, as teachers and everyday actors.

Using my own work as an example, I begin by asking why researchers such as myself can no longer tell you, for instance, about BaAka "pygmy" performance in Centrafrique without thoroughly embedding that telling in my years of research with *particular* BaAka, incorporating in my telling a particularization of that experience. This challenge—the evocation of experience and a critique of that evocation—leads me to consider strategies for bridging contexts of research and teaching and questioning boundaries between "here" and "there," "home" and "the field."

Field-workers who are deeply involved in the life of research (what I call *fieldlife*) are often aware of an implied split between their scholarly work—no matter how humanistic and emotive—and the life they inhabit in the field. Our very being melds with people among whom we learn, and with such involvement comes mutual responsibility and common goals, as well as crises and conflicts. But because of the implied split between life experience and the academy, we must construct scholarly niches and research contexts that fully integrate fieldlife, teaching, and writing. Music and dance research provide especially fertile ground for such efforts, because sounding and moving human bodies in the "field" as well as at "work" are the very sites of both our research and our teaching. Efforts to meld fieldlife and work life tend to create the conditions for activism, where—whether implicitly or explicitly—boundaries between art, scholarship, politics, and daily life are by necessity blurred.

To explore ways in which I've attempted to meld fieldlife and work life, I begin by describing incidents illustrating the world of my own performance research in the Central African Republic (Centrafrique). Weaving together apparently distant worlds, I also evoke examples of my experiences teaching and writing in the United States. These illustrations lead to some broader theorizing about performance processes, activist pedagogy, and the reconfiguration of socioesthetic experience.

What Is Philosophy For?

In the summer of 1992, one year after I'd received my doctorate in performance studies from New York University, I returned to southwestern Centrafrique, the location of my field research since 1986. This was one of many almost annual visits to this region of the equatorial rain forest.

I was passing through Bagandou village with my best friend and field colleague, Justin Mongosso (now my husband), who is a native farmer of Bagandou. We were preparing to leave the next morning on a trek of several days to visit the BaAka ("pygmies") I had lived with during my initial two years of field research. We needed to spend the night in the village center, so that early the next morning we could head south along the trail. Justin was especially keen on catching up with community contacts, and that dark evening he went to pay respects at a nearby funeral commemoration for a distant relative. Justin took with him a copy of my dissertation I had brought to show friends and field colleagues ("Confronting").

Upon his return from the funeral, Justin and I were chatting in the lantern light, when suddenly he asked me, "What is philosophy for?" [A quoi se sert la philosophie?] Apparently, his relatives and fellow villagers had inquired about my dissertation and had read on the front page "in partial fulfillment of the requirements for the degree of Doctor of Philosophy." I was surprised by his question—after all, he had been an integral part of my research process, and I was confident that he understood my work. I responded at first by clarifying that *doctor of philosophy* is simply a generic term for a doctoral degree. But his question sparked concern in me that people might be wondering whether my work had any practical purpose in a world where work means helping to feed, shelter, heal, and educate people. So, I added that philosophy is, generally speaking, about understanding better our lives and the world we live in so that we can live more consciously in this world. In that sense, in fact, my performance studies degree was sort of in philosophy. Justin seemed satisfied with that answer, but I was left with a redoubled awareness of a question that is always with me: What should be the concrete effects and applications of my research?

A Fieldlife Body

Three years later, in 1995, I visited Centrafrique for the last time before completing the book manuscript based on my research *(Seize)*. This description, excerpted from that manuscript, is here meant to convey

BaAka women dancing Njengi (1995). The spirit mask is in the center. *Photo by Michelle Kisliuk.*

something of how my fieldlife body—resonating on several levels—was and is placed among other bodies. My narrative voice is the vector in this case, literally melding "here" and "there" in the telling.

> After a relaxing stay at Justin's farm, the two of us headed through the forest toward his mother's caterpillar-season camp, located on a path I had never taken. . . . As we hiked, there was a constant pittering of tiny caterpillar droppings falling from high in the trees—along with an occasional caterpillar or two, which we gathered in leaf packets for an eventual meal. It was the height of the rainy season, and we were periodically soaked to the skin along the way. After two nights on the trail we reached the caterpillar camp where Justin's maternal relatives were gathered for the abundant season. They fed us amply with manioc, meat and sautéed caterpillars.
>
> The next day while chatting with local BaAka, we learned that there would be an eboka (a dance) that very night—barring rain—and that the dance would be Njengi. This revived spirit dance had apparently caught on with a furor in this area. It had been three years since I'd seen Njengi, and I had never seen the Njengi spirit mask, so I was particularly excited. That afternoon we hiked for forty-five minutes, and soon we could hear the singing and drumming echo through the forest from a distance. As we entered the host camp, the first thing I noticed was the spinning raffia mask. A line of women, leaf skirts bobbing, taunted Njengi by jumping

toward the twirling raffia, playfully advancing. Njengi suddenly dropped to the ground, completely still, then just as suddenly was up and twirling again. . . .

As darkness fell the singing intensified with yodeling, and I decided to join the dancing. The women and girls were happily surprised as I fell into line with the step-twisting circle. The singing intensified, and I sang with the woman next to me, imitating her part. Many BaAka in this region did not know me, since my research had been in a different area, so during a brief break in the dancing I explained that I had lived with a neighboring group for several years. They recognized me then as Masoï (my BaAka name), the white woman they'd heard about who had learned BaAka dances. I wanted to be sure they knew that my interest in joining them was not trivial, and added, probably too eagerly, that I'd been initiated into the women's dance, Elamba. The woman beside me said something earnestly that I did not at first understand. I was surprised to realize later [after listening to the tape-recorded conversation] that she had asked me to please not touch her with any Elamba ancestral sorcery (a power I now wielded as an Elamba initiate). . . .

In the morning Justin and I headed back on the trail toward the farm, me traipsing behind him as we began our two-day trek. Thunder boomed in the distance, hounding us for hours but not catching us yet. . . . Later the thunder was accompanied by wind and lightning, which reminded me of the day before when I had taken a flash photo during the Njengi dance; BaAka girls had ducked and plugged their ears expecting thunder to follow the flash. Fully battered by rain, we trudged into the village, a soggy and limping sight for villagers dry under their awnings. There we found shelter before moving on.

Those are the last words of my ethnography, meant not to conclude but to continue beyond the text, back into life.

A Melding of Worlds:
BaAka Dances in Santa Barbara and Charlottesville

I juxtapose that scene by moving to a scene in May 1995: I had been leading a drum and dance ensemble at the University of California at Santa Barbara (UCSB), and after one quarter, we had established a strong ensemble. At the end of that year, the UCSB African Drum and Dance Ensemble was invited by the combined choirs at California Polytechnic, San Luis Obispo, to perform with them during a concert of "African and African American Music." I decided to teach these choral students to perform some BaAka music and dance; this was my first opportunity to teach in depth some of the songs I had learned in Centrafrique.

Two of my own students from Santa Barbara, Neysa and Megan—outstanding dancers in the group—approached me a few weeks before the show and asked to be initiated into Elamba. Only women and girls who have been inducted into Elamba can perform this particular dance. The induction process involves tiny razor cuts made at strategic points in the body (back of the neck, back of hips, sides of knees, and feet). Into the tiny cuts is rubbed a mixture of ash from special trees, palm oil, and palm salt. (I still had some of this mixture saved from my last visit to Africa; the BaAka women who had taught me expected that I would in turn induct my own students.) At that moment there was an undeniable melding of worlds, literally at the site of the bodies of my students—and with this palpable reality came a sudden fear on my part of the risk and responsibility of importing this tradition, the same feeling that returned when in 1999 I inducted into Elamba six students from the University of Virginia. This feeling echoes the moment when the BaAka woman asked me to please not put a curse on her; I had a sudden realization that my actions could have serious consequences, perhaps beyond my ken, and that I had better be fully aware of the implications of my actions. But in what sense are the dances I teach in America still the "same" dances as those I had learned in Africa? What can or cannot change in order for a practice to retain its identity? Answers to these questions are always contingent, of course, and I take up this issue again later.

Firsthand, embodied experience that students in the United States can have with BaAka music and dance facilitates an awareness of both macro and micro politics of "here" and "there" that resonates both politically and aesthetically. My current teaching and performing with students at the University of Virginia melds worlds and simultaneously opens new, immediate possibilities for meaning, replete with complex problems. Student Kelly Gross of the University of Virginia (UVA) ensemble writes about learning to sing intricate BaAka songs:

> I smile as I sing. . . . The polyphonic texture is so wonderfully lush and thick, that sometimes I can hardly differentiate the various parts we have learned. Many of us are creating new melodies and complementing the overall texture with improvised melodies and yodels. The themes cycle again and again with some overlapping parts and variations. After dropping down to a lower register . . . , I hear the lower melody immediately resonate in my ears. . . . My eyes search the lips of others until I find Laura's and find that she's singing the same melody. Her smiling eyes lock with mine. (Gross 1)

Moluebe, a BaAka girl, dancing Elamba in a forest camp in the Central African Republic (1992). The BaAka singers are on the camera side, not shown. Traveling merchants from the capital city look on in the background. *Photo by Michelle Kisliuk.*

Mary Lucey, an undergraduate student, dancing Elamba in the formal concert hall at the University of Virginia (1999). *Photo by Matthew Walden.*

The ethnically mixed ensemble at the University of Virginia has formed a living community. The circumstances of learning, performing, and thinking together allow us to begin looking at important issues of identity, such as "race" and representation at the university and in Virginia (the state that was the first seat of the Confederacy). The festering wound of the racist history of the United States is present here, and this performance community—with bodies that are dancing and singing and embodying issues of self and other—brings to the surface immediate questions that might otherwise stay in the theoretical realm. First, we rehearse privately, forming an initial community. Then, we perform publicly, generating a wider community—and a ripple of change begins to affect our social realities. One African student, Netta Apedoe, expressed it this way in a poem:

> Us coming together and making sense
> Looking like a quilted community
> And finally showing them how it's done.

During one performance outdoors on the eve of Halloween, we sang and danced BaAka women's dances while my video of BaAka dancers projected abstractly across our moving bodies and across Thomas Jefferson's pillars at the university's rotunda. This juxtaposition of worlds many people found exciting and liberating. Kelly Gross describes another transformative performance:

> I felt one of these incredible moments of performance at its peak, where I was giving my all and was simultaneously feeding the immense accumulated and collective energy of the group. . . . My arms were tightly interlocked over the shoulders of the dancers on either side of me, and . . . we came so dangerously close to one another that we collided, collapsed, and exploded into laughter. . . . It was an exhilarating, spontaneous, and unchoreographed moment. (6)

Students in my classes have mentioned that they have taught the songs and rhythms I'd learned in Africa to their friends and that their experience of performing this "far away" material informally "at home" made for extraordinary moments of communion, friendship, and transcendence through performance.

Why Embodiment?
Field Research and Teaching as Participation
Returning to the question: why a focus on embodiment, or more broadly, performance? Because we are coming to thoroughly understand that research (and teaching, and "art" making) *is* personal history, a history for which we are politically and aesthetically responsible, we also understand that we fundamentally affect and are affected by our engagement with people and the world. When we commit our bodies to practice and presence on various levels, and in so doing examine the qualities and complexities of that participation within our thinking and writing, we cannot presume to stand either outside or

BaAka women dancing Dingboku (1989). *Photo by Michelle Kisliuk.*

Members of the UVA African Drumming and Dance Ensemble dancing Dingboku (1999). *Photo by Matthew Walden.*

above the subject of our research — but instead become embedded in it
and implicated by it, just as we do in live performing.

How can it be, then, that this seemingly transparent equation has
been largely missing — except in boldly grassroots or radical intellectual and artistic contexts — missing from colonial, then postcolonial,
modernist, and bourgeois expression, both intellectual and artistic?
One answer is centrism run amok; the scholarly and institutional ver-

sions of centrism: ethnocentrism (in particular, elite Eurocentrism), classcentrism, extending into gendercentrism or patriarchy. The perpetuation of all of these centrisms is served by the split between "mind" and "experience" that I mentioned above, because such a split disorients the sociopolitical immediacies that would challenge the status quo. What I hope to highlight here is how embodiment (the commitment of bodies) disrupts those centrisms that are served by dualistic thinking. Interactive performance, embodied teaching and learning, as well as ethnographic poetics and experiential narrative are realms in which mind/body dualisms are disassembled, and by consequence, related dualisms such as art/scholarship and self/other also become blurred or collapse. When dualistic thinking shifts to multiplex thinking, there is no longer one center but many, ever shifting centers.

World-Melding in a Rain Forest

As with the students in Santa Barbara and Charlottesville, the world-melding interactions I have had with BaAka were and are largely about alternatives. I have written elsewhere of the multiplex performative consequences of the presence of evangelists in the BaAka region ("(Un)Doing"; "Musical"; *Seize*). To introduce that issue briefly in terms of the notion of world-melding, I offer this example from my field narrative:

> Most BaAka do not understand what writing is, but hearing others speak about the Bible—the most prevalent writing around—they have come to see the printed word as having mystical value in itself. When I was living with BaAka in our Bagandou camp, Duambongo, my neighbor, perused an issue of *Newsweek* given me by a Peace Corps volunteer in town. Duambongo thought the magazine must be powerful simply because it was mbeti, meaning "letters" or "words," and he assumed that these were mbeti ya nzapa, "god writing," as missionaries translate "the Bible." I tried to explain the difference between "god writing" and Newsweek by telling him that Newsweek is simply news (messimo). I illustrated the "newsy" aspect by pointing out the photos in the magazine, some of which BaAka could relate to; examining one photo of a figure skater, Kwanga identified the tutu as a malamba, a raffia skirt that BaAka women wear.
>
> I had several of these kinds of discussions with my camp-mates. For me they were attempts to situate myself and my BaAka hosts in relation to the wider world as I saw it—and to convey information that might help prepare them to interpret the influx of elements from that world now bidding for their allegiance. Sometimes, though, the gap between worlds seemed too wide. Mbouya

and Tina enjoyed pretending to speak French. Tina once looked at the Newsweek (upside down), making "French" sounds: "c'est parce que, oui, oui, oui, c'est tout? Ah, bon." It seemed part mockery and part poignant effort to show that if he wanted to, he could be like those people (villagers and white people) who read and speak French. When I tried to explain that Newsweek was not even in French, I became frustrated; in the long run it did not seem to matter.

But the discussions did become more esoteric. While I was reading a novel, Ndanga came to ask me whether I was reading "god writing" or "news," since I had already pointed out the difference. I said that in this case it was not quite either one, but added that "god writing" has something in common with the novel in that they are both stories (misao). I emphasized that the novel, like "god writing," is not real in the sense that news is real. He did not seem to be following me, so to illustrate my notion of the difference between "reality" and fiction or legend, I tried to use the example of the animals in BaAka gano legends, saying that animals don't really talk, but in gano we pretend they do. Ndanga protested that the animals in gano did in fact talk. He informed me of a BaAka legend about the time when Komba (god) separated animals from people. Once upon a time, animals and people were equal, and all could talk. Then one day there was a big dance and Komba made the animals into how they are now. All gano apparently come from that transitional time. Only then did I see that for Ndanga, legend and my idea of "reality" were not separate things. . . .

I tried another tack to express my perspective, saying that now, in the present, animals do not talk, but we can pretend they do. Ndanga again protested, saying yes, for example, chimpanzees talk, "hoo, hoo." He had a point, so instead I picked up a fork nearby and used a funny voice, making it move and talk. Ndanga found this comical—I had never noticed BaAka (or any other Africans I know) anthropomorphize objects for fun. I still do not know if Ndanga saw my point, but we both enjoyed the exchange.

Global events and transnational movements such as colonialism and contemporary evangelism have uniquely *local* consequences that are often manifested, and sometimes transformed, through performance, and I describe a BaAka performed response to evangelism later in this essay. But first I want to emphasize how in the process of world-melding the negotiation of many, ever shifting centers and aesthetic allegiances is performed interactively within communities impacted by colonialism and globalization.

The Fixed/Mixed Dialectic

In restructuring scholarly and creative institutions, I have developed some strategies for teaching students to think critically about their aesthetic values; such strategies allow us to understand the relational and ever shifting underpinnings of those values. One of these strategies is to introduce a concept that I call the *fixed/mixed dialectic*—that is, a concept that explains how aesthetic allegiances are often determined by where an individual or group is placed in relation to the shifting or relative stability of their perceived world. The politics of culture for individuals and for groups is very much about finding and renegotiating a dynamic balance between "fixed" and "mixed." In terms of teaching BaAka performance, the dialectic shows up, for example, when teaching/learning an ostensibly unchanging "it" (a melody, a dance step) we are then to perform. What does it mean if the singing sounds different coming from my students than on my recordings of BaAka singing the "same" song? When do I know I have "taught them" to sing BaAka style? Is BaAka style, in fact, a sound product or a social process—sometimes, but not always, fused?

In order for our efforts to feel legitimate—"authentic"—we must balance the obvious mixedness and contingency of the route by which these songs/dances came (through me to these students)—a radical shifting of contexts—with a (temporarily) fixed idea of "the song and the dance." Of course, one could argue that all cultural material is "mixed," yet we must "fix" those materials temporarily in order to use them, in order to see them and reenact them. BaAka have, it seems to me, mastered this socioesthetic dialectic, since each performance of "a song" can sound quite different from all other performances of that song. Yet, each dance form and song keeps its distinct identity (based in particular rhythmic relationships, dance steps, melody stylings, and paths of transmission), while slowly evolving into new or "offspring" genres (Kisliuk, *Seize*).

This microperformance dialectic becomes even more complexly layered within the visibly transplanted (mixed) macrocontext in drastically different teaching/performing circumstances. Does the "it" in this case need to become more fixed to balance these mixed circumstances? Or should the style of singing simply meld into local aesthetics? But then, to what degree will local musical habits take over, erasing the value of learning a new aesthetic and tipping the dialectical balance between fixed (comfortable) and mixed (different)? We know that styles and materials always shift and meld, despite efforts to faithfully restore them (Schechner). The challenge, then, is to respond to the ever changing fixed/mixed balance among "materials," unity/identity and skill of performers, and the particular and immediate social moment.

The Object(ive) Subjectively Conceived

110
Michelle
Kisliuk

I've found that a visual aid helps to illustrate what I call "the object(ive) subjectively conceived" (see figure). This model is helpful for visualizing the paradigm shift I am exploring—mapping a way to transcend subjective/objective, dualistic thinking. It is a model that illustrates adaptation to ongoing change and interaction, while allowing correspondences among overlapping perspectives to become visible. I encourage readers to draw on top of this printed model to illustrate particular relevant examples. The middle circle can be any example that might be seen empirically as a "thing" or an "it"—from a dance style, to a melody, to a story, to another person or group—or any topic for potential performance ethnography. The outside circles are various perspectives from which individuals or groups perceive the "thing" (which is not inherently a "thing" but conceived as such strategically). An important aspect of using the model is to focus on the lines or links *between* the inner circle and outer circles that depict the *mutually constituted reality*—the interaction that results in an "object(ive) subjectively conceived."

The model is meant to illustrate:

- *Contextualized value* as opposed to absolute value.
- *Contestation,* or argument. Egalitarian groups like BaAka are experts. If it's not contested, it's either dead or numbingly despotic.
- *Ongoingness,* the continuous re-marking, remaking, and reenactment of multiple boundaries of identity.
- *A conceptual shift away from dualism* that resonates with feminist thought, anticolonial movements, relativism, diversity, and a per-

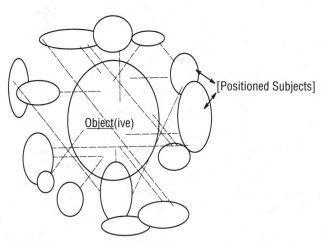

The Object(ive) Subjectively Conceived

formance paradigm, whether in live performance, writing, or other creative action.

- *An egalitarian socioesthetic* as opposed to a hierarchical worldview in which "difference" must translate as either inferior or superior. In an egalitarian worldview, difference is lateral, socially and politically contingent, and *positioned*.

For ethnographers, the model works as a reminder to describe as many perspectives and links in an ongoing complex as possible, while staying aware that the whole picture is infinite and ever changing. Our descriptions will therefore always be partial and limited to the perspectives to which we have momentary access; looking at the model, each positioned subject has a partially obstructed view. Being explicit about one's perspective necessarily implies vulnerability and partiality.

Positioning

I would like to bring together some of the issues I have been addressing so far and to elaborate this idea of positioning by addressing two interrelated areas: politics performed, and ethnography of performance/performing ethnography *as* poetics. I am not suggesting these concepts are in themselves "new," but what is perhaps innovative is a *deliberate linking* of each of these cultural-discursive strategies as part of an interdependent process.

Politics Performed

It is not a coincidence, given the through-line of this inquiry, that I chose to learn with BaAka forest people or "pygmies," whose culture blends an egalitarian performance style with implicit egalitarian social values.

But actually working with and learning from BaAka moved me much further in this direction, in part because of an objectifying precedent of writers and performers representing so-called pygmies as quintessentially romantic—a theme spanning from the ancient pharaohs down to pop music productions by "Deep Forest" and "Zap Mama." Conversely, an equally dehumanizing characterization of pygmies as savage or akin to animals has been perpetuated by colonial-minded Europeans and by many of the BaAka's African neighbors. Also, there has been a precedent of engaged writing about African forest peoples, first by Colin Turnbull in 1961 and then by a series of Turnbull followers who tend to reproduce romantic and/or "savage" paradigms. I have, therefore, been especially concerned to undo such objectifications. In my research and writing, I address the idea of *multiple modernities,* a concept designed to counteract the legacy of representations depicting BaAka as either utopian or savage (Kisliuk, *Seize*). This conception of modernities as multiple and positioned can be mapped onto the object(ive) subjectively conceived model above, as each person or group shapes an aesthetic of modernity based on local experience, and they place themselves in the center. A final excerpt from my narrative provides the example of such politics performed:

It began during a long dry season in 1988, when rumors started to circulate in my home camp that some neighboring BaAka thought BaAka dances were "satanic." Then suddenly Elongo and others influenced by the evangelists refused to participate in BaAka dances and started accusing other BaAka of being satanic. A split developed between those who had been mildly interested before, but were now becoming suspicious of this evangelical craze, and others who were following what Elongo and an increasing number of his cousins and friends were saying.

Several years later, however, BaAka had begun to find a solution to this rift: a new dance form had begun to develop: "The God Dance," it was called. I watched as dancers, mostly children and teenagers at first, moved in a circle, using steps traditionally used by their non-pygmy villager neighbors. The singing style and drum rhythms were in the style of Bolemba pygmies—neighboring pygmies who now live like non-pygmy villagers and who no longer speak their own language. Many BaAka adults stood by, some joining in the dancing, others watching enthusiastically and singing along. Songs from the Grace Brethren Church missionaries were preceded and followed by Bolemba-style interpretations of hymns from various Christian sects represented in Bagandou village, including Baptist, Apostolic, and Catholic. They not only blended all that into the same dance, but also mixed in Afro-pop snippets in Lingala (from radio tunes from Zaïre and the Congo). A man called out a solo line singing "alleluia" and adding a few disconnected words in Sango (national lingua franca), while the chorus responded in Bolemba-style harmonies with an initial "alleluia" followed by pygmy singing-sounds.

I was confused about this transition from hymns in "church" to dancing, and I asked a man whether, as some claimed, one of the American missionaries, named Barbara, had taught them this dance. He said yes, and when I asked incredulously if she actually dances, he answered in the affirmative, demonstrating by imitating her bouncing body movements as she played the guitar to accompany hymns. Barbara and the Grace Brethren do not allow dancing in their religious practice, but since no one was present to enforce a European-style distinction between music and dance, the hymns had soon become the basis for a new dance form.

As I watched and listened to the performance, I saw this developing expressive form, the "God Dance," as a means of addressing modernity. In an effort to reinvent themselves as competent in a changing world, these BaAka were claiming any 'otherness' that surrounds them and usually excludes them, and mixing it into a form they could define and control. I was concerned, however, that some BaAka were trading-away their pride in distinctively BaAka expressions for an idea of the modern. . . .

By 1992 the controversy had settled and when I returned for a visit, my old friend Djolo explained to me then that the "God Dance" is just one among many dances; they could dance their own dances and still "pray to god." They had placed the "God Dance" within a BaAka system of value, poised uneasily within a wider, dynamic repertoire vying to define an emerging identity.

This excerpt can only hint at the complexity and creative tension in this performance and research context. But it gives a sense for what I am hinting at theoretically: the ongoing re-marking of socioesthetic boundaries and the crucial, if sometimes hidden, connection between performance, difference, and the politics of identity.

Ethnography of Performance/Performing Ethnography as Poetics

By "poetics," I mean simply the vitality of "life," or that writing ethnography means writing life. Writing or performance work steeped in ethnographic research must be as vital as the life that inspires it. The means to that vitality is poetics, including an evocation between "here" and "there" that brings us to a heightened awareness of the immediacy of those correspondences.

To that end, I encourage interactive, performative writing with at least three levels of *conversation* (literal or metaphorical), each of which needs to be addressed (see Kisliuk, "(Un)Doing"). The first is an ongoing conversation between the field researcher and the people among whom she or he works. The second level is the researcher's "conversation" with the material of performance, such as song, dance, storytelling, and ideas about politics, social life, and aesthetics. The third level—the ethnography itself—is a re-presentation and evocation of the first two conversations, within an overall metaconversation among the ethnographer, the ethnographer's readers and students, and the material and ideas the ethnographer addresses. I should note that there is no definable border between the field and the space of writing; we write when we are doing research, and we research while we write. An awareness, therefore, that field experience and ethnography are inseparable must infuse both.

In the realm of live performance, the role of conversation is also crucial. We can critique performances in terms of intended and real-

BaAka dancing Mabo, with the Mondimba leaf mask (1989). *Photo by Michelle Kisliuk.*

ized conversations—among performers, among performers and on-lookers, and with the "materials" and what they may represent. When, in 1999, the UVA African Drumming and Dance Ensemble tried to achieve multileveled conversations in an evening performance at the University of Virginia, we found that despite our best effort to trans-form a formal concert hall into an intimate, world-melding environ-

Students at the University of Virginia dancing Mabo (1999). Justin Mongosso dances in the mask (made of plastic decorator greenery). Drummers sit downstage right. The formality of the hall and our efforts to transform it are visible here. *Photo by Matthew Walden.*

ment, the conventions of contemporary theatergoing and moviegoing made our audience seem passive and distant, especially at moments when the house lights were dark. Though the audience had in fact been "with" us, we did not receive their energy, and therefore we labored to fill the large hall with our own energy—not quite relaxed enough to really enjoy our own performance in what could have been a more successful multiplex conversation.

The year ended with more informal performances outdoors, and several students read to us the poems they had prepared for intervals during our formal performance. This one was by Deva Woodly:

This is the center
the pause core
before the pulse
of movement
the kiss of Komba's breath
in these limbs

Sing the stories again
voice breaking
a single sound sent, spiral of sunlight captured,
absorbed and reflected

This energy.
the organic twisting of atoms

to beat; beat again
the space between dwindled
to one ever present
collapse of time.
fingers mating to measure the distance

This moment's music
ours—immeasurable
can't be boxed
sold
squandered.
only passed
mouth to mouth
resuscitation of soul.

Risky Endeavors

The shift that I began this essay by mentioning, a shift toward performance, at its core implies that activist arts and scholarship must be at once grassroots, that is, community-based and community active, *and* by consequence, risky politically, intellectually, and aesthetically. The challenge is how to create such contexts within institutions such as universities, which are by nature conservative and created in part to uphold the status quo of statewide, nationwide, or worldwide power structures. I leave you, then, as researchers, artists, students, and teachers with the task of making spaces where "here" and "there," theory and practice, poetics and everyday life are not separated but intertwined in active, and by necessity risky, endeavors.

NOTE

The title of this essay is a play on the well-known Clifford and Marcus volume, subtitled *The Poetics and Politics of Ethnography.*

WORKS CITED

Apedoe, Netta. "The Oka Community." Unpublished poem. 1999.

Clifford, James, and George E. Marcus, eds. *Writing Culture: The Poetics and Politics of Ethnography.* Berkeley: U of California P, 1986.

Gross, Kelly. "Energy, Interaction, and the Sound Vortex: Performance of BaAka Song and Dance." Unpublished paper, 1999.

Kisliuk, Michelle. "Confronting the Quintessential: Singing, Dancing, and Everyday Life among Biaka Pygmies (Central African Republic)." Diss. New York U, 1991.

———. "Musical Life in the Central African Republic." *Garland Encyclopedia of World Music.* Vol. 1: *Africa.* Ed. Ruth M. Stone. New York: Garland, 1998. 681–97.

———. *Seize the Dance! BaAka Musical Life and the Ethnography of Performance.* New York: Oxford UP, 1998.

———. "(Un)Doing Fieldwork: Sharing Songs, Sharing Lives." *Shadows in the Field: New Perspectives for Fieldwork in Ethnomusicology.* Ed. Gregory F. Barz and Timothy J. Cooley. New York: Oxford UP, 1997. 23–44.

Schechner, Richard. "Restoration of Behavior." *Between Theatre and Anthropology.* Philadelphia: U of Pennsylvania P, 1985. 35–116.

Turnbull, Colin M. *The Forest People: A Study of the Pygmies of the Congo.* New York: Simon, 1961.

Woodly, Deva. "The Dance." Unpublished poem, 1999.

Part Two
*Embodiment
and
Epistemology*

Performance Studies, Pedagogy, and Bodies in/as the Classroom

> We could use our institutional placements to put the body back into thought, to think of pleasures like desire not as a space of absence into which language can't lead us, but as a space of social possibility to which our bodies lead us.
> —JILL DOLAN, "Producing Knowledges That Matter"

It has taken me a long time to realize that, to borrow a formulation of Clifford Geertz, we don't just perform as bodies, we perform in bodies. That this realization has dawned so slowly for me is a reflection of the odd relationship performance has to the embodiments of forgetting and remembrance; I performed as a dancer for at least as long as I have studied performance as a paradigm. Indeed, my identity as a dancer defined me as special for almost half of my life. So, for me, recuperating the body as a site of knowledge through performance and/as training has been something of a long way home, as it must be, to some degree I suppose, for us all.

Over the past ten years, I have solicited performance autobiographies from students in my undergraduate performance studies classes and my graduate seminars in acting theory. I am blessed with an extremely diverse student population, and the details of the autobiographies I receive reflect this. But the absences in these texts also speak. After reading them, I ask my students as a group how many have had some formal dance, martial arts, or athletic training and have had formal opportunities—recitals, exhibitions, games—to demonstrate the results of this training. I have taught nearly two hundred fifty students in these courses since beginning this assignment. Only three of this number presented themselves as having only one of these two elements. Only one student had no formal physical training of any kind. Indeed, the majority of my students were still involved in these activities at the time they negotiated the assignment. Yet, the overwhelming majority of them did not include this information in their performance autobiographies, in spite of working from a very general definition of performance that explicitly included the physical as well as the "textual." I have puzzled over this for a long time. It seems that, to paraphrase Francis Barker, if the spectacular, visible body is the proper gauge of what the bourgeoisie has had to forget, it doesn't particularly relish remembering the trained and marked and constructed body either.

As I observe this "resistance to remember" in my courses, I am simultaneously exploring form, gender, and culture as these emerge in three distinct ethnographic contexts: a regional, semiprofessional ballet company; *butoh,* as practiced by Los Angeles–based Renzoku; and Khmer classical dance, as envisioned by one Cambodian refugee family. I've trained, or attempted to train, in each of these three areas—the enabling fiction that establishes my ethnographic authority in these contexts is physical—and this training has both directly and indirectly funded my sense of what it is to perform in bodies, in "theirs" and in "ours," in the classroom. I would like to use these three contexts paradigmatically to talk about the state(s) of the body in the classroom and how these states intersect with, buttress, and challenge the conventional educational subject. From here, I wish to turn to larger questions: What sort of knowledge is reclaimed by the body of/in classroom performance? How does this knowledge help us interrogate what it means to be subjects and objects of pedagogy as well as subjects and objects of performance?

Donna Haraway observes that "bodies have been as thoroughly denaturalized as sign, context and time." In short, "bodies are not born; they are made" (208). Michel Feher notes that this making generates body as "a reality constantly produced . . . [as] an effect of techniques promoting specific gestures and postures, sensations and feelings and so on" (159). I am interested in these techniques and effects and in using them to explore "body building" in the classroom. It seems to me possible to organize the technologies and effects of this body building according to three axes adapted from Susan Bordo's study of a radically embodied performance, anorexia nervosa. They are: the dualist axis, the control axis, and the difference/power axis (92).

Of these, the dualist axis is the most general and the most attenuated; the epistemological genealogy is well known. Obviously, this split between bodily experience and conceptual life is partly responsible for my students omitting their disciplined bodies from their performance autobiographies. I've seen the obverse of this, too, in many of the dancers with whom I work. In some cases, this manifests itself as a kind of sacred inarticulateness. In others, it appears as a "cultivate[d] sanctimonious muteness, denying what is verbal, logical and discursive in order to champion [a somewhat naive sense of] the physical and the sensate" (Foster xiv–xv).

I want to extend my discussion of the dualist axis a bit further to include not only the division between the mind and the physical body but also that between the mind and the phenomenological body, the body-as-experienced. That is, conceptual life, particularly for the successful educational subject, is held apart not only from the body as body but also and simultaneously from the social practices that change peoples' experiences of their bodies. The ideal educational subject, it seems to me, is one that professes a profound unawareness of the marking and containment of his or her malleable body. Let me suggest that the classroom performance is not a way to heal this split, because I'm not sure what that would mean in pedagogical practice or what it would look like in a classroom performance, but a way to remember it, to make the dualist axis and its consequences at both the physical and the phenomenological levels both vivid and visible.

I am guided in this by the wisdom of Cambodian dance master Somaly Hay and of dancer Sopiline Cheam Shapiro. Cambodian classical dance is framed both as an organic unity and as highly mimetic; ostensibly, the body mirrors the mind/soul as each mirrors nature. This is the illusion the dancers attempt to project, and it is crucial to recognize that, in the artifice of the dance, the audience grasps the simultaneity of both the distance between, and the intersection of, the celestial and the everyday. Yet, for both dancers, this artifice and the technologies deployed by the body in its service are explicit. As a Cambodian dancer performing in Los Angeles put it, "Looks like heavenly dance. Looks like. Means, really, is not. Understand?"

I recently revised my assignment, returning students' autobiographies and asking them to include accounts of their performing bodies and how they were trained and marked. They could do this by telling, by showing, or both but must also account for the medium chosen. Most students write their accounts of disciplined bodies rather than perform them, and this has given rise to discussions about whether or not the choice to write is a further flight from the corporeal. In any case, the process of these revisions becomes extremely emotional, even when done on paper. This emotional work has the character of wry, almost bitterly wistful recollection and recuperation, a way of countering the pedagogical mystification of affect, which holds that

> those in subordinate positions can and must be taught, especially in school and in workplace, that emotional responses such as anger, rage, or bitterness are always inappropriate and unjustified personal responses—forms of emotional stupidity if not psychopathology. (Worsham 128)

As one student noted, in an eloquent reflection on the relationship between the corporeal, the emotional, and the pedagogical:

> For every [gymnastics] trophy I won, there's one line, like the coach saying, 'If your boobs get any bigger or any lower, you'll have to haul them around in a wheelbarrow. Knockers up.' No wonder I don't want to remember this, even the good stuff. I only think about it when I look in the mirror or see myself in a window and see how slumped I am after all those years of [gymnastics] classes. First I think, 'Knockers up.' The same thing. Then I

think, 'Why, when you remember this, do you do it in the coach's voice? Why don't you think, Fuck you. I'll put my knockers wherever the hell I want to?' and stick them right in her face? Why can't I just redo that memory?

Lest our fantasy be that somehow, as educators, we are more aware and outside this axis ourselves, and therefore equipped to serve as neutral facilitators, consider an observation by Edward Said. He is writing here about his experience of Brahms's piano music performed by Alfred Brendel:

> I would not go so far as to say that the various reinscriptions of the Brahms variations had the effect for me of something objective; rather I would say that the music itself was affirmed for me, no doubt much of it, as Gramsci would say, in a muscular-nervous way, because I was able a short time after Brendel's recital, to play it on the piano. That particular physical discipline anchored the other convergences of memory and intellectual history in a practice that was also a discipline of detail. (88)

This is a remarkable statement, it seems to me, not only because it offers the tantalizing possibility of linking the conceptual and the corporeal in and through reperformance but also because of what it implies for us as teacher-observers of performance. For surely our students' performances live in us in this same Gramscian neuromuscular formulation because we are ourselves performers. Yet, rather than anchoring our responses to students' work in our own physical disciplines, we turn instead to the disembodied, ubiquitous evaluation form or to a discussion that remains steadfastly above the neck. I have actually stopped myself from rephysicalizing aspects of a student's performance and turned to written comments or abstraction instead, not wanting, I suppose, to imply to the student that my bodily reinscription was somehow *the* strategy. This now seems rather presumptuous to me. Let me suggest that, in the interest of bracketing and problematizing the dualist axis and its consequences for our students, we explore our own convergences of, and dissonances between, memory, intellect, and the physical on the one hand, and on the other, the practices we have learned to keep our own disciplined bodies silenced and safe, while asking our students to do otherwise.

Elements of the dualist axis permeate the control axis, of course, but here I wish to emphasize both the micropractices of discipline—technique—and possibilities of resistance, not as simple repudiation or evasion of corporeal discipline and training but as the nuanced deployment of these. Donna Haraway observes,

> There is no ground for ontologically opposing the organic, the technical and textual [and] neither is there any ground for oppos-

ing the mythical to the organic, textual and technical. Their convergences are more important than their residual oppositions. (212)

From this perspective, we can move from positions of missionary zeal, as liberators of imperiled, dependent, and vulnerable academic bodies through the utopian practice of performance, to become, instead, walkers in de Certeau's sense—active interrogators of the possibilities offered, both by the path of performance technique and by deviations from it. If the body of the educational subject is the locus, and the object, of particular sociopolitical manifestations of the connection between myths, techniques, and technologies of domination that have much invested in appearing natural and inevitable, then the reconfiguration of technique, of repetition and precision through classroom performance, has the potential to expand our "structures of allowable meanings" of these practices, to explore them as strategies that locate individuals in particular positions or that make available particular corporeal locations in specific convergences of space, time, and power.

Butoh, the transgressive, assaultive Japanese dance antiform, has been instrumental in my own rethinking of technique as the naturalized management of the vulnerable body in classroom performances. *Butoh* was configured as a mode of resistance to the aestheticized body of *bugaku*, classical Japanese dance. Beyond this, *butoh*, as I've experienced it in the work of Melinda Ring, Roxanne Steinberg, Naoyuki Oguri, and Renzoku (collectively known as Body Weather, after the principles of founder Min Tanaka), offers what Feher terms an "ethical/political typology" of the constrained body. *Butoh* is both disciplinary and antitechnical; that is, technique is rigorously framed, attenuated, decentered, and reconfigured intensely, simultaneously. Within the training practices of Body Weather, the ethical/political typology of the body is explicit. Training, in effect, asks: "In the name of what is the body disciplined or styled; [what are the micropractices of this] disciplining and styling; [what are] the goals [functions and effects] assigned to [these] practices" (Feher 165). Or, simply, who has the authority to choreograph his/her own body or the body of another? Melinda Ring puts this another way:

> I finally had to stop going to ballet class after awhile. I kept asking about movements, or trying to almost analyze them. Why turn out? Why is turn out prettier than feet parallel? Why do feet have to be pretty? How many pretty feet are too many? It was a mystery. It was the law. There was no—there was no recourse and no way to appeal—it just was as it was. And I didn't understand it. And I don't think anybody else did, or maybe that it just WAS enough. It wasn't till I worked with Rudy [Perez, former member of the Judson Dance Theater] and then especially

on the farm with Min [Tanaka] that the technique was a problem to be solved. Actually, that is what dance was—how to think about movement and pose problems that the movement and technique solved.[1]

I have begun to play with this same explicit attention to technique as both the "problem to be solved" and the tools to solve the problems in my performance courses. That is, my students and I have become aggressive about asking questions such as, How is the classroom body, the performed body, the body-in-literature framed and disciplined? Why? Can these questions themselves be performed? That is, can we perform our own interrogations and decenterings of performance technique—through exaggeration, perhaps, or parody, or Stanislavskian realism?

My goal here and also in my reading of technique and antitechnique in Body Weather is not to read for simple utopian resistance to the disciplinary imperatives of technique, for I imagine "resistance" in and through classroom performance, and performance generally, as far more complex and subtle and problematic. Feher offers the Foucauldian reminder that:

> the body is at once the object of power—or better the actualizer of power relations—and that which resists power. But again it resists power not in the name of transhistorical needs but because of new desires and constraints each new regime develops. The situation therefore is one of permanent battle [or dialogue], with the body as the shifting field where new mechanisms of power constantly meet new techniques of resistance and escape. (161)

That is, the educational subject is never outside the chain of/as technique, techniques of classroom performance and Body Weather included. Yet, both of these can function to restore remembrance of this process, of this chain, to and through the body. And in this process of remembrance, we can perhaps reimagine physical training in terms similar to those employed by de Certeau in his characterization of "reading as poaching," that is, as those processes "situated at the point where social stratification (class relationships) and poetic operations (the practitioner's constructions of a text [or a body]) intersect" (172). While, on one level, disciplines of training "seek to make the [pedagogical body] conform to the 'information' distributed by an elite," it is equally true that the "weathers of the body," as Oguri would say, "insinuate [the body's] inventiveness into the cracks in a cultural orthodoxy," whether that be the classroom or the *bugaku* stage (de Certeau 172). From this perspective, the complex interrelationship between myth, technique, body, and text in the classroom can more creatively be examined as technologies of the self, as well as technologies of domination, as tactics that

127
*Performance
Studies,
Pedagogy, and
Bodies in/as the
Classroom*

> permit individuals to effect by their own means, or with the help
> of others a certain number of operations on their own bodies and
> souls, thoughts, conduct, and ways of being so as to transform
> themselves in order to attain a certain state of happiness. (Foucault 18)

By now, it is apparent that dualism, control, and my final axis, difference/power, are less axes than concentric circles; it is clearly impossible to discuss difference and power without imbricating dualism and control. Yet, here I wish to sharpen my focus to explore how the difference/power constellation is embodied in classroom performance spectatorship: How does the marked and constrained body of the educational subject look at others, and itself, performing? What sort of knowledge is restored through careful attention to the embodied consequences of looking and being looked at?

Film theory and criticism offer a useful vocabulary to use in discussions of spectatorship that can be extended to the consequences of looking in the performance classroom. Consider, for example, Vicky Lebeau's observation, in a larger critique of the film *The River's Edge*, that

> Insofar as looking is bound up with the process of identification,
> spectatorship has to be minimally social . . . , bound up with social identifications and with fantasies of aggressivity and idealizations that, in turn, are bound up with fantasies of . . . difference. (259)

These social identifications and fantasies of aggressivity, idealization, and difference are safely packaged by and for the educational subject, in part by the erasure of bodies constricted/constructed by such fantasies and such looks. For example, the "neutral" and "obvious" practice of viewing performances by women, by students of color, and by gay and lesbian students constructs "an imaginary [and often unquestioned] symmetricalization in which . . . all appear and [in which all] are treated as though they occupy a common position in relation to each other" and to the institutional hierarchy(ies) that subsume them (259). Thus, we speak abstractly and hygienically about the gaze, but how often do we disembody both the process and the consequences of looking and all these imply—fetishism, exoticism—dare we say, desire—within the audience of the classroom performance? These processes and consequences also mark the body, constrain it, for to paraphrase the text of Barbara Kruger's photo collage, our gaze always hits the side of someone's face (Schneider 104). And sometimes, as teacher-performers, both the gaze and the face are our own. An explicit aware-ness of spectatorship can function, it seems to me, as a radical strategy for problematizing the illusion of homogenization and symmetrical-ization in our classrooms and instead situate difference, multiplicity, and heterogeneity by embodying looking. Consider: "On the one hand, the spectator is fascinated by what he is looking at, perhaps caught up in [a] fiction of totalizing security; on the other, he is subject to the paranoia internal to that fiction—am I being looked at?" (Lebeau 259). And further, How am I being looked at, and how does being looked at in this way etch itself onto my body? Within an audience viewing a classroom performance, the potential for decentering the homoge-neous, unitary educational subject is enticing: "if I am able to look at some [body] looking [and performing], then my looking [and my body] could become the object of a look from elsewhere that I would know nothing about" (259).

I have become far more sensitive to the embodied effects of looking since working with the Pasadena Dance Theatre, a semiprofessional ballet company, and hearing from the young women in the corps the radical gender awareness that comes from accounting for and reading one's own body vis-à-vis spectatorship. The company had an unusually large number of men who, because of their very visibility in an activity gendered "female" (think of Balanchine's dictum: "Ballet is woman") attracted a share of attention that, in the view of many of the young women in the corps, was disproportionate to their efforts and talent. When I asked the women of the PDT to comment on this, they became very animated. The result was a chorus of indignant voices; it was vir-tually impossible to distinguish individual speakers:

> The guys have it so easy—not just in performances but in class
> too. You know they don't wear pointe shoes, that's the main
> thing, so they don't have all this pain—and they don't have a clue.
> And they can be older and fat—well, not really fat, but you know
> a [professional] company will still take them if they're big. . . .
> Bigger . . . Just like even the fat, ugly guys can get dates, but even
> the losers expect the girls to be small. . . . And they don't get
> dropped and hauled around [in lifts, etc.]. And they get all this
> attention: [mimicking] "Oooo guys in ballet . . . Wow! How spe-
> cial!" It sucks. A girl playing football everyone looks at and says,
> "Look at the dyke." And then they look at the guys for real. Here,
> we do all the work and they look at the guys and—forget it if
> there are a bunch of them [male dancers] on stage with you. No
> one sees you at all and no one stares at them like freaks.

It is abundantly clear that the asymmetry of looking has been exhaus-tively theorized by these young women. There is looking, and there is looking, being stared at like a freak and being looked at "for real." It is not just the gaze but how it is deployed and how it codes the bodies gazed at that is of consequence. And though there is considerable time and energy given to "team building" in the company, the team dissolves when immersed in the solvent of spectatorship. None of this, incidentally, was lost on the male dancers, for whom the notion that spectatorship might see a "team," rather than "the guys," was an odd notion indeed.

129
*Performance
Studies,
Pedagogy, and
Bodies in/as the
Classroom*

> What makes PDT special are the guys. Most companies would kill to have us. . . . You just have to say that. Good girls [ballerinas] are easy to find, but guys—that's why we're the show. We're it. [Exaggeratedly pointing to himself with both hands] Look here!!

Like many of us, I suppose, I have asked students in their analytical essays to account for themselves and their decisions as authors of performances. I am now asking how they account for themselves as objects of performance, how they encounter the physical reality of being a body being looked at. I am also initiating, in a much more specific way, discussions of what it means for an audience to look at a particular performer presenting a particular text. The results have been astonishing. Consider one excerpt from a student's essay:

> We have to keep repeating that we are all rubberneckers [drivers who gawk at traffic accidents] on the highway of performance. Not to be snide, but being looked at can be like experiencing a kind of violence. And looking, or having to look can be like being violated. Usually we think of it as the opposite, or think of it as simple, or don't think about it at all. I used to pretend that I had imaginary camouflage as a kid. I needed it because I thought some people in my neighborhood had "death ray eyes." My brother and I would stay up late and tell stories about them, and I couldn't sleep because I would wonder, "What if this was real?" Well, what if it was real? What if the consequences of looking and being looked at were always clearly real? What kind of world and what kind of classroom would that be?

Perhaps, it would be the kind of classroom/world Donna Haraway describes when she insists on "the particularity and embodiment of all vision [rather than] . . . giving in to the tempting myths of vision as a route to disembodiment" (189), a classroom/world of situated, not innocent, knowledges.

We often speak and write in performance studies about the possibilities for performance restoring the body as a site of knowledge. It is paramount to me to explore what knowledges we think we are restoring. I have suggested here that, for me, classroom performance restores the knowledge of what we, as bodies in the classroom, are subject to:

specifically, to constraint, construction, and situated spectatorship. To suggest that the performance classroom might heal the mind-body split, reframe technologies for masking the imperiled body, and recuperate spectatorship is naive, I think. Or at least my goals are a bit more modest. Bruno Bettelheim observed that psychoanalysis explains why we go crazy, not why we survive (qtd. in *How Nice*). I'm not sure that performance explains this either, but I believe that it can frame how we, as embodied educational subjects, survive and what we survive. And if, in this "how" and "what," there is the potential for what Freire calls "conscientization" (20), and in turn, within this the possibility of imaging new, insistent subject positions, perhaps this is not so modest an undertaking after all.

NOTES

This essay is for my students, who continually and irrepressibly reinvigorate the relationship between performance studies, pedagogy, and bodies in/as the classroom.

1. All quotations not cited to a published source are taken from field notes.

WORKS CITED

Barker, Francis. *The Tremulous Private Body: Essays on Subjection.* New York: Methuen, 1984.

Bordo, Susan. "Anorexia Nervosa: Psychopathology as the Crystallization of Culture." *Knowing Women: Feminism and Knowledge.* Ed. Helen Crowley and Susan Himmelweit. London: Open UP, 1992. 90–109.

de Certeau, Michel. *The Practice of Everyday Life.* Berkeley: U of California P, 1984.

Feher, Michel. "Of Bodies and Technologies." *DIA Art Foundation Discussions in Contemporary Culture.* Ed. Hal Foster. Seattle: Bay, 1987. 159–65.

Foster, Susan Leigh. *Reading Dancing: Bodies and Subjects in Contemporary American Dance.* Berkeley: U of California P, 1986.

Foucault, Michel. "Technologies of the Self." *Technologies of the Self: A Seminar with Michel Foucault.* Ed. Luther Martin et al. Amherst: U of Massachusetts P, 1988. 16–49.

Freire, Paulo. *Education for Critical Consciousness.* New York: Continuum, 1987.

Haraway, Donna. *Simians, Cyborgs, and Women: The Reinvention of Nature.* New York: Routledge, 1991.

How Nice to See You Alive. Dir. Lucia Murat. Women Make Movies, 1989.

Lebeau, Vicky. "You're My Friend: River's Edge and Social Spectatorship." *Camera Obscura* 25–26 (1991): 251–96.

Said, Edward. *Musical Elaborations.* New York: Columbia UP, 1991.

Schneider, Rebecca. *The Explicit Body in Performance.* London: Routledge, 1997.

Worsham, Lynn. "Emotion and Pedagogic Violence." *Discourse* 15.2 (1992–93): 119–48.

Deep Embodiment

The Epistemology

of Natural Performance

8

Nathan
Stucky

The study of common sense knowledge and common sense activities consists
of treating as problematic phenomena the actual methods whereby members
of a society, doing sociology, lay or professional, make the social structures of
everyday activities observable.

—HAROLD GARFINKEL, *Studies in Social Interaction*

If performance studies is to be informative about the ordinary phenomenon of human performance, it ought to be able to deal with the
details of actual performances; especially, it ought to be able to account
for the routine structures of performance as practiced not only on the
stage but in daily life. That is, performance studies should be able to
address the commonsense performance of "ordinary" individuals engaged in everyday activities. Performance epistemology, coupled with
conversation analysis, offers an experiential knowledge of the intricate
organization of human interaction. As sociologist Harvey Sacks points
out, "the world you live in is much more finely organized than you
would imagine" (414). The method discussed in this chapter leads the
student performer to bring the bodily experience of another person
into sharp focus.

This work begins with the performance inherent in "ordinary" human interaction, especially apparently mundane conversation, which,
as Sacks and others have explained, turns out to be highly structured
and organized. In order to investigate this mode of producing knowledge, I turn to *everyday life performance* (ELP), a type of performance
that involves the student in a careful and deep examination of empirical performance data.[1] In the process of ELP, the student actor virtually
shares the breath of another person.

Conversational Performance

Conversational performance writes the experience of one body on another like a palimpsest of embodiment. For more than a decade, I have
been experimenting with conversational performance in my teaching.
In the past few years, some of this work has developed in a university
class entitled Conversational Performance, a course that explores "ordinary" human communication as and through performance.[2] The
course is grounded in the work of conversation analysts, such as Sacks,
Emanuel Schegloff, Gail Jefferson, and Wayne Beach. The theoretical
underpinnings of the course derive from the works of Gregory Bate-

son, Erving Goffman, and others. Especially important is the pivotal work of the late Robert Hopper who, starting toward the end of the 1970s, began to investigate performative connections between literary language and everyday talk. For Hopper, "the term *conversational dramatism* joins the performing arts to criticism informed by empirical study of conversational interaction" (181). Hopper's continuing influence is felt in the use of the term he coined, *everyday life performance*. The idea of ELP is to tape-record naturally occurring interaction, transcribe it carefully in the manner of conversation analysts, and then learn to perform it by carefully replicating the intricate detail, the paralinguistic and interpersonal complexity, of the original.

Although the method for creating ELP performances is developed in more detail elsewhere,[3] a brief overview here provides an introduction:

> The basic process for staging natural performance [or ELP] involves five steps: recording, transcribing, analyzing, rehearsing, and performing. Performers are urged to think of the transcript and the recording as two versions of the same script. The general pattern involves repeatedly playing the recording while following the transcript, then reading aloud with the recording while following the transcript until the performer is able to perform the segment using only the transcript. As rehearsals progress, the performers try variations on the above approaches until the "scene" is learned. The ordinary complexity of speech (when rehearsed into the scene) does not sound much like "acting" but rather like people just talking. (Stucky, "Toward an Aesthetics" 178)

It may be helpful to compare ELP to the critically acclaimed work of Anna Deavere Smith, whose one-person shows, *Fires in the Mirror* and *Twilight: Los Angeles,* also seek in some way to replicate the real-life performances of others. Smith tape-recorded her interviews with neighborhood residents in New York and Los Angeles, respectively, and then fashioned collage performances built on her portrayal of these "real life" characters. Smith's highly praised virtuosity included her remarkable ability to represent the voices of her interlocutors. Smith's method was to make recordings of her interviews and then, in her words, to "find the material that will feel best on my body. I lie on the floor with the headphones on and start repeating it and repeating it. . . . This is not an intellectual thing. I really have to wear these words" (qtd. in Tate 101). Smith plays all the parts, shifting costumes along with her changing accents and movements. While Smith's performance style is reminiscent of some elocutionary platform performances of the early twentieth century, inasmuch as she listens carefully to recorded talk and tries to replicate what the "original" speakers sounded like, her technique is similar to ELP.

A comparison with method acting may also distinguish ELP. In the latter, the "psychological" and internal elements of characterization emerge only after careful examination of empirical evidence. In method acting, Constantin Stanislavski's "magic if" asks, "what would I do *if* I were this character?" The method actor's process begins with the actor's empathetic and imaginative capacities. By contrast, ELP may be understood through a rough analogy to Bertolt Brecht's *Verfremdungseffekt* (alienation, to make strange), drawn from Brecht's study of Chinese acting. In Brecht's theatre, the actor may step out of character to comment on the action of the play. Brechtian acting, not devoted to an illusion of character, recognizes the performer as a present "I." This presentational theatrical mode shares with storytelling the acknowledged presence of the speaker, the actor, the teller of the tale. Similarly, the ELP actor does not represent himself or herself to be the character; instead, there is an ongoing sense of both self and other. The narrative accountability foregrounded in ELP, while similar to some presentational forms, is typically masked in Western representational theatre, television, and film. I want to be clear that I'm not proposing ELP as an substitute means of actor training, although it clearly has value for actors; rather, ELP works to reveal the intricacies and nuances of human interaction. It is an embodied study of interpersonal communication.

The ELP actor is openly performing an elaborate quote. The performance, paradoxically, may seem to audiences as among the most realistic performances they have witnessed. Beginning acting students seldom achieve the levels of realism routinely seen in ELP. The ELP performers are doing close copies of real life through a rigorous method. The results are often astonishing to performers as well as audiences. However, the frame that bounds the performance identifies its source. This latter point is important. In the very first ELP presented before a theatre audience *(Believe Me)*, the frame was difficult for some to recognize. The advertising posters encouraged audiences to "Listen in on relationships as they develop and fall apart," but that oblique cue didn't prepare the audience for what they were about to witness. When student actor Lori Johnson took the stage in the first scene, she began to perfectly reproduce talk that was full of carefully rehearsed stops, stutters, starts, awkward pauses, awkward phrases—the stuff of real life. Some audience members initially thought she was fumbling her lines. Actually, she was doing precisely what the recording and rehearsals asked. She was giving a very accurate quote of a real-life performance.

Subsequent public performances have experimented with more direct clues to the audience about the origins of the material. In general, it helps to frame the material explicitly as drawn from recordings of naturally occurring talk. Keeping the audience uninformed makes them think they are witnessing very fine method acting; letting them know the truth problematizes the experience. This performance "actually happened." It is not fiction, not the invention of a playwright, not something that can be set aside. It is a stubborn reality. Of course, in the classroom, where this technique has already had a long run, the class members all participate in the process; they learn how it works. In the classroom, the full benefits of this performance become apparent. There, the focus is not just on the technique but rather on what is revealed through the technique.

In classroom performances, I recommend that the audience become familiar with all, or at least part, of the tape. Sometimes, the entire class studies the same recording. Sometimes, the performers will play the tape recording before performing the scene so that the audience can hear the original voices. Conversation analysts make claims on the basis of primary data; playing the tape gives the audience access to the available evidence. The actor, in the position of analyst, is showing findings to an audience as well as inviting the audience to enter into the study. With ELP as a base, the class can move to consider some fundamental questions of the data, such as those typically asked by conversation analysts: What is getting done? How is it accomplished? In my ELP classroom, these discussions often lead to questions of cultural critique and social action as we shift our talk from the empirical "what" to the interpretive "why."

A Performance Example

It is near the end of a semester. Two students are in the process of performing a final project. Their performance is of a conversation that was recorded off the radio and then transcribed to form a script. In that recording, a young woman named "Pam," age thirteen, is on the phone with a male late-night talk show host, "Jim."[4] Both of the students acting the scene are male. The actor playing Jim is about twenty-two, with a medium height and build. Jim sits at a table with a microphone, a soft drink, and some papers. The actor playing the young girl is in his midthirties, about five feet eleven inches and one hundred eighty pounds. He is sitting on the floor holding a pillow and a telephone. For a few minutes, we hear the original tape; then the actors start their scene. Both students take care to reproduce the paralinguistic details of the original tape-recorded interaction. The segment of transcript below, written in a simplified version of conversation analysts' transcription, points to audible sounds in the tape.[5] It is not "cleaned-up" or "corrected." As part of their training, the students learn the transcription system. The excerpt is from the last few moments of the scene ("I'm an Alien").

Pam: Oh. By the way, guess what. I'm gonna fly::

Jim: You're gonna fly.

Pam: Yeah, because one of my friends, she has this book on astro-projection and you fly

yo sh:sh really do fly

(.3)

hhh. hh. hh

Jim: Oh my Lo::rd. What is your name again?

Pam: hehe .hhh my name's Pa::m. (.) I think.

Jim: [Pam

Pam: and you know (.2) so my friends call me wab because you know what upside down and backwards, that's what it spells.

(1.5)

Jim: Pam- I'm gonna have to let you go now.

Pam reluctantly hangs up the phone. The scene ends. Classmates applaud the performers and prepare to discuss what they have witnessed. At first, there is some discussion about precision and accuracy, the extent to which the performers replicated the tape. But then talk moves to the experience of this performance, what the students learned about the people on the tape and about themselves in the process, what they learned about the structure of human interaction and about the accomplishment of people performing themselves in just an everyday, ordinary way. In a subsequent writing assignment, one of the actors described his experience showing an acute awareness of the physical demands of the performance, and significantly, the challenge of understanding another human being.

> Performing Pam in the classroom presentation that I did with Allan was, certainly, a challenge. Perhaps, foremost, it was a challenge because Pam's 13 year old girl's body has very little in common with my 34 year old man's body. But our bodies do have some things in common and it was by considering what those things were that I was finally able to understand and perform Pam.
>
> . . . We both engage our bodies to communicate the clustering of emotions that are bundled in our everyday performance. . . . I found Pam's conversation sinking into my skin as I worked on the performance. Phrases that she used and the way she produced them have become part of my personal lexicon. During the rehearsal stage as I began to notice this occurring it became easier for me to imagine how Pam would use her body as she said, "re::ally funny." As I began to use my body with Pam's conversation it became easier for me to empathize with her.
>
> It was empathy that helped me most to perform Pam. Before I

began to understand Pam with my body, I didn't feel the responsibility that is associated with performing someone else's real story. But empathy helped me feel that responsibility. It helped me to look deeper than the surface of the conversation to discover something closer to her soul.[6]

What this student refers to as "empathy" begins with a complex alignment grounded in a specific art of performance, an art that reveals traces of performance praxis as ancient as the bard and the rhapsode, as precise as the Kabuki, as technically demanding as ballet. The performer models ideal behavior, actions perhaps easily suited to another body, but by working with his or her own resources, the performer engages in a familiar, unnatural act. Conversational performance (as well as some other modes of performance) allows the performer to *act as*, not *act as if*. It differs from the Stanislavskian "magic if." It proposes, instead, a kind of Brechtian pointing: "I'm showing you what this character/person did." The actor in the above example comes to know through his body: "As I began to use my body with Pam's conversation it became easier for me to empathize with her."

Theorizing the Natural Performance

Beyond a very technical mimesis, the result for the performer and for the classroom audience indicates the possibility of transformation, beginning with the performers themselves. Of course, the audience does not mistake the actor for the character (although the "realism" of the performance can be compelling). There is no pretense of characterization in this event, yet there is a very precise behavior strip that follows the predetermined pattern of another person's prior performance (i.e., a "first order" performance).[7] If this is mimesis, what is copied? What do we imagine we see? What is the experience of the performer? The objective of the assignment only incidentally involves the "theatrical" elements of presentation. Essentially, the experience uses performance as an investigatory tool. The act of performance is the study of the interactional moment of an other body, an other human experience.[8]

Despite the rigors of careful copying, mimesis always leads to alterity. Mimesis is at least an illusion; perhaps, it is delusionary when we believe we have captured the thing, when we have "got it." Because even when we can produce the thing in such a way as to "fool" the audience that it was real (and for the ELP audience it can be), for the actor, the craft of performing with such care leads to specific insights that cannot erase the model. As Michael Taussig argues, "the two-layered nature of mimesis [involves] sentience and copying" (80).

In using the terms *theatre, performance,* and *everyday life,* I think it is important to distinguish what I mean, especially by everyday life. Alan Read maintains an opposition between theatre and everyday life:

"Theatre does not tease people out of their everyday lives like other expressions of wish fulfillment but reminds them of who they are and what is worth living and changing in their lives everyday" (103). A separation such as Read's assumes that there is something called "theatre," and there is something called "life," and that these are distinct and different. One lives life, one does theatre. Like many others, I am interested in blurring the boundary between the traditional concept of performance as something that happens on stage, set apart from the mundane actions of ordinary life.

I have elsewhere described *natural performance* as "the process which takes naturally-occurring (first-order) performance as the basis for a subsequent re/performance" ("Toward an Aesthetics" 169). The concept of *natural* in this performance category suggests that it is available to any speaker in ordinary circumstances. Natural performance includes everything from the simple reperformance of an offhand conversational quote to the more intensely rehearsed, fully embodied ELP. Natural performance is predicated on the observation that the seemingly mundane details of human interaction reveal remarkably intricate refinement and coordination. Humans plan, practice, and rehearse as well as habituate themselves to performance strategies that produce a daily art of high detail. What continues to astonish is that, with virtually no exceptions, anyone can do it. The people I meet perform every day; and when they enter the classroom as students, they already have most of the equipment they need to explore performance in a more self-reflexive manner. This grounding for performance epistemology arises not from formal education or specific training but is inherent in human play and the performative skills involved in ordinary human discourse. Extended investigation into the communicative possibilities of human interaction illuminates and extends the daily lived knowledge of performers.

When a person accomplishes "ordinary life," the variety of skills that are utilized demonstrate natural performance expertise. Among these are broad skills in rehearsing, concentrating, composing, and controlling body and voice. One can also identify specific skills, such as characterization, doing voices, expert timing, maintaining focus, gesture, and many other components of the actor's art. Theatrical performance, in many of its forms, draws on the strategies invoked by ordinary speakers in their daily routines and in mundane conversation.

Performance Epistemology

Acts of conversational performance (especially ELP) open the way to profound knowing. Careful phenomenological description can (arguably, at least) point toward this knowing. However, in the most profound sense, your body really has to be there to know. The knowledge gained from deep embodiment is ineffable; it uncovers nuances we cannot fully express, evokes things unique, personal, and intimate. *Deep embodiment* (a term evoking Clifford Geertz's *thick description* or *deep play*) has to do with total immersion, using all of the evidence available, getting inside. In ELP, deep embodiment is a rigorous engagement through study and enactment. The process of embodying an other, a text, a persona, or a character makes possible radical understanding. The phrase "performance as a way of knowing" points toward this process by implicating the body as a site of knowledge. Performance as a way of knowing means developing "felt knowledge," a kind of insight unique to the performer.[9] I find myself drawn to ways in which the body can learn from interrogating other bodies through enactment.

Precedents for this work can be found in a long history of theatrical performance involving impersonation, characterization, presentation of another's fictive or real presence, or the oral interpretation of a text. In advising the performer on the preparation of a performance of Joseph Conrad's "The Lagoon," Wallace Bacon writes:

> Read the passage aloud, trying to feel the details of the scene. The sun is *dazzling,* making an *intense glitter* on the water of the river. . . . Look closely at the clues to muscular tension and relaxation, and see whether you can sense in your own body muscular responses to these images. (13)

Indeed, Bacon considers this work "an art of enactment, of embodiment, of becoming" (xvii).

Over the years, a number of young playwrights and cinematographers as well as actors and students of rhetoric, interpersonal communication, and performance studies and others have taken courses where ELP was a primary mode of inquiry. For many of these students, the work provides startling insight into the microscopic details of human interaction. Do we really sound like this? How do we know when it is our turn to talk? When is an overlap not an interruption? In this sense, the work of ELP continues Harvey Sacks's search for order in the details of human discourse. For many, though, the performance component is a difficult encounter. The subject is unyielding. The audiotape or videotape presents a historical reality; it exists as a constant measure of the immutable other. Unlike a written text, say, a drama or a poem, which allows the actor considerable license in performance, in ELP the other cannot be romanticized, possessed, generated, or subjugated. The actor's body must accommodate the other, not conquer it.

How It Feels

I listen to the tape recording over and over. I try to make my mouth follow what I hear. I read the transcript and speak along with the tape. What seems important here is the phenomenon of the body. My body.

My bodily experience as an agent moving through time and space. As I try to organize my movements, move my mouth, extend my limbs, the body tells me something about what it feels like to move in new ways. My habitual movements become shifted into other habitual movements, or the other's habitual movements. I in/habit an/other's space. I let an/other's movements become my habit. In this shifting, I am, in Richard Schechner's phrase, "not me . . . not not me" (112, ellipsis in original). I move my mouth, I organize my vocal apparatus, I speak combinations of syllables invented by some other human, I try repeatedly to move into this other space. Will I ever get it? Ultimately, I know I cannot actually move there, but I move somewhere "different" from where I was. This intense mimesis requires less of make-believe or escape than it requires concentration. Like a dancer or musician who attends to the steps or the music until a certain level of mastery allows the body to take over, I become habituated to this performance because I am habitual. With sufficient practice, my body begins to learn new habits. I feel different. I feel that I am dreaming, dancing, breathing with another. I am performing an *other*.

Another Way It Feels
When one is concerned with precision, it can also feel downright frustrating. Sure, sometimes I might "become the other," but sometimes I'm reminded of my feelings as a young violin student, struggling to reproduce the beautiful tones of my teacher yet repeatedly falling short. My fingerings were insufficiently precise, my bowing awkward, the final sound reflecting a need for more practice. Like the work of the musician, ELP can be difficult. While most everyone possesses the basic skill for this, ELP takes us to a new level. Many of those who can whistle a tune would struggle at the piano or violin. Pure honesty in ELP requires an informed, embodied appraisal, a disciplining of sinew, bone, and aspiration. Creativity, in the way one commonly uses it to mean "self-expression," is not foregrounded in this work. Without wishing to eliminate the need for performer responsibility though, we might remember the nature of natural performance as a quotation. When we quote another person in ordinary conversation, we typically do so easily. We know how to accomplish these ordinary performances, these seemingly simple acts. With ELP, the level of difficulty may substantially increase, but the shift is in degree, not kind. To some extent, I am more likely to remain aware of the other and of myself than I might be were I performing a character in a play. In ELP, I "become" the other character, but I don't make it up.

Performance as Analysis and Deep Embodiment
I know of no more rigorous analysis of human action than the deep embodiment of natural performance that seeks to understand another

person though the body of the performer—to breathe another's breath, to know the rhythm, the inflection, the feel. Where ecstatic performance (or psychological performance) encourages a leap, a trancelike seduction into an imagined other (this is, at times, true for psychological realism as well as many other traditional theatrical forms), natural performance demands a study of the "actual," the presence, the stubborn details of a historically real other. The rewards for the performer differ from those of traditional theatre. In fact, the use of natural performance as theatre, while demonstrably viable as an entertainment mode,[10] is surpassed by its power as a pedagogical tool for investigating self and other through deep embodiment. Deep embodiment is at once critical scholarship and empathy.

The stubborn details drawn empirically from historically real others work to mitigate stereotyping or essentializing an "other." One of the great advantages of this work is that it is always, necessarily, particular, not universal. The ELP actor works with a particular human being, a particular voice, in a particular moment. Generalizations that seek to suggest racial, class, ethnic, or gender categories are unhelpful or pointless. The director never can say, "People like your character do this or that!" Instead, the director or actor must look to the specific evidence. I do not mean to suggest that the actor necessarily comes to admire the character/person performed or to like the things said. Rather, the actor learns something important about what it must feel like to do what that person did. Useful critical responses subsequently gain depth and complexity unique to this performance work.

When the performer successfully moves through the work of ELP, there is a strict attention paid to the empirical details of another's prior performance. This is why you can't perform stereotypes in ELP. The fact of that prior performance is immutable. ELP does not ask for inspiration in the romantic sense; it asks for inspiration in the sense of breath. ELP demands focus on the real, the particular, the individual. There is no room to generalize, to universalize, to essentialize. When the actor is making the exact sounds of the subject, those sounds are just what they are, and they are a window into another person in a unique and powerful way. This is not to say that the audience cannot make essentializing moves, but audiences are always characterized by their individual responses.

The ELP performances described here depend on conversational data (recordings of natural talk), but in a broad sense, "natural performance" is a daily phenomenon. People routinely perform others and themselves in informal ways. So, ordinary human interaction carries the seeds of the more focused and rigorous study required by ELP.

A hierarchy of resources, or data, provides a basic idea of the information that might be available to a performer: (1) recordings of natural interaction (videotape or audiotape) that preserve some relatively stable records of historical behavior; (2) face-to-face interaction in which the recording is done by memory (but which has a rich sensory dimension not available on the tape, e.g., smell, touch, and other information); (3) textual reproductions in which the performer has only a written script; and (4) reportings of others, once removed. These first three types have various levels of detail, various amounts of information, so that a finely grained conversation analysis transcript may have more of some kinds of information than a play script. In the final type, the other is filtered, so that we may say that what is actually given is a performance to serve as the basis for a performance.

An additional resource for deep embodiment is the performer's own body, a body that acts in accordance with what it can do and attempts to meet what an other body has already done. The information/feeling/insight/knowledge built into the performing body is at the core of the experience. With novice performers, the first challenge is to engage the other body, since many students have been schooled toward the premium reward of "self-expression." But naturally, such engagement is in the body of the performer. We can draw here on the groundwork established by such writers as Leland Roloff and Wallace Bacon, whose tradition builds on the taking in (of a text), and in Bacon's term, *outering*.

One of the recurrent values of this work is the likely recognition that one cannot simply "walk in another's shoes." This rigorous mimetic approach ultimately tells something about difference. The difference is an exposure that raises awareness, rather like Drew Leder's phenomenological inquiry. Marked by his training as a physician, Leder builds on examples of the body's dysfunction: "when the body is rendered opaque through loss of function, we become aware of it as alien presence" (82). Through a similar awareness, natural performance makes the actor's own body opaque. When working to inflect a phrase, to breathe, or to pause as heard on the tape recording, the actor's own physical apparatus becomes apparent.

The empirical body/presence of the presumed historical real challenges everyday actors with the task of rigorous inspection. "The other" (any other, even the historical self) resists all but the most fortunate performance. The approach described here is humbling at least for its revelations. What the performer encounters is not his or her imagination but the archive of a previous body. Such acting requires creativity as well as discipline. This form of mimesis is paradoxical in that it forces introspection as well as expression. The actor does not "make the character his or her own" in the way the phrase is commonly used. Instead, the actor "simply" acts like another. Ultimately, though, ELP is easier to do than to describe. Students grasp this approach with joy and amazement at what they can do. They suddenly have a whole new way of understanding the structure of human interaction. Students who do not consider themselves performers or actors give remarkable performances that intrigue, captivate, and (importantly) engage their audiences. The engagement leads to critical discussion. What did the original speakers accomplish in their talk? What did we learn about the structure of their interaction? What did we learn about them as human beings? What did we learn about ourselves? I have seen the radical transformative power of this performance in ordinary classrooms, where the epistemological significance of performance is at once personal and social. As a performer along with my students, I've come to respect "performance as a way of knowing," especially as a way to understand everyday performances of "ordinary" people. As Robert Hopper projected, conversational dramatism joins the performing arts to criticism through the empirical study of conversational interaction. Everyday life performance, with its capacity for deep embodiment, demonstrates one way in which a performance studies pedagogy can lead to a better understanding of human communication.

NOTES

1. For a discussion of "everyday life performance," see Hopper. See also chapters by Joni L. Jones and Eric Dishman in this volume. For an explanation of "natural performance," see Stucky, "Toward an Aesthetics."

2. This course in conversational performance, which attracts both graduate and undergraduate students, was jointly created by Phil Glenn, Bryan Crow, and the author.

3. For descriptions of ELP methods, see Gilbert; Hopper; Randall; Stucky, "Toward an Aesthetics" and "Unnatural Acts"; Stucky and Glenn.

4. The names of the recorded speakers and the actors have been changed.

5. In this simplified transcription, various uses of *h* signify laughter. A colon indicates a stretched sound. Pauses are indicated in parentheses in seconds and tenths of seconds. Square brackets indicate the beginning of overlapping utterances.

6. Quoted by permission from a student writing project in the author's Conversational Performance class.

7. In natural performance theory, each performance is an "original." See Stucky, "Toward an Aesthetics" 170–71.

8. Denzin discusses this work as performance science, an attempt to blend social sciences with performance (108). Denzin's overview is helpful, although I am not convinced by his assertion that these performances do not engage in "cultural critique" (114). There, it seems to me, he misses the important point of selection of texts in the process; the role of juxtaposition and arrangement, with their inevitable critical and aesthetic impact; and also the pedagogical contexts of these performances. Nevertheless, Denzin indicates helpful comparisons of ELP with other performance approaches.

9. I am indebted to my colleague Ronald Pelias at Southern Illinois University, for whom the phrase "performance as a way of knowing" is a touchstone of embodied performance theory. Pelias attributes his use of this phrase to his graduate teachers Leland H. Roloff and Joanna H. Maclay (ix).

10. Several theatrical performances have been created, borrowing on the techniques discussed here. In addition to *Believe Me,* these include *Conversation Pieces,* dir. Bryan Crow, Southern Illinois U, Carbondale, 30 Apr., 1–2 May 1987; and *Naturally Speaking,* dir. Nathan Stucky, Louisiana State U, Baton Rouge, 28–30 Apr. 1990.

WORKS CITED

Bacon, Wallace. *The Art of Interpretation.* 3rd ed. New York: Holt, 1979.

Believe Me, I'm Lying, Believe Me. Dir. Nathan Stucky. U of Texas, Austin. 8, 9 March 1985.

Denzin, Norman K. *Interpretive Ethnography: Ethnographic Practices for the 21st Century.* Thousand Oaks: Sage, 1997.

Geertz, Clifford. "Deep Play: Notes on the Balinese Cockfight." *Myth, Symbol, and Culture.* Ed. Geertz. New York: Norton, 1971. 1–37.

———. "Thick Description: Toward an Interpretive Theory of Culture." *The Interpretation of Culture.* New York: Basic, 1973. 3–37.

Gilbert, Joanne R. "Inspiration and Conversation: Breat(h)ing the Other." *Text and Performance Quarterly* 13.2 (1993): 186–88.

Hopper, Robert. "Conversational Dramatism and Everyday Life Performance." *Text and Performance Quarterly* 13.2 (1993): 181–83.

"I'm an Alien." Transcribed conversation. Author's collection. Southern Illinois U, Carbondale. SIUC.NS.4.95.

Leder, Drew. *The Absent Body.* Chicago: U of Chicago P, 1990.

Pelias, Ronald J. *Writing Performance: Poeticizing the Researcher's Body.* Carbondale: Southern Illinois UP, 1999.

Randall, Deleasa M. "Staged Replication of Naturally-Occurring Talk: A Performer's Perspective." *Text and Performance Quarterly* 13.2 (1993): 197–99.

Read, Alan. *Theatre and Everyday Life: An Ethics of Performance.* New York: Routledge, 1993.

Roloff, Leland H. *The Perception and Evocation of Literature.* Glenview: Scott, 1973.

Sacks, Harvey. "On Doing 'Being Ordinary.'" *Structures of Social Action: Studies in Conversation Analysis.* Ed. J. Maxwell Atkinson and John Heritage. Cambridge: Cambridge UP, 1984. 413–29.

Schechner, Richard. *Between Theater and Anthropology.* Philadelphia: U of Pennsylvania P, 1985.

Stucky, Nathan. "Toward an Aesthetics of Natural Performance." *Text and Performance Quarterly* 13.2 (1993): 168–80.

———. "Unnatural Acts: Performing Natural Conversation." *Literature in Performance* 8.2 (1988): 28–39.

Stucky, Nathan, and Phillip Glenn. "Invoking the Empirical Muse: Conversation, Performance, and Pedagogy." *Text and Performance Quarterly* 13.2 (1993): 192–96.

Tate, Greg. "In *Fires in the Mirror,* Anna Deavere Smith Wears Her Words." *Village Voice* 21 July 1992: 101.

Taussig, Michael. *Mimesis and Alterity: A Particular History of the Senses.* New York: Routledge, 1993.

Action, Structure, Task, and Emotion

9

Phillip B.
Zarrilli

Theories of Acting, Emotion,

and Performer Training

from a Performance Studies Perspective

Born out of the practical time-specific demands of "the profession," theories and practices of acting are usually inward-looking and genre/period/context specific. By "theory of acting," I mean that each time an actor performs, he or she implicitly enacts a "theory" of acting—that set of assumptions about the conventions and style that guide his or her performance. Informing any particular theory of acting are specific assumptions about the body-mind relationship, the nature of the "self," one's state of mind or consciousness, the presence or absence of emotions/feelings, and the performance context. As one is trained and acculturated into a system of acting practice, these assumptions often remain at the periphery of consciousness and seem "natural" until challenged.

Central to the ongoing debates about the nature and practice of acting, as well as the concepts of body, self, person, role, and character implicit in any particular theory, paradigm, or practice of acting, "stands the question of emotion" (Roach 11).[1] The "question of emotion" in contemporary Western actor training, especially in the United States, is configured around the commonplace tendency to assume an emotion is a spontaneous eruption of feeling. Young actors often confuse their own commonplace personal/emotional life experiences with those of the characters they are asked to play. Since both one's personal emotional life and acting involve intense "feelings," and since characters are often analyzed using a psychologically based set of assumptions about behavior, this confusion is not surprising. Given their practical concern with performance, most commonplace theories of acting and the emotions do not reflect metatheoretically on the nature, process, practice, or phenomenon of acting/performance and of emotion within that process.

The problem of emotion in Western acting received its earliest and still quintessential metatheoretical expression in Dennis Diderot's infamous 1773 statement of the paradox of acting—"If the actor were full, really full of feeling, how could he play the same part twice running with the same spirit and success?" (qtd. in Cole and Chinoy 162). As Joseph Roach explains, Diderot was the first to approach acting "as a craft rather than as a diabolic or sacred mystery," and therefore, to him do we owe "our concept of the actor's art as a definable process of creating a role" (117–18). Diderot, speaking through "The First," concludes that the actor is "best when he imitates anger. Actors impress the public not when they are furious, but when they play fury well. . . . What passion itself fails to do, passion well imitated accomplishes" (Cole and Chinoy 170).

In spite of the nuances of Diderot's complex and lengthy reflection on acting in light of "vitalistic materialism" (Roach 116), Diderot's statement of the paradox as a paradox and his conclusion, at least on the surface, accentuate the type of dichotomy between reason and emotion, body and mind, still reflected in much thinking about these terms. When reason becomes exalted, and emotion is denigrated, the result is an unfortunate oversimplification, since "the relationship between the two terms is much more complicated" (Woodward 3).

As I am a performance theorist who makes use of the interdisciplinarity of performance studies *and* a practical theatre-maker who trains actor/performers and directs, this essay is my metatheoretical reflection on how three, seemingly quite different perspectives might converge to shed some light on the question of emotion in acting.

Theories of Performance and Theatre
Acting as Process and Practice in the Performative Moment
One of the most important modes of theorizing theatre is through the more comprehensive notion of "performance." *Performance* can be defined as one mode of social, cultural, aesthetic, and/or personal praxis through which experience, knowledges, discourses, and meanings have been and are constantly (re)negotiated and (re)positioned through daily and/or extra-daily performance practices.

In all performative events per se, performers and spectators alike could be described as materializing (sub)culture, context-specific ways of experiencing the performative moment. Here *practice* implies both the performer's as well as the spectator's active *engagement* in the *process* of performing and/or spectating; it captures the experiential component of the process (Zarrilli, "What Does It Mean"). But many of our current critical theories and methodologies have not taken sufficient account of the body/experience/emotion at this site of materialization of experience and meaning in the theatrical performative event, either from the perspective of the performer or the audience. While more materialist/constructivist accounts—whether those of semiotics, structuralism, new historicism, anthropology, or feminist theory—have provided long-needed critiques of reductive and essentialist ways of thinking, I would agree with philosopher Robert C. Solomon, who recently argued that "what tends to get lost in social construction theory is subjectivity, experience, the irreducibly personal aspect of emotion" (273). It is through the experience-generating body-self in practice that one's self, agency, power, and emotions are potentially "disciplined" and/or "transformed."

These are "technologies" of the body in Foucault's sense, practices through which "humans develop knowledge about themselves" (18). Training in voice, acting, movement, and the like are specific psychophysiological techniques practiced to shape and potentially "transform" the practitioner to attain a certain normative and/or idealized relationship between the "self," one's "agency" or "power" (often in the form of virtuosity), and/or behavior. In this sense, actor training, acting, as well as spectating are "incorporating practices" through which the *bodymind* (as I refer to it), and therefore experience and meaning, are "culturally shaped in its actual practices and behaviours" (Connerton 104).

Embodied practices are those modes of doing through which everyday as well as extra-daily experiences, realities, and meanings are shaped and negotiated.[2] As discussed by Mauss, de Certeau, and Bourdieu, everyday practices include such habitualized and routine activities as walking, driving, or engaging in hygienic practices. Extra-daily practices are those practices—such as rituals, dances, theatre training and performance, the recitation of oral narratives, meditation and/or religious practices, martial arts—that require the practitioner to undergo specialized body-training in order to become accomplished in attaining an often virtuosic state of consciousness, body, agency, and power. Extraordinary energy, time, and resources are often invested to create cultural specialists, whose embodied practices are the means by which personal, social, ritual, aesthetic, literary, and/or cosmological "realities" are created, enacted, and experienced. Similarly, though usually in a less obvious manner, time and energy are often invested in acculturating spectators in how to experience and appreciate performances.

But modes of extra-daily cultural practice such as acting and spectating are not *a* practice that is reducible to its obvious set of virtuosic body-techniques or ideal mode of engagement; rather, modes of embodied practice exist as a set of potentialities inherent in the complex *set* of practices, discourses, and representations through which a practitioner's experience of practice is historically and contextually negotiated. Through entrainment, embodiment, and/or acculturation complex, extra-daily cultural practices and performances "structure the structure" of available experiences and meanings (Kapferer 202). A performance "score" is the structure of potential actions that postulates itself (and its ideal audience) in the process of its creation, whether in workshop or rehearsal and/or by convention/tradition.[3] When considering "performance" more broadly, the actor's "score," or what the actor 'does' onstage[,] may range from a psychologically motivated realistic character, through a character-structure into and out of which the actor steps on a moment-to-moment basis, to the sequential playing of multiple roles, to the playing of roles or sequences of action which require the development of a specific relationship to the audience as a part of one's score, to the playing of multiple personae, to the enactment of tasks without any characterological implications. For the actor, whatever the actions to be performed, these actions are the 'material' conditions of his or her work. (Zarrilli, Introduction 21)

One of the most important models of practical performance research focusing on embodiment and "what the actor does" when performing a score is the work of Eugenio Barba. Barba researches the "material bases" of the performer's art—those "bits of good advice" and/or "principles" (but not laws) that are "useful for [extra-daily] scenic practice" (Barba and Savarese 8). This research is a practical form of metatheoretical inquiry since, unlike specific theories or practices of acting, it looks more broadly at "principles" (but not laws) of performative behavior.[4] The focus on practical "bits of advice" narrows the sociocultural and contextual frame from ethnographic inquiry to the confines of an intercultural, transnational training or laboratory space where a new working vocabulary and paradigm of the psychophysiological principles of performance are practically explored. Barba's research has called attention to the dynamic psychophysiological nature of such important "principles" as "balance," "dilation," "energy," and "equivalence," which can become *points of departure* for practical performance work. Implicit is an understanding of the importance of the performer's virtuosic actualization of a particular psychophysiological state or condition.

Whatever the structure (of training, workshop, or performance) and whatever the score of specific actions, at a metatheoretical level, structure is never static but is always *in a process of negotiation*. Bourdieu calls this openness a form of "tactical improvisation" (Jenkins 51). The view of improvisation and process adopted here is multifaceted; tactical improvisation occurs both "within" a specific process of practice, such as acting or actor training, as well as between practice as received and the horizon of its possibilities that stretches toward an "undetermined" future. It is within this potentially undetermined future field of the possible that the individual practitioner constantly (re)constitutes his or her own practice and that the spectator shifts his or her expectations, thereby subtly or overtly shifting and re-creating experience, its paradigmatic formations, and discursive constructs.

Victor Turner described the potentially transformative nature of these "open-ended" processes as "subjunctive" in contrast to the "indicative" (244), explaining that "Subjunctivity is possibility [and is] concerned with supposition, conjecture, and assumption, with the domain of 'as-if' rather than 'as-is'" (265). Such open-endedness is characteristic of many modes of contemporary actor training and performance that stress being "in the moment." David George similarly views all performances as characterized by "their temporality, ephemerality, ambiguity, specificity, their restless improvisation, their haunting by shadowy options, [which] make them events or at best processes" (19). When considered from the perspective of performance, "for all too long theatre has been categorized as a form of representation when [at least in the moment of performance] it was actually an experiment in creative alternatives" (23).

For the audience, too, possible meanings lie in the processual experience of the performative moment. At a metatheoretical level, the inherent indeterminacy, singularity, irregularity, and therefore "improvisatory" qualities of the performative moment are often occluded for spectators, especially in formal or "traditional" theatre contexts, where the virtuosity of performance "hides" the indeterminacy the actor may experience in the moment. Reception is both individual and collective. And any act of reception is active, even when an audience appears to be passive or when the process is "unsuccessful" in attaining an ideal-typical mode of aesthetic/experiential engagement.

When acting is viewed as a process, practice, or set of actions, it invites consideration of the specific tasks or actions in which the actor is engaged. But what are the "tasks or actions" in which the actor is engaged when portraying "emotions," and what is the nature of this "engagement"? To understand the "emotional" tasks or actions that constitute an actor's performance score, I turn to the specific example of Kerala, India's *kathakali* dance-drama, where "the emotions" are so obviously present in the use of facial expression.[5] I do so with the understanding that explaining emotion in *kathakali* is necessarily an interpretive task of translation "from one idiom, context, language, or sociohistorical mode of understanding into another" (Lutz 8). My translation covers three perspectives from which we can examine the emotional states of being/doing exemplified in *kathakali:* analysis of these states as enactments and representations of a South Asian understanding of the emotions, as reflected in its epic characters; analysis of the emotional states *(bhava)* of psychophysiological embodiment from the point of view of the actor; and analysis of the modes of spectatorial practice of experiencing these emotional states *(rasa).*

Structure, Task/Action, and the Psychophysiological Embodiment of "Emotion" in Kathakali Dance-Drama
As South Asian scholar June McDaniel points out, Vedanta, the classical yoga of Patanjali, and Ayurveda all in their own way "provide a ba-

sis for [a] negative view of emotion" (45). This fundamentally negative view of emotion in everyday life is found throughout *kathakali* dance-dramas, where its epic heroes suffer to "excess" such effects as over-weening pride, separation from their lovers, or the scourge of cosmic anger. I begin with an example from *Nalacaritam, First Day,* one of the most famous plays in the South Indian *kathakali* dance-drama reper-tory. There is a moment in which the actor playing the male hero, Nala, embodies the following verse as it is being sung by the onstage vocal-ists: "Having heard [the sage] Narada's words, and the words of other travellers, Nala's mind, already immersed in thinking about Damay-anti, became pained by his longing for her" (Varryar). In performance, this verse is rather simply enacted and does not employ *kathakali's* highly codified language of hand gestures used to deliver first-person lines; however, it requires the actor's consummate skill in "interior act-ing" as he subtly embodies *cinta bhava*—a state of being best translated as "reflecting." Nala's active state of "reflection" is about his love for the beautiful heroine of the play, Damayanti—an act that causes him "pain" because he is unsure whether his budding love will be assuaged.

Working within the "sense of appropriateness" *(aucitya bodham)* to the dramatic context, the actor assumes a physical attitude of thought-ful reflection. Nala's state is subtly conveyed to the audience through the actor's use of his eyes and facial expressions, both of which are in-fused with the "emotional" resonance of the moment through subtle and skillful manipulation of his breath *(prana vayu)*. At the culminat-ing point in the Malayalam verse and as the onstage vocalist slowly sings, "it happened, his mind was pained by sorrow," on a quick catch-breath, the actor moves his right hand to his chest as his eyes look up at the sky, and then, slowly following the trajectory of the gradual ex-halation of his breath, his eyes trace a line downward toward the ground as he heaves a deep sigh, and his facial expression assumes a pained sorrow *(soka bhava)*. The actor playing Nala lingers thought-fully on his beloved, taking sufficient time to allow this performative elaboration of Nala's inner mental state to be relished by those con-noisseurs in the audience who know the story and Nala's state of mind well enough to "taste" both his act of reflection and the resultant pain in an aesthetic experience of *rasa*. Nala's reflective state of mind then gives ways to sorrow. For the actor playing Nala, embodying the state of *cinta bhava*, or "reflection," necessarily involves psychophysiologi-cally moving through this temporal progression from reflection, to sorrow, to pain.

The *kathakali* actor's score is a detailed series of psychophysiologi-cal elaborations of the base text *through time*. Full psychophysiological embodiment of these detailed states of being/consciousness/emotion *(bhava)* involves years of intense training and ideally results in the actor's ability to engage his bodymind fully in each specific action in his score (Zarrilli, *Kathakali Complex*). The amount of time it takes to enact a line like the above is much longer than the "real" time it would take to either speak the line or behaviorally enact it. This is so in part because the "mood" is the relatively languorous elaboration of "reflection" (sorrow/pain). In addition, because this particular line is much less set than usual and relatively open to the actor's individual interpretation, performance time is determined by how long the actor takes to psychophysiologically complete his interpretation.

As described above, each state in turn is embodied and realized as the actor focuses externally on specific points while delivering hand and facial gestures and engages his "inner eye" (attention, or perceiving consciousness in-the-moment) as well as breath/energy *(prana-vayu)* in what he is doing. As G. S. Warrier explains, "You get the entire emotion on the face. Then the actor practices what is called concentrating the thought there, and gives it wind *(vayu)*. It's one of the great secrets of acting. . . . It gives nervous control."[6] For the actor, his own "concentration of thought" *is* the psychophysiological concentration of both his breath and field of visual/mental focus in what he is doing in each moment. For example, as the actor moves his right hand to his chest, and as his external focus goes upward, he is not "thinking about" or "reflecting upon" either his own (actor's) state or condition of sorrow or that of the character; rather, "sorrow" *is* his active engagement through time of his inner energy/breath *(prana vayu)* in the embodied act of focusing his gaze and placing his hand. In this particular example, "nervous control" is the virtuosic actor's ability to modulate his breath and focus through time so that the audience might have their own (aesthetic) experience of the character's "emotional" state of sorrow.

The fundamental assumption that, as McDaniel writes, the "terms for emotion and thought, mind and heart, are not opposed" (43) applies both to Nala's representation as a character on stage as well as to the actor psychophysiologically embodying the role. McDaniel goes on to explain that the term *mana*

> means both mind and heart, as well as mood, feeling, mental state, memory, desire, attachment, interest, attention, devotion, and decision. These terms do not have a single referent in English, and must be understood through clusters of explicit and implicit meanings. (43)

The "structuring of structure" is the actor's psychophysiological score, and the specificity of the *kathakali* actor's task of constantly directing his focus and breath reflects the engagement of the actor's *manasa* (mind/attention/heart) in the act of performing each "emotional" state *(bhava)* in turn. In this sense, the actor trained through a corporeal discipline learns to "direct" his or her "passions" as he or she learns to control the breath. The performative elaboration of "emotional states," such as Nala's, goes far beyond a simple representation of his emotional behavior. It is precisely these "negative" states of mental/emotional excess embodied on the *kathakali* stage that the ideal herosages like Nala should overcome.

Central to *kathakali* dance-drama and a number of India's other performing arts is the Sanskrit notion of *rasa*—a term too often mistranslated simply as "emotion" and actually meaning sap, juice, flavor, color, or residual essence as experienced by the audience. In the above example, as the actor psychophysiologically embodies each progressive mind/emotional state *(bhava)* through his cultivated ability to engage his entire bodymind, the audience "tastes" each state in turn. These states enhance the ideal audience member's experience of the subtler nuances of the primary *rasas* around which *kathakali* dance-dramas are loosely organized—for *Nalacaritam*, "love in union and separation." The actor's task is to use his virtuosic psychophysiological abilities to embody and thereby "carry forward" *(abhinaya)* these states for the audience's pleasure.

In both devotional and aesthetic experience in South Asia, the participant is gradually acculturated into a state where "raw, 'concrete' emotions can be transformed into aesthetic and religious ones" (McDaniel 43). Because there is no sharp distinction between emotion and cognition, thought is associated with knowledge and discrimination, as well as feelings and imagination (44).

In a 1993 interview, seventy-eight-year-old *kathakali* connoisseur Ganesha Iyer explained his view of the process of aesthetic experience of the emotional states elaborated by *kathakali* actors:

> When the actor enacts certain *rasas*, they are able to create a sympathetic motion in my heart. When he enacts a sorrowful aspect, I do not experience sorrow but appreciate his expression of sorrow. . . . I experience sympathetic vibration. But in some people, they may experience this as a *real* emotion. . . . When a very sorrowful scene is enacted, some may weep. . . . This difference may be due to having a more "intellectual" appreciation, and not "emotional."

Iyer's observations reflect this progression from a state of uncultivated "raw" emotion to a state of "refined" aesthetic experience "of the mind," implying a richer, deeper, potentially more transformative experience.

The South Asian paradigm operative here assumes that any discipline of practice, whether yoga, a performing or martial art, or the aesthetic experience of the ideal *rasika/sahrdaya*, has the potential to transform one's sensibilities of thought/mind/body/emotion. Accordingly, one's sensibilities begin at the grossest, physical, most external level, and through a gradual process of education and cultivation, one moves toward a subtler, more refined, and "internal" or "mental" mode of appreciation and/or action. *Kathakali* is, in this sense, a "theatre of the mind," which is a theatre of the "cooked" and not the "raw" emotions.

Kathakali invites us to see the actor's "problem of emotion" anew. Although in South Asia, it is assumed that everyday emotions are fundamentally negative and involve potentially overwhelming experiences, there is no absolute dichotomy between reason and emotion, mind and heart. There is always a "cognitive" or mental element involved in the representation and performance of emotion. Attention is focused on elaborating mental/emotional states, not reproducing them behaviorally. Attention is also given to developing a state of consciousness or awareness *beyond* emotion and assumed in aesthetic, devotional, and psychophysiological practices. *Kathakali's* version of performing the "emotions" might be described as an "aesthetics of plenitude"—a performative aesthetic *(bhava/rasa)* that assumes that both performers and audience engage the performative event *as a practice*, as an extra-daily way of being/doing attained through cultivation and/or training. Both actor and spectator are engaged in states of consciousness that are "dual" but not dualistic; both enter states of active engagement in which perceiving consciousness is appropriately directed and modulated.

"Character" is equivalent to the sequential set of psychophysiological actions that the actor embodies through time, and the character's "emotions" are more clearly not those of the actors since they begin on the "outside" as physical configurations of the face/hands/body. The actor's task is a psychophysiological one that engages his or her complete bodymind/consciousness in each moment of embodiment.

Precisely because of *kathakali's* "emotional excess," it contrasts sharply with the more "natural" appearance of staged emotion in much contemporary Western character acting. When emotional states are elaborated in nonrealist genres, there is less potential "confusion" of the collapse of the actor's own private emotions with those of characters because there is not the same equivalence of time and behavior.[7] The performers of nonrealist genres more obviously modulate and elaborate the psychophysiological embodiment of emotion through either their vocalization or a gestural line of action.

The "Question of Emotion" Revisited:
Western Perspectives from Diderot and Psychology
In the final part of this essay, I briefly return to Diderot as well as to more recent Western studies of emotions in acting to reflect on how the cognitive element of acting and recent cognitive theories of the

emotions shed light on the structure and emotional engagement of the actor in traditional, formal character acting in the West. The paradox of Diderot's "paradox of acting" is that behind the apparent dualism is a subtle understanding and explanation of the psychophysiology of the actor's process that attempted to account for both the "experiential" and "cognitive" components of emotion. As Joseph Roach explains, the "inner model" of the character serves "as a kind of linear matrix and template: it structures sequences of passions" (133) as an "art-in-time" (153) to be absorbed by the actor through rehearsal *(repetition)* to the point where the score is performed "spontaneously." Diderot's "insistence that mind and body are inextricably interwoven in the same web of nervous fibres, which can be shaped into patterns of response by repetition" (Roach 157), parallels *kathakali's* dual consciousness without dualism and looks forward to the work of cognitive psychologists.

In her study of emotions and acting, psychologist Elly Konijn views emotions *not* as residing "solely in a person's inner self" but as existing and arising

> from an interaction with the environment. Contemporary cognitive theories of emotions hold that emotions are functional reactions regarding an individual's well-being with respect to his concerns in coping with environmental demands and in establishing relationships. ("Actors" 133)

In this view, "the situational meaning structure forms the basis of an emotional experience and defines a specific emotion." Therefore, Konijn carefully distinguishes between four, quite different domains of "emotion" that converge in acting: the "private," daily, primary, or "prototypical" emotions such as anger, sadness, love, and hate, which the individual experiences in daily life; the "task emotions" of the "actor-craftsman"; the "intended emotions" that constitute the actor's "inner model" or the performance score/structure, developed through the actor's imagination and/or determined by genre or convention; and the "character emotions" as performed and received by the audience (133).

In daily life, or in realist modes of representation that presume to re-present behavioral responses to everyday emotions, "regulation of emotions . . . [is] usually directed at reducing the negative or distorting side effects of emotional experiences" (Konijn, "Actors" 133). But the situational meaning structure and therefore the actor's "task-emotions" are quite different from those experienced in "daily life" or represented in realist theatre. The professional actor's task concerns acquiring "skills and techniques to cope with environmental demands" of acting, which in turn leads to demonstrating competence as a professional before a highly critical and evaluative audience—a performance situation, which is both "difficult" and "urgent," resulting in "high intensities of emotion" (Konijn, "Emotions" 3–5). In acting, as in other high performance situations, "challenge" becomes "a central emotion," and when "balanced by the skills of the actor, this leads to the optimal experience of flow and concentration, focusing on what needs to be done" (6–7).

Therefore, for Konijn the actor is not what might be described as a "bundle of feelings" but rather, following Diderot, an "actor-crafts-man" ("Actors" 133) whose "emotional" experience of acting is deter-mined by the situation in which the actor performs his or her task. Consequently, in stage performances,

> there is no actual need to arouse emotions in oneself as an actor
> in order to convey character-emotions convincingly. The func-
> tion of task-emotions therefore is to contribute to the illusion of
> spontaneity of character-emotions and to achieve presence on
> stage. ("Actors" 134–35)

In Konijn's terminology, the actor's "private emotions" may be involved along the way in the training or rehearsal process as the actor impro-vises, negotiates, and develops the "inner model" of the character's "intended emotions," eventually scored and performed as the "charac-ter-emotions." The "character" is the structuring of that set of actions (character-emotions) that the actor must embody during perfor-mance, and the process of creating the inner model is the "structuring of the structure of action" to be performed before an audience.[8]

Helpfully, Konijn also differentiates between the experience of a novice and that of an experienced, virtuosic performer who gradually "shapes" the actor's task-emotions through training and/or practical experience ("Emotions" 8). Although the expression of character-emo-tions is reflected in facial expression in particular and shaped by the conventions of particular genres, whether realism or *kathakali*, the "task-emotions do not have characteristic facial expressions"; rather, they are noticeable in the actor's relationship to the specific task of em-bodying the performative moment—"a sharp readiness, an increased awareness, presence, tenseness, alertness, excitement, warmth, goal-orientedness, and so on" (9). For Konijn, this process of shaping the "task-emotions" is a positive process of development. Konijn's con-clusion parallels both Barba's differentiation between "daily" and "ex-tra-daily" behaviors noted earlier, as well as the process of virtuosic, or superior, "cultivation" of awareness/concentration/consciousness through psychophysiological practice.

What are the implications of this convergence of perspectives drawn from performance studies for actor training and acting? Exam-ining performance as a process, we see acting as one form of perform-ing that possesses a score or structure actualized as it happens through the bodymind's engagement in the performative moment. Actors should be trained both to recognize and actualize not only a character-based model of acting but a variety of performance scores or structures that extend their range of performance skills, such as improvisation and devising new work (Oddey). Within their training in character-based acting, actors should be able to differentiate between and actualize quite different performance scores and actions of a variety of dramaturgies.

The performative moment, scored and structured by convention, in training, and in rehearsal, *aims* toward (virtuosic) actualization of a structured order but can never be existentially so. Even in "traditional" approaches to performing dramatic texts, the apparent "stability" of the dramatic text belies the instability of the actor's *act* of performance that, as Gantar asserts, "is best defined as a messy, essentially unstable phenomenon whose main attributes are, first, sensitivity to even the smallest disturbances, and second, abundant uncertainty" (541). This view is reflected in Konijn's definition of the task-emotions in acting. Therefore, the performative moment is always poised between the ideal actualization of a structure and its potential dis-order—a disorder that always threatens to become pandemonium. Contemporary modes of actor/performer training should necessarily take account of this "existential reality" in the structuring of training toward performance; therefore, training should include ways of allowing the actor to inhabit this existential state of "dispossession and difference" where "anything might happen."

Konijn's model of emotion and acting calls for techniques of training through which the actor's task-emotions are both recognized as different from the prototypical and performed character-emotions and then cultivated, shaped, and developed so that the actor is able to attain a "sharp readiness, an increased awareness," and so on. Such awareness is evident in a *kathakali* actor's performance, as described above, and in Roach's description of the optimal state Diderot expected actors to possess, with a "freedom of mind, a calm at the center that persists despite whatever paroxysms the body suffers outwardly" (Roach 148). Similarly, Yasuo Yuasa's research on the body and bodymind relationship eventually led him to describe the practitioner as developing an experiential sensitivity to the internal circulation of *ki* (breath-energy), becoming a "*ki*-sensitive person" whose psychophysiological awareness is experienced as "a *self-grasping sensation of one's body*, that is, as an *awareness* of the whole of one's body" (qtd. in Nagamoto 60). Yuasa asserts that the *ki*-sensitive person, through cultivating disciplines, activates "a mediating system that links the mind and the body" (59). Extensive training in psychophysiological techniques can develop and attune the bodymind toward an intuitive ability to better inhabit this moment, to explore the variety of performative principles that are part of the dynamic experience of the embodied performative moment, *and* to engage and modulate any performance score psychophysiologically.

NOTES

1. The "question" or "problem" of emotion continues to be one of the most important and vexing because the question and nature of the emotions remain open to debate in various disciplines and from multiple perspectives. Even within particular disciplines such as psychology, "most writers have disagreed in their definitions of emotion, often describing different phenomena" (Ekman 9).

2. Barba and Savarese's distinction between "extra-daily" and daily practices is useful since it calls attention to the similarities and differences between habitualized modes of daily practice and virtuosic modes of embodied practice, such as performance.

3. Modes of ongoing training, such as Grotowski's paratheatrical work and workshops, each possess their own inherent "score" and processual horizon of expectations.

4. Barba and Savarese clearly differentiate their use of the term *theatre anthropology* from other anthropologies and insist that it denotes "a new field of study applied to the human being in an organised performance situation" (5).

5. As should become clear in the following discussion, instead of *kathakali,* I could just as easily have discussed opera or melodrama, arguably the two Western genres closest to *kathakali,* since both could be described as "exaggerating" the emotions and using a "psychophysiological" approach to embodying the emotions.

6. See also Zarrilli, "What Does It Mean" and *Kathakali Dance-Drama,* chap. 4, for a further discussion of the details of this process.

7. There *are* debates in Kerala today about the degree to which the actor's own personality and experience come into play in performing *kathakali.*

8. Neuroscientist Susana Bloch has developed research on the training of emotional expression for actors. Bloch ultimately reaches the same conclusion as Konijn that "actors do not need to 'feel' the [character] emotion they are playing but must produce the correct effector-expressive output of the emotional behavior" (Bloch et al. 214). Although Bloch's research is highly significant, unlike Konijn, she has yet to articulate an overarching theory of emotion in acting found in Konijn's fourfold delineation of "private," "task," "intended," and "character" emotions.

WORKS CITED

Barba, Eugenio, and Nicola Savarese. *A Dictionary of Theatre Anthropology.* New York: Routledge, 1991.

Bloch, Susana, Pedro Orthous, and Guy Santibañes-H. "Effector Patterns of Basic Emotions: A Psychophysiological Method for Training Actors." *Acting (Re)Considered: Theories and Practices*. Ed. Phillip B. Zarrilli. New York: Routledge, 1995. 197–218.

Bourdieu, Pierre. *Outline of a Theory of Practice*. Cambridge: Cambridge UP, 1977.

Cole, Toby, and Helen K. Chinoy, eds. *Actors on Acting*. Rev. ed. New York: Crown, 1980.

Connerton, Paul. *How Societies Remember*. Cambridge: Cambridge UP, 1989.

de Certeau, Michel. *The Practice of Everyday Life*. Trans. Steven Rendall. Berkeley: U of California P, 1984.

Ekman, Paul. *Emotions in the Human Face*. 2nd ed. Cambridge: Cambridge UP, 1982.

Foucault, Michel. "Technologies of the Self." *Technologies of the Self: A Seminar with Michel Foucault*. Ed. Luther H. Martin. Amherst: U of Massachusetts P, 1988.

Gantar, Jure. "Catching the Wind in a Net: The Shortcomings of Existing Methods for the Analysis of Performance." *Modern Drama* 39.4 (1996): 537–45.

George, David E. R. "Performance Epistemology." *Performance Research* 1.1 (1996): 16–25.

Iyer, Ganesha. Personal interview. 1993.

Jenkins, Richard. *Pierre Bourdieu*. New York: Routledge, 1992.

Kapferer, Bruce. "Performance and the Structuring of Meaning and Experience." *The Anthropology of Experience*. Ed. Victor W. Turner and Edward M. Bruner. Champagne: U of Illinois P, 1986. 188–206.

Konijn, Elly. "Actors and Emotions: A Psychological Perspective." *Theatre Research International* 20.2 (1995): 132–40.

——. "Emotions on Stage: A Task-Emotion Theory of Acting." Unpublished manuscript, 1997.

Lutz, Catherine A. *Unnatural Emotions*. Chicago: U of Chicago P, 1988.

Mauss, Marcel. "Techniques of the Body." *Economy and Society* 2.1 (1973): 70–88.

McDaniel, June. "Emotions in Bengali Religious Thought: Substance and Metaphor." *Emotions in Asian Thought*. Ed. Joel Marks and Roger T. Ames. Albany: State U of New York P, 1995. 39–63.

Nagamoto, Shigenori. *Attunement Through the Body*. Albany: State U of New York P, 1992.

Oddey, Alison. *Devising Theatre*. New York: Routledge, 1994.

Roach, Joseph. *The Player's Passion: Studies in the Science of Acting*. Ann Arbor: U of Michigan P, 1993.

Solomon, Robert C. "The Cross-Cultural Comparison of Emotion." *Emotions in Asian Thought*. Ed. Joel Marks and Roger T. Ames. Albany: State U of New York P, 1995. 253–300.

Turner, Victor. *On the Edge of the Bush: Anthropology as Experience.* Tucson: U of Arizona P, 1985.

Varryar, Unnayi. *Nala Caritam, First Day's Play.* Unpublished translation by M. P. Sankaran Namboodiri. N.d.

Warrier, G. S. Personal interview, 1993.

Woodward, Kathleen. Introduction. *Discourse* 13.1 (1990–91): 3–11.

Zarrilli, Phillip B. Introduction. *Acting (Re)Considered: Theories and Practices.* Ed. Zarrilli. New York: Routledge, 1995. 7–21.

———. *The Kathakali Complex: Actor, Performance, Structure.* New Delhi: Abhinav, 1984.

———. *Kathakali Dance-Drama: Where Gods and Demons Come to Play.* New York: Routledge, 1999.

———. "What Does It Mean to 'Become the Character'? Power, Presence, and Transcendence in Asian In-Body Disciplines of Practice." *By Means of Performance.* Ed. Richard Schechner and Willa Appel. Cambridge: Cambridge UP, 1990. 131–48.

Performing the Mystory

A Textshop in Autoperformance

10

Michael S. Bowman and Ruth Laurion Bowman

> If I were really just expressing myself, I wouldn't think that people would be that interested.
>
> —LAURIE ANDERSON, QTD. IN JOHN HOWELL, *Laurie Anderson*

In their survey of alternative or experimental performances now featured in many theater and performance studies classes, Linda Park-Fuller and Ronald Pelias point out that a substantial number of such performances tend to focus on, or derive from, personal or autobiographical material (126). Furthermore, the autoperformance mode, which commonly "compresses into a single presence the protagonist-author-director-performer" of the piece (127), figures prominently in many of the alternative performance types they describe.

While using performance as a means to explore the self, or alternative "selves," has been a staple of performance art in the United States since the 1970s, introducing autobiographical or autoperformance work in the performance classroom presents a number of challenges as well as opportunities. In addition to the usual problems of teaching an art—balancing the pedagogical need to codify, simplify, categorize, and even routinize our subject matter against art's tendency to resist or disrupt codification, simplification, and so forth—Park-Fuller and Pelias note that autoperformances often raise difficult questions of evaluation and appropriateness. If we ask our students to work in the autoperformance mode, then presumably we will need to develop some criteria for evaluating their compositions as well as their performances. And if those compositions are about personal or autobiographical matters, how do we establish a context for prudent levels of self-disclosure or an appropriate classroom standard of decorum and tact? Park-Fuller and Pelias remind us that very few performance teachers are experienced in such matters, and they recommend that more research be devoted to these issues so that in the future "talk about these performance events will gain greater sophistication" (138).

In what follows, we attempt, primarily through an account of an autoperformance project we have used in our own classes, to illustrate how we have tried to work through the pedagogical issues identified by Park-Fuller and Pelias. Drawing primarily on theories of textuality, especially Gregory Ulmer's ideas about "textshop" and "mystoriogra-

162
Michael S.
Bowman
and Ruth
Laurion
Bowman

phy," our project seeks to contribute to the current theoretical and pedagogical work on personal experience narratives and autobiography in performance studies, by adopting what might be considered a more impersonal, intertextual approach. Its basic move is to shift from a "readerly" to a "writerly" stance in regards to performing personal or autobiographical materials. Instead of asking students to reproduce the personal experiences, events, or narratives of their lives in a performance, it requires them to rewrite those experiences.

To some extent, of course, any autobiography or autoperformance rewrites the life it may seem merely to represent. In many cases, however, the fact of rewriting is disguised in the act of performance. That is, the "natural" performance aesthetic (Stucky) that operates in many autobiographical and personal narrative performances, like most forms of realism, often conceals the traces of its own constructedness.[1] The mystorical approach, by contrast, seeks to foreground its own artificiality, to demonstrate its rhetorical self-consciousness. Instead of inviting students to give a performance in which they might "express themselves," such that the performance could be (mis)construed as a straightforward reflection of some already-existing self, the mystory seeks to establish a metonymic or allegorical relation between the self and the performance. Because the mystory is typically built as a collage or assemblage of textual/experiential fragments, and because it seeks to recode or reaccentuate those fragments intertextually or semiotically in the performance, the mystory performance becomes an occasion for inventing new knowledge of the self, rather than merely reproducing what is already known.

Rationale

Ulmer insists that neologisms such as *mystory* and *textshop* are sometimes necessary due to misunderstandings that occur when discussing a pedagogy based on contemporary theories of textuality, theories that some may feel have little practical value to pedagogy or to the field of performance studies. Like Ulmer, though, we believe that the vanguard arts and contemporary theory might help us make performance studies an equal partner with other divisions of knowledge in the university. As Ulmer explains, "The need for a textshop emerges out of the difficulty students have understanding our object of study . . . exclusively by means of analytical modes of thinking and writing borrowed from the social sciences" ("Textshop" 113). Having worked with Ulmer's approach for several years, we are convinced that it is often unproductive to study performance an-aesthetically, with methods borrowed largely from the social sciences, despite the efforts of many of us (ourselves included) to do so. While students often come to a performance studies class because they are intrigued by the beauty and power of performances they have seen, they sometimes leave such courses having discovered that performance is just psychology or political science by other means, or worse, that it is something worth studying but not worth doing. Certainly, the urge to politicize or demythologize performance is beneficial, but the question arises: How might performance studies classes also take into account the inventive strategies of texts and performances they encounter and learn invention from the performing arts, without forsaking interpretation and criticism? The textshop, as Ulmer describes his pedagogy, is designed toward such ends.

Roland Barthes's well-known essay "From Work to Text" provided Ulmer with a name for his "textshop," and Barthes's distinction between the *readerly* and the *writerly* offers it a rationale and a statement of value.

> Why is the writerly our value? Because the goal of literary work (of literature as work) is to make the reader no longer a consumer, but a producer of the text. Our literature is characterized by the pitiless divorce which the literary institution maintains between the producer of the text and its users, between its owner and its customer, between its author and its reader. This reader is thereby plunged into a kind of idleness—he is intransitive; he is, in short, *serious:* instead of functioning himself, instead of gaining access to the magic of the signifier, to the pleasure of writing, he is left with no more than the poor freedom either to accept or reject the text: reading is nothing more than a *referendum.* (*S/Z* 4; emphasis in original)

In Ulmer's view, a textshop should be designed to supplement (not replace entirely) a readerly performance studies classroom, where text and performance are taught as specialized knowledge or skills, with a writerly laboratory, where our subjects are approached with the pleasure of "amateurs" (a term whose respectability Barthes attempted to revive).

Ulmer describes the textshop as a humanities laboratory in which the students attempt to reproduce experiments in vanguard literary art. He asks us to think of a laboratory in one of the "hard" sciences: In learning the science, students not only read about some idea, they also are expected to reproduce the experiments themselves, until they reach a point in the advanced stages of their education when they begin to confront problems that have not yet been solved ("Textshop" 117). Similarly, a textshop would teach experimental or vanguard autobiographical writing and autoperformance as ideas that have changed (or are changing) our view of culture, and it would assume that students cannot be expected fully to understand those ideas until they ex-

164
Michael S.
Bowman
and Ruth
Laurion
Bowman

periment with them, practice them. The point in both the science and humanities labs is to produce a person capable not only of reciting the history of invention or analyzing the inventions of others but of inventing something. The lesson should be that imagination and imitation are both integral parts of invention.

The textshop, then, complements traditional "readerly" courses or units in theory, which frequently ignore the fact that theory has influenced the practice of the arts as much as it has the interpretation of the arts. In a textshop, the two principal ways that theory is assimilated into the humanities—by critical interpretation and by artistic practice—are considered to be of equal cognitive and pedagogical value. Our remarks, in this essay, focus on just one side of the assimilation of theory by performance studies—the side of production—featuring Ulmer's notion of the mystory. Ulmer's approach may itself be considered as a critical methodology operating at a macro level, capable of testing theory itself, for such is the function of the humanities experiment. The relevant question is not "if the theorists are right, what might be the meaning of this text/performance?" but "if the theorists are right, how might a text/performance be composed?" The experimental setting of the textshop is designed to promote the practice of autoperformance itself as methodology productive of knowledge and understanding.

The Mystory Project

"Mystory" is Ulmer's name for a mode of creative research appropriate to a postliterate age, one that would result in a multimedia text, such as a video or a performance, rather than a more traditional expository essay. As a neologism, *mystory* is comparable to another familiar neologism, *herstory*, which seeks to excavate and represent the collective story of women suppressed in patriarchal history. In a similar vein, mystory attempts to uncover and trace the story of the "self" that is buried or enciphered in a variety of "other" historical discourses. In particular, mystory alludes to (and seeks to incorporate) the following forms:

- History—as both a story of the past and a professional discourse that enables and constrains how the past is represented
- Mystery—as both a popular culture genre (detective fiction) and an analogy for scholarly research (drawing significant conclusions from seemingly inconsequential clues)
- My story—as emblematic of the autobiographical imperative in contemporary art and the attempt to relate to one's research materials personally in recent "confessional" and "performative" scholarly and critical writing[2]

More broadly, *mystoriography* can be defined as an attempt to conduct and represent research in terms of three general domains of discourse: the professional (any branch of formal knowledge or expertise); the popular (including both contemporary pop culture forms, such as music or television, and more traditional resources, such as family lore, community stories, oral histories, etc.); and the personal (individual memories, experiences). In short, the mystory assumes that identity is enciphered by means of certain dominant institutional discourses. Researching and writing one's mystory is thus an attempt to decipher one's identity by tracking down and interrogating specific texts from these discourses.[3]

The project described below may be adapted for use in a variety of performance studies courses (as well as nonacademic contexts). We have used variations of the assignment in courses at all levels, from introductory-level performance of literature classes to graduate seminars in performance theory. We have also used variants of the project successfully in professional development workshops with groups of nonstudents who had no prior performance experience. The project detailed here is taken from an intermediate-level undergraduate course in which most students have had some previous performance experience, either an acting class or a performance of literature class.

Although the specific aims of the project vary from course to course or from context to context, the basic pattern of development follows a standard sequence of learning activities: reading, group discussion, research (archival and fieldwork), writing, and performance. In the beginning, we give students examples of mystorylike autobiographical texts to read and videotapes of autoperformances to watch. At this time, they also receive a handout describing the lab project: to research, write, and perform their own mystory, using the three general categories of discourse outlined by Ulmer, as well as the models discussed in class. The basic objective of the project, to put the matter in other words, is for the students to perform like the texts and performances we study, rather than to perform from them. The research and writing components of the assignment help the students avoid some of the less interesting possibilities of the project that sometimes develop, such as the desire to perform an extemporized personal narrative or the belief that the mystory is an "anything goes" assignment. That the experiment adds a performance element to Ulmer's mystoriography also exploits a property of performance art that tends to be underrepresented in much scholarly writing: its ability to delight and entertain an audience.

The focus of the project often shifts from problems of meaning and interpretation, as students confront texts and performances that strike them initially as all but indecipherable, to matters of wider historical,

166

Michael S.
Bowman
and Ruth
Laurion
Bowman

social, or aesthetic interest as they begin to research and write their own mystories. Although the project is not designed primarily to improve student performance skills, the performances of the mystories often turn out to be among our students' strongest. One reason for this may very well be that the mystory project is usually done at the end of a semester, after students presumably have gained more experience rehearsing and performing (for us). But another reason, judging from their testimony, is that many students want to perform the mystories they have researched and written, and so they will frequently devote more time and energy to rehearsals and preparations. Because most students begin the project skeptical of the whole performance art enterprise, we perceive the marked attitudinal shift in many of them to be one of the most important "outcomes" of the assignment.

In the intermediate-level performance class, the mystory exercise is the last of four major units covered in the semester. The course as a whole is designed generally to (re)introduce students to basic principles of aesthetic form. In a performance class, of course, such principles are presented as modes of thought and action, rather than as a set of terms or concepts to be "covered." The first half of the course is designed to help students recognize and understand aesthetic forms in both art and life, while the second half is intended to help students learn to think and act in or with such forms. In the first unit, we review such elementary formal components of drama and narrative as plot, point of view, character, and dramatic structure. In the second unit, poetic concepts like image, metaphor, metonymy, and rhythm are reviewed, and experimental or avant-garde techniques such as collage and assemblage are introduced and explored. The third unit grounds the exploration of narrative and dramatic forms in performances of literature, while the mystory unit is presented as extending poetic and avant-garde principles into the domain of "nonliterary" texts such as personal narratives and autobiographies.[4]

Reading and Discussion

The fundamental methodological principle in Ulmer's textshop is the Barthesian notion that every text contains a set of "instructions" for making another text. This writerly approach to reading or "audiencing," while applicable to any genre or mode, is quite useful when dealing with avant-garde texts and performances, for many students find such things meaningless or nonsensical. Because their customary ways of decoding texts and performances do not seem to work as well with experimental or avant-garde forms, we have found it to be a relatively simple matter to bracket or defer the question of meaning and shift their attention instead to how such texts are made. The initial phases of the project seek thus to prepare the students by: introducing examples of vanguard autobiographical texts and autoperformances; elucidating the text's "instructions"—its principles or techniques of composition, and the effects achieved thereby—in group discussions of those texts and performances; and codifying those principles into a model or "relay" for students to follow as they research, write, and perform their own mystories. Hence, the guidelines for producing a mystory in a given context or class will depend in part on the texts and performances that are studied as models.

One text we have used successfully in this project is N. Scott Momaday's well-known autobiography, *The Way to Rainy Mountain*. Momaday's text has several attributes to recommend it for use in an undergraduate course or unit on autobiography and autoperformance. First, most of our students seem to like reading the book, even though they also say that they do not understand it. Second, the book's compositional pattern is relatively easy for students to decipher, once we draw their attention to it. And third, Momaday's text is a good model for what we hope to achieve in an autoperformance project, because it constructs the self as part of a collective order, intertextually articulated in myth, history, and personal experience.

In discussing what they find enjoyable in the book, students commonly mention three features of the reading experience: that they learned something about Native American (Kiowa) history and culture; that they appreciated the author's respect for the traditions and stories of his people; and that they found themselves reading the book in fits and starts. Students note that although the book is relatively short, it takes nearly as long for them to read as a book twice its length because, as one student put it, "you have to stop and think: it's not big, but it's deep." Many of them describe being put in a pleasantly soporific state while reading it—relaxed, contemplative, "daydreaming." Others report that, because the book does not seem to have a linear plot, they skipped around in it, reading some sections several times, while skimming over others. Such perceptions account in part for their feelings of incomprehension: If it takes them so long to read such a short book or to figure out how it should be read, then they (or the author) must be doing something wrong.

The dissonance they experience in reading the book can be invaluable for pedagogy. In articulating what they do not "get" about the book, they often reveal, implicitly or explicitly, their presuppositions about how art, autobiography, or narrative is supposed to be constructed. Such discussions can have a powerful critical effect. In trying to reconcile the pleasures they experience with "not-understanding," they articulate for themselves a distinction between making aesthetic effects and explanatory effects. Because much of their previous schooling in the arts has asked them to translate the former into the latter—

168
Michael S.
Bowman
and Ruth
Laurion
Bowman

for example, writing plot summaries, character analyses, and so forth—a text like this one, which resists such translation, can provide that initial moment of distantiation or alienation for us to propose rethinking and experimenting with how an autobiography "ought" to be done and renegotiating the effects it is "supposed" to create, by focusing our attention on how Momaday assembled his text instead of worrying about what it means.

Indeed, the real value of the mystory experiment begins to emerge at this point. While many students worry that they did not understand the book, all of them are struck by the book's compositional pattern: its thirty-four, three-paragraph "chapters," interspersed with drawings by the author's father, bracketed by an introduction and an epilogue. The students also are able to grasp the basic method used in writing each of the thirty-four "chapters": the first paragraph is from Kiowa mythology, legend, or oral tradition (i.e., Ulmer's popular discourse); the second provides a more "objective" ethnohistorical gloss of some aspect of the legend or myth (professional discourse); and the third recounts authorial anecdotes or memories related to the matter addressed in the first two paragraphs (personal discourse). Although there is some ambiguity about the speaker(s) in/of these paragraphs, the introduction explains that the source of the myths is the author's grandmother; the ethnohistorical matter correlates with scholarly works such as James Mooney's *Calendar History of the Kiowa Indians* and Elsie Clews Parson's *Kiowa Tales;* and the personal anecdotes represent the author's impressions while traveling from Montana to Oklahoma after hearing of his grandmother's death.

Once such matters are articulated in discussion, students can begin to correlate the fragmented, impressionistic, collagelike style of composition with the effects they experienced; yet, while most of them can explain its rationale and identify its main features and its intended effects (eventually), they do not yet believe any of it. That is, while *Rainy Mountain* produces a pleasurable, aesthetic effect in many of the students, they are skeptical of their own capacity to produce such effects themselves by imitating its procedures.

The assignment asks them to do just that, of course: to research, write, and perform a mystory, using (in this example) Momaday's text as a model or relay for discovering/inventing the self by imitating its procedures. We do not ask them to adopt Momaday's point of view or to use precisely the same kinds of materials in their mystory but to draw on the resources of their own heritage or culture, their own developing sense of professional discourse, their own memories and experiences. While we expect students to begin with the three general categories of discourse identified by Ulmer and to use examples of each in their compositions, the individual and his or her training, experience, and heritage will determine what kinds of personal, professional, and popular discourse will appear in the mystory. At a minimum, then, their compositions and performances will be comprised of three different texts or textual/experiential fragments. But because we usually require the performances to be fifteen to twenty minutes in length at this level, the compositions inevitably include many more than three.

Research and Writing

The research and writing of a mystory can begin at virtually any point in the student's life, and there are advantages to having students begin at an arbitrary moment in order to avoid their launching into traumatic personal experience narratives. For that reason, we usually recommend that students start their research by looking for a popular or professional intertext, or else we will place some additional constraints on the archive of personal materials that may be consulted. With *Rainy Mountain* as our model, for instance, we might stipulate that the personal material be restricted to an occasion of mourning, such that the purpose of the mystory becomes one of honoring or memorializing the connections and continuities that link the individuals in time and space. Or we might suggest that the personal archive be centered on some trip or journey (real or metaphorical), with the stipulation that the journey be represented in a series of "snapshots" or "souvenirs"— visual images or artifacts that the performer incorporates in the performance either through actual photographs, slides, or material objects, through performed "poses," or through verbal descriptions— rather than through a conventional narrative of the trip.

On other occasions, with other texts serving as our primary model, we have asked students to begin by writing a "vita minor," as Ulmer calls it (*Teletheory* 209), which is a listing of all the skills, talents, competencies, or areas of knowledge and expertise that do not appear on the individual's "official" vita or resume and that would be considered irrelevant by prospective employers. Generating such a fragmented list of attributes as the vita minor prompts students to understand and appreciate themselves differently from the predominant life-story they are trying to construct in college. In many instances, they find only traces of some former self that they had ignored or forgotten and that the mystory assignment might help them to recover.

Finally, on still other occasions, we have used an even more arbitrary mechanism for constructing the personal archive, by restricting students to such things as might be found in a keepsake drawer or a shoe box of mementos and souvenirs, or else by focusing on a particular skill from their vita minor that they would like to share with the class in the manner of a "How-to" speech. The point in all these cases is twofold: to distance them from any tendency they might have to

170

Michael S.
Bowman
and Ruth
Laurion
Bowman

equate the personal archive with personal anecdotes, and to effect an attitudinal shift such that "the personal" becomes a central part of the mystery to be investigated in the research, rather than the alibi offered in response to the research questions.

No amount of the usual arguments used to demonstrate the genius of Shakespeare or other artists to students will convince a class that a mystory will be an important work of art—or any kind of "art" at all. The procedure seems too easy to follow; anyone could make a mystory, even themselves. Of what value could such things possibly be? But of course, the autoperformance initiative, like much avant-garde art, is located precisely within this issue: the invention of a democratized art practice accessible to everyone, against the capture of art by concepts of genius or specialization. The value of the mystory experiment is not so much in the product but in the process of creation, just as much of the value and power of autoperformance as practice cannot be comprehended externally but only through experience. It exists precisely for the user as actions, and it is writerly through and through.

Performing the Mystory

The "proof" comes after the experiments have been completed in the lab, when the students find themselves amazed by their own work and the work of their peers. The performances are especially helpful and revealing in this regard because they allow everyone to experience each other's work. Having been quite (properly) skeptical that the selection and juxtaposition of textual/experiential fragments—the basic formula for composing a mystory—could produce anything interesting or memorable, the students are surprised to find themselves laughing and crying, cheering and applauding each other throughout the performances, as well as replaying favorite phrases or moments to each other as they leave class.

One student, whose inspiration was to extend the mystory method of composition to the "text" of a woodworking project, quite stunned one class with a performance about his progress from childhood to adolescence to manhood within the scene of his family's wood shop. The performance juxtaposed professional advice on safety, tools, and carpentry, following the popular format of such television shows as *This Old House*, with anecdotes that the performer had solicited from his friends and family members about various incidents that had occurred in the family's wood shop over the years, all within the framing action of demonstrating how to build a table. The demonstration became "dangerous" in the performance context—contrasting with the family anecdotes about the performer's fastidiousness regarding safety—in that the constraints of time and space made it impossible for the performer to follow his own advice about safety in the shop and the care and attention that must be given to carpentry and woodworking projects.

Another level of risk developed from the final kind of discourse that the performer incorporated into his mystory. Interspersed with the family anecdotes, safety lessons, and the woodworking demonstration was another series of short confessional anecdotes that were critical of the performer's own tendency to put on "macho faces" as he grew older—for example, former girlfriends who had accused him of being insensitive, and his stupid propensity to get in drunken brawls with other males over trivial matters. After reporting one of these self-critical remarks, the performer would interview the audience to find out just how far a man could go in terms of constructing a more sensitive or feminine "mask" for himself. When the audience members told him that they would not think him less a man if he carried a purse, wore makeup, and so on, he would proceed to modify his "mask" accordingly, such that by the end of the performance his appearance was somewhat androgynous, as well as grotesquely comic. The performance as a whole illustrated the performative lesson regarding the importance of role-playing and mask wearing—as well as the importance of a particular institutional discourse, with its own system of practices (its own scene, agents, logic, form, media, and proofs)—to the performer's learning a masculine identity, while at the same time offering a critique of the identity he had been performing during his early adulthood.

Ulmer suggests that the proper (i.e., writerly) response to a mystory should be the desire to produce one's own. In most classes in which we have used the assignment, we have found students to be even more anxious than usual as the due date for the performances approaches. But after seeing the first two or three of them, they are eager to see more of them—and to perform their own. The mere fact that each performance is usually so different from the others, perhaps in contrast with other assignments they do in school in which the products (exams, essays, performances) tend to be more similar, surprises many of them, especially since they were all following the same procedural outline.

Evaluation

This raises the question of how we evaluate the mystory performances. The criteria for evaluation are similar to those that might be used to determine the success of an experiment in a chemistry or physics lab. Did the procedure produce the expected results? When the ingredients were mixed, did the solution explode or turn solid? Does the mystory in performance possess the qualities of the model or not? Remember, the goal is not to invent a new, never-before-seen performance form

172
Michael S.
Bowman
and Ruth
Laurion
Bowman

but to replicate an important kind of textual and performance experiment whose results are now known. The undergraduate students in the humanities lab are not expected to invent a new form of literary or performance art any more than their counterparts in the chemistry lab are expected to find a cure for AIDS.

In short, experimental creative or imaginative projects function with the same features of identifiable criteria as do analytical assignments. The student's work must have the qualities we discovered during the initial readings and discussions of, in this instance, mystory. To the extent that it falls short of manifesting these properties, it is a less successful experiment and may be graded accordingly. Thus, it usually turns out to be a relatively easy matter to "grade" the projects, for in our experience, most college students are capable of following procedures and using models and hence do quite well on these exercises. The evaluation, in short, is done in formal terms, based on a set of criteria established in our class discussions. It does not entail a judgment of students' personalities, of how "off the wall" they can be, or of how traumatic or dramatic their lives have been, as some students early on fear it will be.

Student responses to the assignment, in terms both of their completed projects and their comments on the process, have been overwhelmingly positive. In many cases, as we indicated earlier, a student's performance of the mystory will turn out to be his or her strongest work in the class, and one indication of student responsiveness to the assignment is the care and attention students give to refining and polishing their mystory performances. More importantly, though, many students have reported being "carried away" by the research component of the assignment, of setting off on the trail of some more or less specific item, only to encounter along the way other equally interesting, though unforeseen, materials and experiences.

At its best, the assignment can be transformative, reconnecting the student with his or her culture, family, and heritage in a vital, immediate way. One young woman of Cajun descent reported in the class discussion following her performance that her background had always embarrassed her. Her family and neighbors had seemed to her to be uneducated, backward country people; her grandparents spoke only French, while she spoke only English, which caused additional problems when she was growing up; and she had always thought that she would have to leave home, escape her background, if she were to "find" herself. The mystory project allowed, even prompted, her to go home again. She had been studying French in college and had managed to interview, albeit clumsily, her grandparents and other French-speaking relatives during the course of the project. (It was, she said, the first time that she had ever had anything like a direct conversation with her grandmother.) She also began to develop an interest in the history of the Louisiana Cajuns as a result of the research she had done and wanted now to learn more about these people among whom she had been reared. In doing the project, she testified, she "found" herself in a most unexpected place.

Finally, to produce an autoperformance using the mystory technique teaches at least one lesson that could not be learned in any other way—that however difficult many experimental or avant-garde texts or performances may be to understand, they can be relatively easy to make. This insight, Ulmer suggests, might serve as an axiom for the avant-garde generally and as the motto of the pedagogy of the textshop: Easy to make—Hard to understand ("Textshop" 127). By applying analytical thinking to one's own experiment, treating it as if another had made it, the student becomes familiar with the difference between making aesthetic effects and explanatory effects. But the understanding of autoperformance itself, or even of the productive act from both sides, is only part of the goal of the project. Its further goal is to discover a way for performance studies to contribute more directly to a cultural pedagogy. The textshop in autoperformance explores the possibility that the creative imagination is as educable as critical thinking and that the former facility may be as important as the latter in helping students locate themselves in the story of their community, family, region, or nation.

NOTES

An earlier version of this essay was presented at the Performance Studies Formations conference, Northwestern University, March 1996.

1. For an explanation of "natural performance," see the essay by Nathan Stucky in this volume.

2. Since we began teaching the mystory, Ulmer has included his own version of the mystory writing project for undergraduate-level students in the most recent edition of *Text Book* (Scholes, Comley, and Ulmer chap. 5). Jarrett offers another extension of Ulmer's ideas, using jazz as a compositional model for writing the mystory.

3. In some instances, Ulmer refers to four different institutional discourses, rather than three: family, entertainment, school, and discipline (*Heuretics* 193–97).

4. On some occasions, we have reversed the final two units in this course, approaching "nonliterary" texts through conventional narrative and dramatic form and using a mystorical approach to performing literature (cf. Bowman and Kistenberg).

WORKS CITED

Barthes, Roland. "From Work to Text." *Image-Music-Text*. Trans. Stephen Heath. New York: Hill, 1977. 155–64.

174
Michael S.
Bowman
and Ruth
Laurion
Bowman

———. *S/Z: An Essay*. Trans. Richard Miller. New York: Noonday, 1974.

Bowman, Michael S., and Cindy J. Kistenberg. "'Textual Power' and the Subject of Oral Interpretation: An Alternate Approach to Performing Literature." *Communication Education* 41 (1992): 287–99.

Jarrett, Michael. *Drifting on a Read: Jazz as a Model for Writing*. Albany: State U of New York P, 1999.

Momaday, N. Scott. *The Way to Rainy Mountain*. Albuquerque: U of New Mexico P, 1969.

Park-Fuller, Linda M., and Ronald J. Pelias. "Charting Alternative Performance and Evaluative Practices." *Communication Education* 44 (1995): 126–39.

Scholes, Robert, Nancy R. Comley, and Gregory L. Ulmer. *Text Book: An Introduction to Literary Language*. 2nd ed. New York: St. Martin's, 1995.

Stucky, Nathan. "Toward an Aesthetics of Natural Performance." *Text and Performance Quarterly* 13.2 (1993): 168–80.

Ulmer, Gregory L. *Heuretics: The Logic of Invention*. Baltimore: Johns Hopkins UP, 1994.

———. *Teletheory: Grammatology in the Age of Video*. New York: Routledge, 1989.

———. "Textshop for an Experimental Humanities." *Reorientations: Critical Theories and Pedagogies*. Ed. Bruce Henricksen and Thais E. Morgan. Urbana: U of Illinois P, 1990. 113–32.

Teaching in the Borderlands

11

Joni L.
Jones

To survive the Borderlands
you must live *sin fronteras*
be a crossroads.

—GLORIA ANZALDÚA, *Borderlands*

The performance studies classroom is my space of resistance within the academy. It is where I hope to effect social change. Teaching at an institution where a market economy governs most educational policy and where the legacy of discriminatory admissions procedures result in a student population that is 4 percent African American and 15 percent Latin American, I am compelled to find oppositional strategies in my teaching.[1]

Through such teaching, the classroom becomes a borderland, a liminal space capable of disrupting the social order. The borderlands are porous, shifting, and contestable; they are *sin fronteras*. In the epigraph that opens this essay, it is especially appropriate that Gloria Anzaldúa invokes the term *crossroads* in her description of this volatile and contingent space, because the crossroads is the domain of Èṣù, who must give safe passage. Èṣù, the Yorùbá "principle of indeterminacy" (Euba 2), presents the traveler with options, sometimes irrevocable choices. The traveler, like the student and the teacher, is presented with possible paths in an unfamiliar forest and can choose recklessly or wisely. Èṣù silently works with the traveler to determine her or his fate. Though Èṣù may obscure key details that would aid in your decision making, ultimately you will determine which road speaks to you.

Students come to a distinctive crossroads when they enroll in my course, Performance of Dramatic Literature. In this course, the classroom serves as a laboratory for the exploration of race and ethnicity. I focus on African diasporic literature, using Paul Carter Harrison's *Totem Voices*[2] as the anthology of plays from which the students will select their performances. Cross-cultural performance is a very particular border crossing. The borderland is not a "no man's land"; rather, it is a specific place to reside. Young blonde women perform Yorùbá deities, Latinos play South African musicians, Asian American women play African American teenagers, and of course, my African American students explore, through their bodies, worlds they find both familiar and new. This is often a painful time, full of complex discussions of archetypes and stereotypes, construction of identity, and our mutual complicity in the continuation of oppression. Performance forces these issues to become more than intellectual challenges, because the students must literally put the issues inside of themselves as they embody the characters. In doing so, they are challenged to respond specifically to a vital and vibrant world. They enter a borderland in which they must challenge the construction of the self along with the construction of the other. Dwight Conquergood explains the malleable nature of identity in the borderland:

> Borders bleed, as much as they contain. Instead of dividing lines to be patrolled or transgressed, boundaries are now understood as criss-crossing sites inside the post-modern subject. Difference is resituated within, instead of beyond, the self. Inside and outside distinctions, like genres, blur and wobble. (184)

The students interrogate the construction of their self-identities as a necessary component of exploring the characters as others. Performance inevitably shifts one's molecules and makes one new. The course provides the environment for that regeneration to occur.

Self and Other

> This sharing of self with other, this matching of self with other, is a profoundly human activity which, in the richest sense of the word, *educates*. (Bacon, "Case for Interpretation" 22)

In the Performance of Dramatic Literature course, my intention is to provide the students with an opportunity to discover new body memories. These memories may contribute to their self-performance repertoire or may rest in their psyche as an invisible though present addition to their selves. The philosophy of the course harkens back to 1960s oral interpretation classes and beckons toward a radical revision of the future. The course rests on the basic assumption that performance changes the performer, thereby changing the world. In this classroom, the bard, the troubadour, the jongleur, the masked performer is indeed a potential threat to the world order, for in this classroom, the students and I learn the possibilities of our humanity. It is here that we explore, as Paulo Freire states, "humanization . . . [as] the people's vocation" (25). In this performance course, I am not interested in actor training. I suggest, with great humility, that at its best, the course is human training.

When the students in the course take on cultures they believe are other than their own, they expand themselves through the bodily incorporation that is performance. In this way, performance is like an intimate relationship in which one opens to another and is in the process irrevocably changed. In describing the profundity of this experience, Wallace Bacon discussed the performer "matching" with the literature so that the performer comes to have a "sense of the other," an acknowledgment of otherness and a joining with an other (*Art* 40). Indeed, performance is sense making in which the self must relinquish center stage in order to fully respond to and embody an other.

Throughout this essay, I have included several examples of exercises that create the space for students to literally play with cultural constructions. The exercises help create what Lawrence Grossberg calls "radical contextualism." In discussing the relationship of culture and power, Grossberg writes that "cultural studies, in its theoretical practice, might be described as a theory of contexts, or, in its political practice, as the practice of making contexts" (5). I borrow Grossberg's language to describe what happens in the performance classroom. Through the exercises and performances, the students make cultural contexts. Vocal warm-ups that include singing gospel songs and improvised signifying, physical warm-ups that include the group creation of a step routine and African American jump rope rhythms, along with the performances and the sampling of exercises presented in this essay all serve to root the course in an African diasporic context. The playing is critical to an embodied understanding of culture; the playing puts the theories of embodiment into practice.

The body has a set of learned and repeated behaviors that constitute the performance of the self, what Pierre Bourdieu calls *habitus*. Bourdieu writes, "The habitus tends to ensure its own constancy and its defense against change through the selection it makes within new information by rejecting information capable of calling into question its accumulated information" (61). In my course, the students confront information they would ordinarily reject in their everyday bodily practice. The self is asked to take on a different habitus, complete with the specific details of this other and the distinctive history inscribed onto that other. Many of the students, most of whom are not theatre or performance studies majors, see the unique and ingrained performance of themselves for the first time.

> *Journal assignment:* After reading Horace Miner's critique of cultural description, "Body Ritual among the Nacirema," students should assume the role of an anthropologist and write about some aspect of U.S. culture. This is particularly effective before reading Wole Soyinka's *The Strong Breed* because the exercise encourages the students to see Soyinka's characters as people responding to their specific cultural norms rather than "foreigners" engaged in "weird" practices. The exercise reminds students that all cultures are constructed and adaptable.

An initial step toward performing across cultures is the awareness of the self as a social and individual construction. This awareness allows for the possibility of a flexible and diverse self-presentation while not minimizing the decidedly material ramifications the construction carries.

> *Exercise:* Students pair with someone they do not know in the class. On a sheet of paper, they write down three things they "know" about their partner. They may not ask each other questions but must fictionalize a reality for the partner. They must go beyond physical attributes and speculate about birthplace, birth order, academic major, leisure activities, study habits, and other such traits. All students then write down the reasons that led them to their speculations. The students discuss with each other what they wrote. As a class, the students and the teacher talk about the performing self and the ways in which we communicate, even unintentionally.

As the students become more aware of their habitus, they move toward what Drew Leder calls "dys-appearance" (86). For those in good health, much of the body exists in a state of disappearance; we are unaware of our hip joints, our arm muscles, or our eye ligaments until illness brings them to our attention. During times of illness, the otherwise unmarked and therefore unnoticed parts of our bodies make a loud appearance as dysfunctional features. Our habitus has been disrupted as we consciously experience parts of our body that, prior to illness, did not seem to exist. In performance, the body experiences a similar dys-appearance. When soft-spoken students perform loud, angry characters, the voices that ordinarily serve them well are suddenly deficient. They must use their vocal folds in ways that go outside of their usual physical practice; they must discover ways to incorporate the characters into their own bodies. They can begin by masking the features of their self-performances that open a space for the acquisition of the characters inside, around, and through their selves. The masking of self also allows the audience to find the characters within the performers.

> *Journal assignment:* Find a picture that looks like the character you are going to perform. Be certain the picture is consistent with the race/ethnicity, gender, and age of the character. Attach that picture to your journal and describe what you will have to do to your self-performance in order to come close to the picture. Be specific in discussing your self and the adjustments you will have to make.

When a European American woman in the class performed an African American male while wearing red nail polish, lipstick, and a long, bouncing ponytail, she was so committed to her performance of her self she was not able to find a "sense of the other." She was not willing/able to put herself aside to allow someone else to come through. Bourdieu explains that habitus is a product of history and "ensures the active presence of past experiences, which [are] deposited in each organism in the form of schemes of perception, thought, and action" (54). The character, then, is rooted in a particular set of behaviors and history, and that history must also be brought to the performance. The student described above was not taking the character's reality or history into account when she chose to display the details of European Americanness and her femaleness in her performance of an African American male.

> *Exercise:* Based on an exercise developed by Augusto Boal, the students write their name and an adjective that is an opposite of themselves on a piece of paper. The class is divided in half, with one half standing (Group A) and the other half sitting (Group B). The facilitator collects the papers from Group A and gives them to Group B so that each student in Group B has a sheet of paper. Group A walks around naturally while each member of Group B closely watches the student whose paper they are holding. Group B is asked to take note of posture, eye contact, pace, angle of head, proximity to others, length of stride, and other performance features. Group A then performs the adjectives they wrote on their papers; Group B pays keen attention to the details of this performance. Group A is asked to sit, and Group B now begins to walk like the person they were observing. They also perform the assigned person's opposite, just as that person performed it. Students attempt to see themselves as performed by someone else. As a class, the students discuss what it feels like to see one's self performed, what the distinctive features of their self-performance are, what the limitations of performing someone else are, and what adjustments must be made to perform outside of the self.

Performance insists on a heightened awareness of self, if the performer wants to create a character that is more than just a subtle shift in the self-performance.

> *Journal assignment:* Complete the attached Self Inventory. For each character you perform in class, note the points of difference and identification between your self and the character based on this inventory.
>
> *Self Inventory*
> 1. Physical Self
>   What are three of your typical gestures?
>   How do you maintain eye contact with friends?
>   What are three of your unique vocal qualities?

2. Emotional Self

How do you physically respond when you are angry?

What things consistently make you smile?

When you cried last, what was it about?

3. Spiritual Self

What spiritual activities do you engage in each day? each week? each year?

What happens after death?

How do you feel about Christmas?

4. Intellectual Self

What was the last book you read that was not assigned for a class?

What course, book, or person most expanded your thinking?

What does "intellectual rigor" mean to you?

5. Artistic Self

In what activities are you the most creative?

If you had to choose a career in some artistic field, what career would you choose?

What poem is particularly meaningful to you?

6. Artifactual Self

What is your favorite costume for attending class?

How do you typically adorn your body?—jewelry, glasses, lotion, makeup?

How much time do you spend in the morning with hair care?

7. Cultural Self

What are your family's most memorable traditions?

What style of language do you speak at home? with friends? writing in a personal journal?

What are your affinity groups?

stereotype *n* **1 : a plate made by molding a matrix of a printing surface and making from this a cast in type metal 2 : something conforming to a fixed or general pattern;** *esp* **: a standardized mental picture held in common by members of a group and representing an oversimplified opinion, affective attitude, or uncritical judgment (as of a person, a race, an issue, or an event)**

In order to make the distinction between the self and the other apparent, performers are likely to focus on points of difference rather than points of identification. In this way, performance mirrors one of the developmental stages of infancy in which the baby first begins to differentiate self from all other things in the universe. Sander Gilman discussed the implications of this differentiation:

As the child comes to distinguish more and more between the world and self, anxiety arises from a perceived loss of control over the world. But very soon the child begins to combat anxieties associated with the failure to control the world by adjusting his mental picture of people and objects so that they can appear "good" even when their behavior is perceived as "bad." (17)

The infant then divides the world into that which is "good," or can be controlled, and that which is "bad," or outside of the self's control. The self is similarly divided into the good self that is free of anxiety and the bad self that is anxious because it is aware of what it cannot control. Those things that produce anxiety must be controlled by making them stable and predictable, like inanimate objects. This is the beginning of the formation of a stereotype.

Stereotypes are an important way in which the brain organizes material. We know that an object is a chair because we have encountered objects similar to the one in question, and we were able to sit in them. We do not spend much time wondering whether or not the chair will support our weight, or begin to move across the room, or make music when we touch it. This same generalizing occurs with people. Just as stereotyping makes the chair predictable, stereotyping people converts them into stable and predictable objects. Stereotyping becomes a way of controlling an other. Gilman explains the crucial relationship of self to other:

> Stereotypes arise when self-integration is threatened. They are therefore part of our way of dealing with the instabilities of our perception of the world. This is not to say that they are good, only that they are necessary. . . . for the nonpathological individual the stereotype is a momentary coping mechanism, one that can be used and then discarded once anxiety is overcome. . . . [The nonpathological individual] is able to repress the aggression and deal with people as individuals. (18)

Stereotypes and the self form a symbiotic union in which the very act of individuation relies on the formation of stereotypes. A self free from anxiety and fear has less need to maintain rigid stereotypes but instead creates porous and flexible categories. The lines of demarcation that bound the stereotype, the other, flow around and through the lines of the self. Self and other share the same membrane; they are linked in a mutually defining relationship.

stereotype *vt* **1** : to make a stereotype from **2 a** : to repeat without variation **b** : to develop a mental stereotype about

stereotyped *adj* lacking originality or individuality *syn* see TRITE

Performance relies on stereotypes to communicate. Stereotypic choices, the understood rules of behavior, create communication between performers and audiences. Indeed, the mark of an extraordinary performer is often how she or he manipulates the stereotype. In this course, performance stereotypes must be allowed to live. They reveal where the performer is in his or her conceptualization of blackness and how the performer sees the self in contrast to the other. When playing a scene from Charles Fuller's *Zooman and the Sign*, an Asian American student, performing an African American urban teenager who has just killed a little girl, adopts a swagger, an angular body posture, and a loud voice; some might argue that the student is relying on media-driven stereotypes of African American males. For the performer, these choices are markers of blackness, signs chosen to communicate in the sort of shorthand in which performance always participates. These markers may constitute the "gaps," what Anna Deavere Smith calls the distinction between "the real person and [his or her] *attempt* to seem like them" (xxxvii). Rather than shy away from this distinction and the possibility of creating stereotypes, Smith honors the gap. She explains, "I try to close the gap between us, but I applaud the gap between us. I am willing to display my own *unlikeness*" (xxxviii). Performance provides a space for reveling in difference.

archetype *n* 1 : the original pattern or model of which all things of the same type are representations or copies : PROTOTYPE
archi- *or* **arch-** *prefix* 1 : chief: principal 2 : primitive : original : primary

The notion of performing stereotypes can be problematic for African diasporic drama in which the playwrights have created characters as archetypes. Indeed, Femi Euba sees African diasporic drama itself as having an "archetypal function" (12). Northrop Frye defines *archetype* as "a typical or recurring image" (99), and M. H. Abrams writes that archetypes are "a set of universal, primitive, and elemental patterns" (11). Because stereotype and archetype both rely on identifiable and recurring patterns, the line between an archetype and stereotype is not always clear. Paul Carter Harrison discusses the importance of archetypes to African-based aesthetics:

> The inclination to testimony is the direct outgrowth of blacks attempting to overcome the rifts of consciousness created by regionalism and elitism so as to identify the tracings of a collective

ethos, a sense of common purpose. Thus, archetypal characters are more vital for public testimony than individuated characters pursuing their personal assessment of reality. Like the blues singer, archetypes provide potent communal references that illuminate the social landscape. (xlii)

Harrison talks of the "testimony of Zooman" and says he is "not a tragic hero but rather a demonic force inviting a social critique" (xlvi). These descriptions situate Zooman among archetypes rather than among "individuated characters pursuing their personal assessment of reality." While Harrison seems to be making an intellectual distinction between stereotypes and archetypes, such distinctions are not always performed in clear ways. When a student performing Zooman wears baggy pants and a baggy, hooded sweatshirt, folds her arms across her chest, and leans heavily to the side, it is difficult to determine whether or not this is a stereotypical or an archetypical performance. Even more complex are the performance choices students might make when they choose to perform any of the Yorùbá deities in Pepe Carril's *Shango de Ima*. Is it stereotypical or archetypical when a student performs Shango, the deity of thunder, while wearing red cloth and beating a drum? Studies of Yorùbá cosmology frequently state that Shango is associated with the color red, and that he is the patron deity of drummers. When helping students differentiate between archetypes and stereotypes, perhaps it would be useful to consider Carol Pearson's observation:

> The *stereotypes* are laundered, domesticated versions of the *archetypes* from which they derive their power. The shallow stereotype seems controllable and safe, but it brings then less, not more, life. The archetype behind it is full of life and power. (xvii)

While the drum and red cloth of Shango contribute to the manifestation of this deity as an archetype, these performance choices alone do not insure an archetypical performance. To achieve an archetypical performance, one must create an embodiment that is "full of life and power," one that feels "original" and "primary" rather than "trite."

Differentiation between the self and the other is an important step in the performance process. Performers should be encouraged to explore the stereotypes that come to them, rather than reject them as inappropriate or offensive. Attempts to suppress the stereotype are often futile; the body will display the images embedded in the performer's psyche. Suppressing the stereotype also negates the possibility of moving through the stereotype, because suppression eliminates dialogue. If students are not permitted to explore the stereotype, they are less likely to see the ways in which the stereotype is an extension of self-identity, a way of protecting the self from a "bad" world.

While the performance of stereotypes is a necessary beginning for those students who have placed the other within the safe confines of a stereotype, ultimately the nuanced performance with detail will give the character dimension. Working through the stereotype assists the student in balancing the power relationship between the self and the other. The student must decenter the self by paying close attention to the other. The detail yielded through close attention helps the student move toward a more physically and emotionally complex performance. Psychologist Susan T. Fiske argues that "people in power stereotype in part because they do not need to pay attention, they cannot easily pay attention, and they may not be personally motivated to pay attention" (621). In the Performance of Dramatic Literature course, I employ two strategies to encourage the students to pay attention.

Methods of Embodiment:
Everyday Life Performance (ELP) and Improvisation

> Dramatism demands critical practices that obliterate distinctions between life and art. From Burke to Goffman to Schechner to Turner to Conquergood, dramatistic writers testify that life and drama are one. (Hopper 181)

Embedded in and woven around our everyday practices are the principles that govern our lives, what Michel de Certeau calls the "text of society" (167). While the students in Performance of Dramatic Literature do not have the time to conduct the extensive fieldwork required to fully immerse themselves in such texts, they can listen closely to personal narratives of real people, which are the repositories for cultural practice. Personal narratives are the stories of persons who are, by virtue of being human, connected to culture(s). Giving full attention to personal narratives not only encourages the performer to understand the cultural underpinnings of such narratives; it also gives the performer ample detail for creating specific, rather than stereotypical, performances.

> *Exercise:* Students bring to class a portable tape recorder and a cassette tape. They are paired with other students in the class and move around the room or the building so that they can find a somewhat private space. One at a time, each student in the pair tells her or his story while the partner records the story. The stories can be guided ("When did you first realize your racial identity?" "What was the best thing that happened in high school?" "Where were you when you heard about the O. J. Simpson verdict?") or the stories can flow from the students' interests ("Tell your partner about your favorite movie.") After each partner has told her or his story, they exchange tapes so they are able to

walk away with the tape of their partner's story. The students
practice the stories and present them in class fully clothed as
their partner.

Everyday life performance, developed by Nathan Stucky and Robert
Hopper, is an important tool for exploration of the self and an other.[3]
ELP grew from a methodology in conversation analysis in which researchers painstakingly transcribed taped conversations. The transcriptions noted the length of pauses, the inhalations of air, the bend-
ing of vowels, as well as pitch, volume, rate, and tone. Stucky and
Phillip Glenn describe the potential of ELP:

> One objective of our work is to help students understand fictional
> language as a form of natural expression which is just as available
> to them as their own oral idioms. We encourage students to rec-
> ognize literary qualities in their own natural speech and in litera-
> ture. Once the imagined barriers between these supposedly dif-
> ferent uses of language begin to break down, students have a
> better chance of engaging the literature through performance.
> (193)

The skill for detail and close attention that the students learn from ELP
can be applied to the development of their fictional characters. Like the
real persons in the ELPs, the characters should also have a distinctive
breathing pattern, idiosyncratic smacks, clicks, and nonfluencies.
Whereas ELP works well for establishing the general importance of detail, improvisation helps with the specific application of detail to the
character being performed.

**Through spontaneity we are re-formed into ourselves. It
creates an explosion that for the moment frees us from
handed-down frames of reference, memory choked with
old facts and information and undigested theories and
techniques of other people's findings. (Spolin 4)**

Improvisation insists that the students invent a reality. That invention
is inevitably shaped by their experiences, their biases, their prejudices,
and their fears—but it must also go beyond those limitations, because
the invention necessarily exceeds the students' stereotyped understandings of an other. Mary Catherine Bateson sees improvisation as
an especially critical tool in cross-cultural negotiating. For Bateson,
"improvisation is central to living in periods of change" in which we
must become conversant with "a canon of human experience, as con-
trasted with a canon of great books" (118). Through the mutual invention and spontaneous creation of improvisation, students expand their
canon to include cultures they deem other than their own.

Exercise: Students study the roles of Sello, Manana, and John from Zakes Mofokeng's *A New Song*. They should especially note the moments near the end of the play in which Sello and Manana have managed to get the gun from John, a white South African who is holding them captive in their own home. Throughout the play, Sello and Manana, a black South African husband and wife, have discussed what they would do if they could overpower John. The students are to improvise the closing moments of the play, with one significant difference; instead of following the play, which has Manana retrieving the gun and handing it over to Sello, who threatens John but decides not to kill him, the improvisation has Manana keep the gun and decide what John's fate should be. The three performers must now rely on the detail supplied by the playwright throughout the play, their inner sense of human interaction, and their ability to process all of the unpredictable elements of performance. If their initial impulses are stereotypical, these impulses will be challenged as they respond to the spontaneous forces that unfold in the scene.

Exercise: Students examine the lady in yellow's poem "it waz graduation nite" from Ntozake Shange's "for colored girls who have considered suicide/when the rainbow is enuf." Students are assigned the roles of the lady in yellow and other characters described in the poem, such as bobby mills, martin, jerome, sammy yates, eddie jones, randi, and jacqui. They will improvise the party that the lady in yellow describes. The remaining students should create roles for themselves at the party so that the entire class participates. This is a long exercise in which they may or may not follow the details of the party from the play. The extended time should give the students an opportunity to fully examine the characters in varied situations at the party. Many scenes may be happening simultaneously. Because all the students are involved, there will be less tendency to perform for an onlooking audience; the focus will be on knowing how the character behaves in the given circumstances. The teacher should also be a character in the improvisation, thereby reducing further the sense of performing for someone and requiring the teacher to participate as fully as the students.

Creating improvisations around scenes from the plays helps the students to solidify their characterizations and more vigorously interrogate their stereotypes. In one memorable improvisation from *Zooman and the Sign*, a European American student performing Zooman had to enter the home of a little girl he has shot and killed just the day before. During the improvisation, the mother, the father, and the son are grieving when Zooman breaks into the home to confront the family about pushing the neighbors to identify the little girl's killer. The student playing the son leaped to his feet and shoved Zooman to the ground. The student playing the son disregarded the fact that the student playing Zooman was actually a woman. The woman playing Zooman was startled by this aggressiveness but had to regroup and respond as Zooman in the scene. For a split second, she was aware of her "female response" and had to instantly convert that into a "male response" that more appropriately suited Zooman. She quickly got to her feet and charged the son, and the two wrestled for a few seconds. It was exciting to see how the improvisation forced her to a deeper, more specific sense of her character. She discovered something about the performance of herself as female and the performance of Zooman as male. Reliance on a stereotypically male performance alone could not sustain the scene. She had to pull on other resources that took her through the stereotype.

> *Journal assignment:* You are an African American reporter for the *Chicago Defender.* You are reporting on the killing of Toledo by Levee at the end of August Wilson's *Ma Rainey's Black Bottom.* What will be your headline? What details will you include? What language and style will you use? What photo, if any, would you include? This entry should be the newspaper article itself, not a description of what you would write.

Possibilities

Performance makes both identification and difference vibrate at a deeper, more resonant pitch. It does not allow the energetically naive declaration "we're all the same" to hold sway. Doing this would be the same erasure that is found in stereotyping. In the practice of stereotyping, the detail of the individual is overlooked, while in the attempt to universalize, the details of difference are more deliberately ignored. In both, fear exists—fear of no control, of unpredictability, of some pieces of the self too deeply frightening to confront. This fear leads to the construction of an object/other in the case of stereotyping and to an appropriation/incorporation into the consuming self in the case of universalizing. In both processes, we still miss each other—both are broad strokes absent of detail. As teachers and students, we must be willing to do the terrifying work of examining our self-constructions and our rigidly held constructions of others, if we are to create a truly liberatory education. Performance can be a vital tool in that liberation.

All of us in the academy and in the culture as a whole are called to renew our minds if we are to transform educational institutions—and society—so that the way we live, teach, and work can reflect our joy in cultural di-

versity, our passion for justice, and our love of freedom.
(hooks 34)

The body believes what it plays at: it weeps if it mimes grief. It does not represent what it performs, it does not memorize the past, it enacts the past, brings it back to life. What is "learned by body" is not what one has, like knowledge that can be brandished, but something one is. (Bourdieu 73)

NOTES

I would like to gratefully acknowledge the research assistance provided by Jill Carleton in preparing this essay.

1. According to the US Bureau of the Census 1990 summary tape file 3, 11.9 percent of the population of Texas was African American and 25.3 percent was Latino/a. These figures are grossly out of alignment with the student population at the University of Texas.

2. Harrison's text offers the African diasporic perspective that is important to the course; however, only one female playwright is included. William Branch's *Crosswinds* is another diasporic anthology, and it, too, only has one female playwright. More recent anthologies such as *Contemporary Plays by Women of Color* (Perkins and Uno) and *Colored Contradictions* (Elam and Alexander) include many women playwrights but do not give the diasporic breadth that is important to the course. I often supplement Harrison's text with Pearl Cleage's *Hospice*. Because Cleage's play is a one-act, it doesn't add substantially to the students' reading load. Shay Youngblood's *Shakin' the Mess Outta Misery*, Oni Faida Lampley's *Mixed Babies*, and Adrienne Kennedy's *Funnyhouse of the Negro* are also relatively short plays and could be used to balance the number of male playwrights in Harrison's anthology.

3. For a more detailed description of ELP rehearsal techniques, see the Apr. 1993 issue of *Text and Performance Quarterly*, which is devoted to an exploration of performance and conversation and to conversational dramatism. In particular, see Stucky; Juhl; and Randall.

WORKS CITED

Abrams, M. H. *A Glossary of Literary Terms*. New York: Holt, 1971.

Bacon, Wallace A. *The Art of Interpretation*. 3rd ed. New York: Holt, 1979.

———. "The Case for Interpretation." *Renewal and Revision: The Future of Interpretation*. Ed. Ted Colson. Denton: NB Omega, 1986. 15–25.

Bateson, Mary Catherine. "Joint Performance Across Cultures: Improvisation in a Persian Garden." *Text and Performance Quarterly* 13 (1993): 113–21.

Bourdieu, Pierre. *The Logic of Practice*. Trans. Richard Nice. Stanford: Stanford UP, 1990.

Branch, William. *Crosswinds: An Anthology of Black Dramatists in the Diaspora.* Bloomington: Indiana UP, 1993.

Carril, Pepe. *Shango de Ima.* Harrison 47–90.

Cleage, Pearl. *Hospice. New Plays from the Black Theatre.* Ed. Woodie King, Jr. Chicago: Third World, 1989. 45–72.

Conquergood, Dwight. "Rethinking Ethnography: Towards a Critical Cultural Politics." *Communication Monographs* 58 (1991): 179–94.

de Certeau, Michel. *The Practice of Everyday Life.* Trans. Steven Rendall. Berkeley: U of California P, 1984.

Elam, Harry J., Jr., and Robert Alexander, eds. *Colored Contradictions: An Anthology of Contemporary African American Plays.* New York: Penguin, 1996.

Euba, Femi. *Archetypes, Imprecators, and Victims of Fate.* New York: Greenwood, 1989.

Fiske, Susan T. "Controlling Other People: The Impact of Power on Stereotyping." *American Psychologist* 48.6 (1993): 621–28.

Freire, Paulo. *Pedagogy of the Oppressed.* New York: Continuum, 1970.

Frye, Northrop. *Anatomy of Criticism: Four Essays.* Princeton: Princeton UP, 1957.

Fuller, Charles. *Zooman and the Sign.* Harrison 275–329.

Gilman, Sander. "Introduction: What Are Stereotypes and Why Use Texts to Study Them?" *Difference and Pathology: Stereotypes of Sexuality, Race, and Madness.* Ithaca: Cornell UP, 1985. 15–35.

Grossberg, Lawrence. Introduction. "Bringin' It All Back Home—Pedagogy and Cultural Studies." *Between Borders: Pedagogy and the Politics of Cultural Studies.* Ed. Henry A. Giroux and Peter McLaren. New York: Routledge, 1994. 1–25.

Harrison, Paul Carter, ed. *Totem Voices: Plays from the Black World Repertory.* New York: Grove, 1989.

hooks, bell. *Teaching to Transgress: Education as the Practice of Freedom.* New York: Routledge, 1994.

Hopper, Robert. "Conversational Dramatism and Everyday Life Performance." *Text and Performance Quarterly* 13 (1993): 181–83.

Juhl, Kathleen. "Everyday Life Performance and 'the Method' in the Acting Classroom." *Text and Performance Quarterly* 13 (1993): 200–204.

Kennedy, Adrienne. *Funnyhouse of the Negro. Black Theatre U.S.A.: Plays by African Americans: The Recent Period, 1935–Today.* Ed. James V. Hatch and Ted Shine. New York: Free, 1996. 333–43.

Lampley, Oni Faida. *Mixed Babies. Manhattan Class Company: Class 1 Acts, 1991–1992.* New York: Dramatists Play Service, 1992. 15–46.

Leder, Drew. *The Absent Body.* Chicago: U of Chicago P, 1990.

Pearson, Carol. *The Hero Within: Six Archetypes We Live By.* San Francisco: Harper, 1986.

Perkins, Kathy A., and Roberta Uno, eds. *Contemporary Plays by Women of Color.* New York: Routledge, 1996.

Randall, Deleasa M. "Staged Replication of Naturally-Occurring Talk: A Performer's Perspective." *Text and Performance Quarterly* 13 (1993): 197–99.

Smith, Anna Deavere. *Fires in the Mirror: Crown Heights and Other Identities.* New York: Anchor, 1993.

Spolin, Viola. *Improvisation for the Theatre.* Evanston: Northwestern UP, 1963.

Stucky, Nathan. "Toward an Aesthetics of Natural Performance." *Text and Performance Quarterly* 13 (1993): 168–80.

Stucky, Nathan, and Phillip Glenn. "Invoking the Empirical Muse: Conversation, Performance, and Pedagogy." *Text and Performance Quarterly* 13 (1993): 192–96.

Youngblood, Shay. *Shakin' the Mess Outta Misery.* Elam and Alexander 379–415.

Joni L.
Jones

The Dialogics of Performance and Pedagogy

12
Arthur J.
Sabatini

Two friends are on a vacation in a foreign country. They see tourist sites and holy places. They dine, shop, walk, and talk to people. They are having a great time, and on their second night, they go to a nightclub where a comedian is telling jokes. One of the friends starts laughing wildly. The other looks over and says, "What are you laughing at? You don't know this language." "I know," the friend replies, "but I trust these people."

Whom Do You Trust?

From certain perspectives, pedagogy and comedy are related performance genres. ("Take my class. Please!") Pedagogy is the type of performance that is so common, so universally and historically threaded through the human experience that its every feature has been parodied, not least of all by people who have been students. Certain pedagogical types—elders, wise uncles, savvy aunts, Zen masters, nutty professors—are characterized by their distinctly ironic, mirthful, or unintended comic behaviors. Alfred Jarry's bumbling monster, Père Ubu, was modeled after a teacher; performance art with bad or mad nuns are staples in clubs and small theaters. Examples abound. As an institution, "education" operates with codes and processes that are so socioculturally and historically overcoded, they become ready stages for humorous exchanges. From the walking and talking act of Socrates, to the Marx Brothers' antics in *Horsefeathers,* to the most recent high school settings for films and sit-coms, laughing and learning, although seemingly incongruous as behaviors, provide a rich trope for study as performance. Among many similarities, comedy and teaching raise issues about authority, representation, social relations, knowledge, and play. There is also the matter of trust.

Trust aside, for a moment, I prefaced this essay with a joke as a way of playing with the notion that teaching and the study of knowledge can be viewed as comedic. It is not that epistemology is particularly humorous, or that knowledge itself is a joke, or even that the act of knowing provokes laughter. Rather, it seems that regardless of how teachers, philosophers, or scientists approach the subject of what we know and how we know (and how we know we know), and despite good will and rigor, the success of any argument or understanding of a text depends upon the responses of others. And others, even if they speak the same language, are unknowable. Of course, being unknowable does not guarantee that responses will amuse. When knowledge is perceived as a threat, responses can be highly serious, politicized, even deadly. So, it is not the case that epistemology is exclusively comedic. Few laugh at the mere mention of Hegel and Schlegel. But Socrates is witty, and there is joy and laughter, of a sort, in the writings of Nietzsche, whose Zarathustra spake, "we should call every truth false which was not accompanied by at least one laugh." Bakhtin adds to these reflections. In *Rabelais and His World*, a study that foregrounds language, play, and bodies, he says, "Certain essential aspects of the world are accessible only to laughter" (66).

For more than a decade of teaching and thinking about ethics, epistemology, and performance, my most constant theoretical traveling companion has been the Russian thinker Mikhail Bakhtin (1895–1975). Bakhtin's writings fall into a hybrid category between the humanities and social sciences, literary theory and (what is called) sociological poetics. His work has been variously characterized, but I consider it as nothing less than a comprehensive theory of performance, at the core of which is a philosophical epistemology. Inasmuch as I reorient Bakhtin's thought toward performance and performance studies issues, it is because his overarching theorization of *dialogism* or *dialogics* is precisely about language, epistemology, ethics, and performance. Bakhtin accentuates the spatiotemporal relations between selves/others *and* the particularities of culture and history. As will become clear, he lucidly frames human relations in categories familiar to many versions of performance theory.[1]

Bakhtin's work provides a version of an epistemology of performance suited to consideration of performance in general and the genre called pedagogy in particular. In the following, I explore dialogism and allude to Bakhtin's other concepts of *authorship, co-participation, co-experience,* and *utterance* in order to show how they can be useful for analyzing performance and pedagogy.[2] Bakhtin, who did not specify a methodology for investigation of performance, nevertheless provided a general outline of his major concerns. His work continually requires that certain questions be asked, including: Who is speaking? (which can be restated as, Who is performing?) And what is the context of response? Other explicit questions he poses are: What is the *text?* What are the types of discourses being used? How are they used? What is the sociopolitical context of an utterance? What are the boundaries of an utterance? What are the ethical aspects surrounding or implicit in dialogues?

These are crucial questions in the context of a classroom. Issues of textual authority, writing, performance, *and* relationships between students and teachers and institutions are constantly present as we teach and learn. Regarding the specific performance called teaching, other questions prompted by Bakhtin emerge: What genre of performance is pedagogy? What is the typology of discourses that operate in pedagogical situations? What is the relation between student and teacher? Who teaches? What types of knowledge and forms of interpretation exist and are being created in the context of teaching performance studies (historically and socio-ideologically)?

Bakhtin's concepts and ready lexicon consciously inform both the substance and style of my teaching. I am drawn to his philosophical epistemology because it incorporates themes, such as creativity and temporality, that are compelling to me in the context of teaching. Bakhtin's attention to the phenomenology of the body and his notions of alterity and politics augments my predilections in academia. In addition, his approach to art forms and genres accords with my own. For example, Bakhtin has written extensively on the novel, and I use his understanding of the novel to teach fiction and performance studies. What he says of the novel also relates to pedagogy as performance. In the essay "Epic and Novel," Bakhtin argues that the novel evolves with "a certain semantic openendedness, a living contact with unfinished, still evolving, contemporary reality." (*Dialogic Imagination* 7) For me, pedagogy should also operate as if there were no final words.

Of course, anyone who teaches somewhat re-presents the performances of his or her prior teachers or teaches according to familiar cultural and historicized scripts. Which is to say, like participants in rituals, like actors and theatrical traditions, like clients and therapy, teachers and their performances can be comprehended dialogically in the context of *both* society and history *and* in relation to their individualized classroom performances and pedagogical practices.

One decisive result of my awareness of dialogism is that I listen more, especially to noise, laughter, and silences. It might be that as human beings we continuously overhear and evaluate others' knowledge over time, whether or not we fully understand it. Performance, too, pulses with the euphony or din of an epistemology. Or, since I maintain that performance and knowledge are intertwined, epistemological inquiry resonates as performance. What John Cage says of sound also applies to knowledge: It is everywhere. Performance is its present tense. The music you hear *means;* so does the noise. One question that needs to be asked is, Means what? From a dialogic perspective, the answer involves others. Trust me.

Dialogics 101

Dialogism presents the case that language, consciousness, cultural production, individual and social behavior, and aesthetic activity occur within multiple interdependent contexts. On the most elemental level, the image of persons in actual conversations is at the root of dialogism. But for Bakhtin, engagement in dialogue is not simply a matter of turn taking or following conversational rules. Explicit social, historical, and spatiotemporal relationships need to be accounted for. As with subsequent discourse theorists, Bakhtin argues that speakers are *co-participants*, or interdependent interlocutors. Each person in a dialogue—or a polylogue among many people—speaks and answers. Listening is one form of answering. Words, breath, paralinguistic voicings, inner speech, gestures, eye movements, and all other material aspects of a situation, or what he calls *utterance*, are mutually shared and *co-experienced*. Utterance, then, is Bakhtin's term for performance.

Utterances are interconnected, like "links on a chain." As Bakhtin writes in *Speech Genres*,

> Each utterance is filled with echoes and reverberations of other utterances to which it is related by the communality of the sphere of speech communication. . . . Each utterance refutes, affirms, supplements, and relies on the others, presupposes them to be known, and somehow takes them into account. (91)

All persons are mutually, that is, dialogically, implicated in a given utterance. Moreover, dialogical relationships among utterances also occur transhistorically and transspatially. Hearing Mozart's *Così fan tutti* is a situation of utterance. If I am directing or performing in *Così fan tutti*, I am in a different semantic position, and my responses are not the same. Naturally, this applies to teaching situations.

We all unavoidably live with responsibility toward others. Thus, Bakhtin argues, it takes at least two to know and a culture for knowing. More precisely, both culture and knowledge exists on the *borders* between human beings. An epistemology of performance that develops from these assumptions requires constant attention to two interrelated, simultaneous contexts. We should know as much as possible about the specific relations between individual selves and others in the spatiotemporal circumstances of a performance *and* in relation to the particularities of culture and history. It asks that, along with others, we become responsive to epistemology as a performance genre itself *and* that we respond to performance as epistemological. Of course, determining what a person or culture's version of what constitutes knowledge or performance—and their relationship—requires clarification and dialogue. Perhaps, even an entire course.

Epistemology of Performance plus Pedagogy 101
Inevitably, laughter, epistemological inquiry, and pedagogy require close examination of texts, genres, and practices. Performance studies scholarship that draws upon linguistics, anthropology, and theory often includes aspects of social and cultural analysis. However, the degree to which emphasis is placed on questions of performance, specific interpersonal or social relationships, *and* epistemology is, for good rea-

sons, generally slight. First, it is difficult to say what knowledge is. It is also exceedingly difficult to account for what others know. Third, as a field, epistemology is as diverse and polycentered as performance studies. The question, What is knowledge? is no less problematic than, What is performance? To ask, What is the epistemology of performance? doubles the trouble.

Of course, for many theorists, performance studies itself represents an emergent dialogic/epistemological project consistent with other vectors of intellectual inquiry in this historical period. Performance studies investigates an aspect of human experience that has been studied and disciplinized in other categories. It is aggressively interdisciplinary and thoroughly intertextualized. In addition to the important work of theorizing, performance studies scholars readapt, recombine, and reorient the information and insights accumulated in other research. The epistemological issues and controversies in other fields are no less pertinent in the study of performance. This makes performance studies a thoroughly dialogic field, and those of us who teach it reflexively become both the objects and subjects of our own thought and practice.

On this account, Bakhtin's dialogic approach is pertinent because it leads to rethinking epistemology before positing that epistemology is performance or an epistemology of performance. Regardless of methodology or the aims of any inquiry, it is crucial to ask and frame questions and develop supporting arguments. Since Socrates, pedagogy might amount to little more. To that end, and without claiming to be comprehensive, I would propose that there are several axioms that are basic for an epistemology of performance. First, when approaching or categorizing an action or event as performance, distinct systems of reference and meaning pertaining to performance enter into our response or analysis. That is, to invoke the notion of performance, as a theorist, performer, or audience is to represent the event in question as a *text* with certain properties as a *genre*.[3] Genres may be social, cultural, aesthetic, or defined (or misnamed) by participants or observers. Rituals and festivals are genres. Naturally, many social performances mix or cross genres, and often, artistic performances intentionally interrogate the very notion of genre.

As Bakhtin argues in *The Formal Method in Literary Scholarship*, genre is a material fact, and it is inextricably woven into history, cultural practice, and understanding. Epistemologically, performance genres represent modalities of social organization and forms of meaning. "Genre appraises reality and reality clarifies genre" (136). When we conceive of knowledge itself as a social phenomenon, it necessarily depends upon shared recognition and dialogue, if not agreement on basic concepts and genres.

Often, classification projects may prove to be debatable or incomplete. Moreover, the experience of an event will differ from its representation. A second axiom for the study of performance, then, is that exegesis and analysis proceed from representations of performances as texts. Bakhtin's notion of text simply states that texts are what we discuss and study. Utterance designates human events that occur in knowable situations. "Only an utterance has a *direct* relationship to reality and to the living, speaking person (subject)" (*Speech Genres* 122). It is, Bakhtin states, "determined by the actual conditions of the given utterance—above all, by its *immediate social situation*" (*Marxism* 85). Thus, utterance refers to any type of performance or event: from reading a book, to spending a day at the circus, to conducting monkey business in cyberspace.

The problem of the textualization of performances requires as much clarification as that of genre. Factors that need to be considered are: authorship (of utterances *and* texts); the historical situation of performance (the *context*); and how the performance is socially produced and consumed, both immediately and over time. Obviously, these factors involve signifying and communication processes. A third axiom for an epistemology of performance, then, is that knowledge requires a theory of signification and communication.

An assumption of the last axiom is that what we call knowledge requires language and dialogue. It can also, as other essays in the present collection suggest, derive from what the body knows. But Bakhtin's dialogism, as Michael Holquist notes, is "perforce, a philosophy of language" (41). It describes language as a shared, historical material, ideologically charged phenomenon. Language is not merely a vehicle for representing ideas or events or even communicating "messages." It is an ever metamorphosing system that functions through dialogue/performance between two (or more) subjects who engage in (specific) utterances.

In terms of language, each classroom is a community, but not all communities adhere to the same understandings about how to do things with words. In my classes, I assume that students have differing values in relation to their shared language. In addition to racial, gender, and ethnic differences, some students view language as functional and more of a tool than an object, while others value the ludic and ambiguous dimensions of language. Attitudes toward language and authority and truth vary.

We trust each other or not. But following dialogic thought, the emphasis is neither finally on the notion of trust or on trust of oneself or others. It is on the relations between and among individuals, each of whom has a responsibility, and all of whom become the author of their responses. Thinking dialogically privileges relations and relationships, mutual positions, attitudes, and continuing responses, along with their assumptions and transformations.

Pedagogy as Performance Genre and Affirming Authorship

To return to other questions posed earlier: What genre of performance is pedagogy? What discourses operate in pedagogical situations? What is my relation to others as a person and a teacher? What types of knowledge and forms of interpretation exist in the context of teaching performance studies (historically and ideologically)?

From a dialogic perspective, these questions require assessment of the specific utterances that comprised them. As a cultural genre, the college course admits of a variety of institutionally sanctioned performance scripts and activities. Seminars, large lecture courses, and acting workshops are courses. Within each course, it is often (though not always) only the instructor who can *orchestrate* events so as to maximize dominant voices (those of texts, the canon, scholarly authority) or rely primarily on *indirect speech* (selected critical studies; outside source materials), or encourage responsible, open-ended, exploratory dialogue authored by everyone in the class.

Were an outside observer to study my pedagogy over a semester (in my present situation), they would note an interdisciplinarized and multimediated approach to thematically, conceptually, and historically considered subjects. Courses I teach include texts, writings, audio and video selections, and increasingly, Internet-based resources. Performances by students and guest artists occur regularly. The courses variously address theory, language, verbal art, comedy and laughter, and twentieth- and twenty-first-century Euro-American avant-garde and experimental performance traditions. While each class explores manifold issues, the underlying questions are: What knowledge can be found in performance (and art in general)? How do we analyze and value performance as a form of knowledge? What theoretical approaches are useful for understanding performance and its analysis?

Comedy and related genres, I argue/joke, are forms of knowledge. Experimental performance and artistic traditions can be characterized as being about the creation and transmission of epistemological objects, modes, sign systems, and processes. In some cases—experimental music, sonic arts, digital media, and performance—entirely new categories for organizing sound and performance have been introduced, requiring, at least, a reconceptualization of genres, ways of listening and knowing. Similarly, from *Dada* to contemporary multimedia and digital performance art, the project of simultaneous, decentered, polylogic presentation of images and the use of multiple sign systems and media has impacted on our processes of perception and understanding.

From a dialogic viewpoint, it would be necessary to examine syllabi, texts, assignments, media presentations, lecture and discussion notes, and my interaction with individual students in order to determine the particular intellectual and socio-ideological *intonation* or tone present within my courses. Some purely verbal analysis would be necessary as well to see if my voice and utterances contain the interplay of discourses that I think they do! (Every class of mine begins, "Any questions?" which has been suggested as my epitaph. As one student remarked, "it is as if our questions are the lessons." She was right to say *as if*, because, as the theory of dialogism would point out, her questions were among the possible responses to previous utterances).

As students have noted, my speech is marked by an East Coast urban, Italian American upbringing that seems intellectually honed by too much reading and the cultural transformations of the 1960s. In a classroom, I balance a familiarity with peculiar enthusiasms and an unapologetic presentation of ideas in what is generally regarded as accessible terms. References to authors, books, art, performance, popular culture, generational and cross-cultural differences are abundant in most of my talk. Anecdotes abound. I speak rapidly, with lotsa wordplay, longer than I should. Nevertheless, an observer would describe to what degree my classroom is marked by extended dialogue (including instances of written communications, personal conferences) and how the utterances and subject positions of students are disclosed.

While parts of this essay may show it (or not), I value humor and adhere to a long critical and practical tradition that conceives of comedy and comic speech as subversive genres. Comedy, as nearly all theories suggest, results from some form of nonthreatening incongruity, a rupture in otherwise predictable systems of meaning or communication. Such disruption creates a space for alternative responses, voices speaking with other tones. When laughter is involved (as one sign of the comic), the voice and the body temporarily merge in sound and motion.

Comedy aside, the discourses in any classroom are as variable as those in a novel or a sampled recording. The multidimensionality of the voices of students emerge differently in different class situations. A Bakhtinian would assess the relation between myself and students with the premise that, as the institutionally designated authority in the class, my utterances can never be evaluated outside of my role. The fact that I may tell jokes or redirect discussions toward ideological concerns does not mean that the jokes are funny or that there is agreement about the lines of inquiry pursued. In most college classes, students maintain a secret or alternative dialogue among themselves regarding the texts or the instructor. As course evaluations show, they often hold strong opinions about certain issues that instructors are unaware of. This is due to their personalities, attitudes, ages—all the factors that contribute to fleshing out the social circumstances of an utterance. Students in Arizona have different lives from those in New York City; students I taught in the 1970s differ from students in 2001. The music is not the same. But the quality that human beings have in common, as Bakhtin posits, is that we are the *authors* of our utterances, and we are responsible for them.

Each class meeting is an utterance. It is comprised of the many individuals, many *languagedness,* or *heteroglossic* voices of the texts and students. Concurrently, the entire course, as designed by the professor, is an utterance. It is a response to an idea, research, selected texts, a sequence of courses in the curriculum, or a particular period or theme. In a course titled Comedy, reading, lectures, and jokes provide examples of how language and signs in everyday life are ambiguous, and how human beings engage in forms of play that are integral to the pleasure and meaning in laughter. Reading *Rabelais and His World* leads to discussion of what Bakhtin calls the language of the marketplace, the body, the profane, and the marginal languages in different historical epochs. Students' language in everyday life provides some of the texts for examination. When during the course we explore *Monty Python,* the parody of British class consciousness and bureaucratese in skits can be viewed as a struggle among contending forces who play out their ideological positions in shops and government departments or through fragmentation and distortion of national symbols. *Python's* juxtapositions of "high" and "low" cultural images and discourses is hysterical and appropriate for the period but typical of comedic forms. It is a variation on specifically British entertainment traditions ranging from 1920s music hall revues to 1950s and 1960s radio and television shows, such as *The Goon Show, Beyond the Fringe,* and *That Was the Week That Was.* For a given social class, or when their speech genres are considered as utterance, a dialogical consciousness illuminates, among other things, the interplay and stratification of voices, images, and discourses in *Python.* The voices in the classroom become paramount as students become oriented toward *Python's* social, historical, and ideological play. Laughter signifies. As the varied relationships (to *Python,* among students) are exposed, explored, and evaluated, they become utterances that suggest other issues for discussion.

The previous paragraph refers primarily to pedagogic aims. It is also about performance in courses and classes. Instruction includes reviews of methodologies and critical and historical studies that contribute to understanding of performances. My intent is also for students to comprehend the language and semiotics of texts as well as genres and their evolution, varieties, and significance. But it is essential for students to identify their own subject positions in relation to texts and to each other. Their dialogue contributes to the production and consumption of knowledge in a course. After many years of teaching—after dialoguing with Bakhtin studies—my pedagogical approach and techniques are consciously oriented toward accentuating this *polyphony* of voices and their relationships in a class. (Of course, as you have already figured out, my re-presentation of my practice in this text is necessarily monologic, rather than dialogic. That is where you come in . . .)

Naturally, to the degree that any instructor is the first speaker in a course, all subsequent utterance "refutes, affirms, supplements" what has been stated by the course title, syllabus, and lectures. But there are many ways to accent dialogization in a performance studies course through student responses. In the early stages of a course, I ascertain as much as possible about students' backgrounds, interests, and academic pursuits. On many occasions, I have changed some of the content of a course or added materials suggested by students. In courses such as the two-semester sequence The Avant-Garde and Experimental Performance in the Twentieth Century, I have gathered enough materials to *reaccentuate* most sections of the course. I am prepared, with little sacrifice to my general goals of approaching the epistemological and historical content of avant-garde/experimental performance, to address, say, issues of technology, interculturalism, gender, politics, conceptions of the body, and so on.

There are other ways to increase dialogue and heighten students' awareness of their own subject positions and relationships. Professors do this intentionally or inadvertently through shared assignments, in-class small-group discussions, and interactive media projects. Professors with backgrounds in theater and dance have an array of games and exercises for eliciting personal responses. As a teacher of composition and writing for over a decade, I accumulated numerous techniques for organizing critical responses among small groups and creating situations for open discussion and dialogue. I have adapted many strategies for performance studies classes, with the emphasis, these more Bakhtinian days, less on directing students toward completion of final products than on defining subject positions and understanding their places in meaningful dialogues with others.

How do I know what others think of my performances? Examinations, papers, grades, and course evaluations do not fully measure individuals' complete responses to the performance of pedagogical acts. Likewise, evaluating audiences' responses to performance or inquiring into the epistemological dimensions of performance for individuals or a society is a complex task. Performance studies has demonstrated that performances resonate with knowledge. Epistemology as performance is an equally valid arena of study. What others think (students, audiences, societies) and how we develop relationships with them is a dialogic and pedagogic project.

Every era produces the knowledge it desires and the theory of epistemology it needs. In a world of rapid technologization, internationalization, and increasing cross-cultural awareness through information systems, performance studies is focused precisely on the moment of meaning and values of those involved. In a world where communication is dominated by simulacra, virtual reality, and economic and political forces, performance studies asks us to consider the semiosis of cultural and aesthetic events. It calls attention to persons, lives, voices, communities, the body. Dialogic thought intensifies an awareness of the ethics and trust involved in relationships, responses, and responsibility. To me, this sounds like a knowledge worth performing. And to you?

NOTES

1. Bakhtin himself never wrote directly on pedagogy, performance, or performance theory, nor did he define his work as *dialogism* (a term used by Michael Holquist and others). Dialogism or the dialogic principle emerged in Bakhtin's writings after his early studies of art, aesthetics, and creativity.

2. When first introduced, Bakhtin's specialized terms or words, some of which he appropriates (e.g., *text*), are italicized. As with the lexicons of psychoanalysis or semiology, the adaptations of Bakhtin's concepts are often used separately from his overall theorization. This has often limited their meaning and efficaciousness.

3. See Bakhtin's essay "The Problem of the Text in Linguistics, Philology, and the Human Sciences: An Experiment in Philosophical Analysis" in *Speech Genres*. Bakhtin's conception of social and ritual genres has similarities to that of Victor Turner.

WORKS CITED

Bakhtin, Mikhail. *The Dialogic Imagination: Four Essays*. Ed. Michael Holquist. Trans. Caryl Emerson and Michael Holquist. Austin: U of Texas P, 1981.

———. *Rabelais and His World*. Trans. Helene Iswolsky. Cambridge: MIT, 1968.

———. *Speech Genres and Other Late Essays*. Ed. Caryl Emerson and Michael Holquist. Trans. Vern W. McGee. Austin: U of Texas P, 1986.

Bakhtin, Mikhail, and P. N. Medvedev. *The Formal Method in Literary Scholarship: A Critical Introduction*. Trans. Albert Wehrle. Cambridge: Harvard UP, 1985.

Bakhtin, Mikhail, and V. N. Voloshinov. *Marxism and the Philosophy of Language*. Trans. Ladislav Matejka and I. R. Titunik. New York: Seminar, 1973.

Holquist, Michael. *Dialogism: Bakhtin and His World*. New York: Routledge, 1990.

Part Three
Negotiating Borders

Improvising Disciplines

Performance Studies and Theatre

13

Linda M.
Park-Fuller

With every conference I attend, with every book or article I read or write, with every class I teach and workshop I take, I find the field of performance studies shifting, transforming, metamorphosing—in my hands, in my mind, in its relationship to my department, my university, and the world—and my teaching philosophy and practices continue to change, accordingly. What do I tell my students in this time of change?

To teach performance studies, we need to be able to address "marketplace" questions (HopKins; Kendig; Taft-Kaufman, "Embodied Performance") from both our undergraduate and graduate students—questions like "What is it, and how does it relate to theatre (or other disciplines)? What will I learn? Of what use is the knowledge and training I will acquire? What are the benefits to society, to me?" And the question most frequently asked: "Can this learning help me to make a living?"

Discovering new ways to answer our students' questions will necessitate investment from each person who teaches—a project for which this collection of essays lays a solid foundation and toward which we should continue to build. In this essay, I will approach our challenge in five steps. First, I want to address our conceptualization of performance studies by interrogating the prevailing spatial/geographical metaphor that grounds most discussions of the field—not to refute its usefulness but rather to show its limitations and the need for additional metaphoric conceptions. Second, I will draw upon both performance theory and practice to propose the metaphor of "improvisation"—a metaphor that reflects and permeates our work on many levels but does not yet have currency as a trope for conceptualizing the discipline. In the following three sections, I will utilize the improvisation metaphor to discuss pedagogic aspects of our work at the disciplinary level ("Improvisation and Service"), at the local level ("Improvising Curriculum"), and at the most essential level of classes and activities ("Improvisation and Praxis)."

The Geographical Metaphor

206
Linda M.
Park-Fuller

Scholars in performance studies and other fields have made good use of geographical metaphors to help define our disciplines. Increasing references to the terminology of "boundaries and borderlands" that Conquergood notes in relation to ethnography apply to other areas of performance as well ("Rethinking Ethnography" 183–86). Both Worthen and Strine, Long, and HopKins focus on the metaphor of performance "sites" to discuss the philosophy or the development of the field; Strine traces categorical "landscapes" to clarify the cultural matrix in which our discipline operates; Dolan employs metaphors of "location," "maps," "boundaries," and "bridges" to explore identity politics in social, cultural, and disciplinary categories; and both Carlson ("Theatre History") and Stucky ("Re/Membering") in their respective studies on theatre history and performance history refer to boundary lines and walls. These geographical metaphors seem to function in three ways: to serve as a vehicle by which to explain disciplinary insights; to provide a fresh lens through which to view our areas of study; and to assert a bond between performing disciplines and cultural studies.

I have great appreciation for the insights and issues that have come to light through the use of terms that image our work as *charting, mapping, border crossing,* and the like, and I have found such terms to be useful. However, as rich as the images may be, eventually they place us in danger not only of "mistaking the map for the territory" but of being blinded by the sight of *only* maps and territories. Performance disciplines, in their many incarnations, are far too complex to be envisioned only in spatial terms, and geographical metaphors are severely limited in their ability to speak to teaching practices and pedagogy.

When used in relation to *teaching* especially, metaphors of "place" can become dangerously real and dangerously reifying. Teaching and learning occur in physical sites, such as classrooms, buildings, and campuses, which are real to both students and faculty, and in institutional sites, such as departments and colleges, which are often equally as real to us. While we pay lip-service to interdisciplinary philosophies and practices, those institutional and disciplinary divisions are real enough to set up an "us-them" worldview, foster turf wars and messy department splits or mergers, and produce insecure, angry faculty who do not want their boundaries blurred but secured and safe. At this level of everyday struggle to teach, to learn, to hold on to or secure a job, to survive professionally—as a faculty member or as a discipline— boundaries are all too real, and geographical metaphors only serve to reinforce them, inhibiting creativity in teaching and learning.

Even metaphors of "blurred boundaries" and "border crossings" (for all their good intentions) may only reinscribe the demarcations, for a discipline that speaks in terms of boundary crossings still thinks in terms of boundaries. Such terms may be exciting for us tenured professors who can revel in the (secure) "freedom" of an "interdiscipline" (Conquergood, "Of Caravans" 137) or "anti-discipline" (Joseph Roach qtd. in Carlson, *Performance* 189). But graduate students and prospective teachers may find the image of the academic world as geographically bound or unbound to be particularly unsettling. Their situation is extremely tenuous, for they do not yet know where they will find jobs, and therefore, they do not know how to train themselves to succeed in their positions. They do not know in what type of departmental grouping they may find jobs or what possibilities for interdepartmental teaching or research exist. To be sure, some ambiguity exists for all prospective teachers, but performance studies graduates are often fortunate if they find jobs where they can teach a course in their field (never mind their research specialty). Besides their training in performance studies, therefore, they need ample work in at least one related area (theatre, communication, anthropology, business, etc.), and as yet, it is difficult to tell which area(s) might afford the best opportunities for jobs. Their situation is stressful enough; the geographical metaphor only compounds it.

Ultimately, it is the anxiety this metaphor evokes that bothers me most. I have lived all my professional life in the "borderlands" and have seen, and participated in, more than my share of territorial conflicts, philosophical strife, and professional casualties, and I am tired of the battles. Unlike some scholars, who seem to relish the idea of contestations and struggles that the "borderland" metaphor evokes, I seek a gentler analogy, and in Mary Catherine Bateson's works, I find a familiar one. In "Joint Performance Across Cultures," Bateson rejects the "juggling" metaphor often used to describe women's handling of multiple roles.

> By contrast, the metaphor of an improvisational art form, putting together different elements, dealing with the unknown in a way which sustains performance and connects it with other systems of meaning . . . can make us celebrate the uncertainties with which we are beginning to live. (120)

Applying this same metaphor of an improvisational art form to performance studies and reconceiving our discipline in its light is an approach I can relish.

The Metaphor of Improvisation
While a shift in metaphoric conception cannot magically solve the problems associated with the ambiguities of this developing discipline nor provide us with a definitive answer to our students' questions, it can perhaps allow us freedom to explore them in a more playful, provoca-

tive manner, at the same time that we retain an honest recognition of the risks involved. Following Conquergood's observation that "we must draw on *topoi* from among multiple discursive styles and traditions" ("Rethinking Ethnography" 186), and answering Dolan's call for "other metaphors to realign and restructure the objects and subjects of inquiry in our own field" (436), I propose a metaphor of improvisation/composition to augment our trove of tropes—a metaphor of inventive, creative action to complement the popular spatial metaphors— a phenomenological/experiential metaphor to fund the geographical image. Specifically, I use the term *improvisation* to mean improvising as a means of composing, that is, "performing," as the dictionary says, to "make or provide from available materials," and I find the metaphor appropriate in several ways.

First, improvisation is indigenous to performance; we know what it means, and we value it. It also strikes a responding chord in relation to the work of our colleagues outside our discipline. Moreover, while it is associated with literary, choreographed, or scored performances, it is even more integral to the oral tradition—an area of special interest to performance studies scholars. Second, the metaphor of improvisation suits our interests in cultural and identity studies. For decades, performance studies scholars, along with ethnographers and social psychologists, have studied how humans imaginatively perform to create, invent, and transform their cultures and themselves. Conquergood's discussion of the "rise of performance" in ethnography implies that the creative, imaginative, playful, and provisional attributes most associated with *improvisational* performance are highly relevant to human expression and social culture ("Rethinking Ethnography" 187). Similarly, but by the different path of drawing upon speech act theory and the notion of "performativity," performance studies scholars such as Judith Butler show how we improvise our identity. Third, the term *improvisation* has currency in relation to alternative and postmodern performance forms, such as performance art, personal narrative, and reconstructed speech—forms of special interest to performance studies scholars and practitioners. Finally, recent pedagogical studies (Logan; Nudd; Hill) have linked improvisation with teaching tools and methods.

Clearly, the term resonates with several aspects of our research and performance practices. Perhaps most important, however, the metaphor of improvisation may help us to articulate *why* we research—the educational and public service purposes of our work. In the following discussion, I explore performance studies as a postmodern, improvisational discipline, as an institutional course of study, and as a teaching philosophy, subject, and tool. I will attempt to stress performance studies as an improvisational *method* of pedagogy—a method of thought, a method of building curriculum, academic decision making, and teaching/learning, and most of all, a method of service. My observations will be colored by examples from my own experiences teaching in a midwestern state university and in a theatre and dance department that is largely undergraduate and that tends to emphasize practice over theory. I conclude with a response to the hypothetical students' questions.

Improvisation and Service:
Performance Studies as Discipline

Of all the terms used to characterize performance studies, the most intriguing may be Roach's recent appellation, a "postdiscipline" (46). Though he does not explain it, the term *postdiscipline* implies to me that conceiving disciplines as geographically envisioned academic "fields" or bounded "areas" may be moribund, and other ways of imagining scholarship, learning, and teaching are developing. Such a postdiscipline that strives not only to cross borders but to tear down ivory walls and connect with society in ever changing ways seems an appropriate term for describing performance studies. Moreover, this view helps to account for our discipline's evolution that, like an improvisational performance, has rightly used what is at hand (experimental theatre, folklore, oral interpretation, anthropology, rhetoric, conversation analysis) to meet the changing needs of our society and our students. Understanding performance studies as a postdiscipline makes it possible to imagine it not so much as an area or an object but as an act and an agency—as an ever evolving act of service and as a unique manner of seeing the world (its people, art, history)—both improvised through a collection of performance methods (artistic, educational, theoretical, and practical) and designed to help heal society and our world.

Understanding our discipline, in part, as an act of service revives and ennobles those helping aspects of our profession and affords opportunity for increased community work. The inherent link between improvisation and community service has been notably illustrated in writings by Jonathan Fox, Augusto Boal, and others. Drawing on the work of Milman Parry and Albert Lord, Fox's insightful discussion of the oral tradition and contemporary nonscripted theatre demonstrates that improvisation is rooted in community rituals, invites interaction within communities, and often serves as a transformational tool to heal social ills. He also reminds us that improvisation is not mindless but is a sound construction based on formulas, themes, and phrases, and that it belongs to (or "originates with") *all its performers* (together or singly) and only exists in a multiform, rather than uniform, manner (as does our improvisational, communal discipline). Acting out of a Marxist tradition, on the other hand, Augusto Boal also chose improvisation over agitprop drama for its interactive capabilities, and he later shaped it into forum theatre in an effort "to not give solutions, to not incite people," but rather to "let them express their own solutions" (Taussig and Schechner 23). As improvised theatre in Boal's hands serves the spect-actors who participate, so an improvised postdiscipline should seek to serve not an "audience" of students but the spect-actors in our classrooms, academic environments, communities, and the world.

Given such improvisational disciplinary identity, we can appropriately claim to reflect in our manner the objects of our study. We can explore what Conquergood has called "the world as performance" ("Rethinking Ethnography" 190), not only in relation to ethnography but also in relation to art, education, civic service, government, health, and spiritual, social, and physical well-being. We can stop wasting our time and energy, to borrow Carlson's argument, "in the defending of disciplinary turf or in the protection of the presumed purity of any particular area of academic pursuit" ("Theatre History" 96) and attend instead to how our endeavors can help humanity. We can use our performance knowledge and skills to improvise ever shifting and multifaceted disciplinary "production" aimed at serving the world in which we live.

Improvising Curriculum:
Performance Studies in an Institution

Conceptualizing ourselves as improvisational does not mean that performance studies is a method without content. Rather, we seek to study performance in all forms, but the selection and shape of the performance acts and methods studied will change within the context of any given university. To illustrate, I will discuss the process of improvising curriculum with examples taken from the program at Southwest Missouri State University.

Usually, curriculum develops by updating what already exists and adding new courses to fill gaps and embrace new disciplinary trends. At SMSU, the performance studies curriculum includes three courses that originated as oral interpretation courses: Performing Literature, Scripting and Performing, and Scripting and Directing. These popular courses fit well into the larger departmental emphasis on practice, and as the discipline has progressed, they have undergone considerable change.

In the current incarnation of these courses, in addition to teaching students "how" to interpret, perform, and direct literary texts, we probe the activities themselves. Students still learn about interpreting literature, but now we explore the act as an improvisational, intertextual process (Scholes; Long; Bowman "Performing Literature"; Bowman and Kistenberg; Allison and Mitchell). Similarly, we still study, adapt, improvise, and compose performance texts, but we are now including many more types of texts (as described, for example, in Stern and Henderson; Park-Fuller and Pelias; Gray and VanOosting; Stucky, "Performing Oral History"; Pelias, *Performance Studies*). Moreover, students still present or direct performances but often as an expression of social discourse or as a method of inquiry as well as an artistic act; our discussions now turn to questions about political realities, ethics, the process of engagement, or the classroom as a social community as often as they turn to address the performer's skill or the text's structure (Pelias, "Empathy"; Bowman, "Toward a Curriculum"; Taft-Kaufman, "Other Ways"; Logan).

In addition to altering existing curriculum, we have dropped some courses and added others to fill the needs of our students. A first-year general education course was added to introduce students to social and cultural aspects of performance. We added a graduate seminar in performance to acquaint students with contemporary theories in performance studies, particularly theories of identity, culture, and postmodern art. Both of these courses require students to conceive of performance as a method of investigation or as a method of reporting research, in addition to an aesthetic performance. Naturally, students are required to read and write extensively in all performance studies courses, but we are also committed to the teaching of performance *through* performance whenever we can.

While the above curriculum evolved improvisationally and intradepartmentally, in the addition of a new general education capstone course section, Exploring Community Well-Being Through Performance, course planners came not only from theatre but from nursing, education, social work, health, sociology, communication, and management, among other departments. Described in my essay "Towards an Interdisciplinary Performance Studies Course," the proposal arose in response to a window of opportunity that appeared when our university was granted a statewide "public affairs" mission. The process of developing this course was quite complex—partly because it was a new concept, partly because it involved so many people, and partly because we insisted that our section center on a set of performance methods (personal narrative, theatre of the oppressed, trigger scripts, playback theatre), while the topics changed according to the expertise and interests of the teaching teams and enrolled students. In spite of the complexity of the project, our proposal won approval as well as funding for teacher training.

The point is that curriculum changes to address the needs of students in society. In this case, performance faculty working with other colleagues to meet the real needs of people in real situations developed an interdisciplinary educational model with *performance at its core*, and that, in turn, benefited and stretched the department of theatre, the university, and the community in general.

In addition to improvising curriculum, improvisation serves the academy in other ways. Nudd has shown how forum theatre techniques have been used to train graduate teaching assistants for the classroom. Similar improvisational techniques may provide a method for institutional decision making and for resolving professional conflicts. Departments and colleges might establish student and faculty improvisational groups, similar to Augusto Boal's legislative theatre groups, that could pose problems and generate ideas about common efforts. Working improvisationally allows groups to present numerous resolutions in a playful, interactive, provisional manner that encourages spontaneity and teamwork among group members. At the same time, opportunities for shifting leadership arise, which, in turn, create more democratic decision making.

To be sure, the idea of an improvisational discipline may not attract the immediate respect of all faculty and administrators. Those given to argument may see in the metaphor only negative connotations that signify lack of preparation, laziness, "winging it," or "faking it." But farsighted colleagues who truly care about making significant changes in the academy and the world will take the time to understand the complexities and potentials of a creative process that works. Performance studies can play a significant role addressing those needs by developing new service pathways that complement traditional theatrical outreach and by exploring innovative strategies for decision making within departments and other academic units.

Improvisation and Praxis:
Performance Studies as Learning Experience

Improvisation is an excellent metaphor for performance studies in the classroom and in activities. Here, in the arena that drew many of us to this discipline and that remains the source of our pleasure in teaching—the arena of learning about and through performance—the concept of improvisation seems a "natural." Yet, the dominant concept of teaching, what Paulo Freire calls the "banking" concept of education—where students are the depositories and the teacher is the depositor—still holds a formidable vise grip, even within performance disciplines. Unfortunately, teaching performance is no protection against dehumanizing classroom practices that promote a "superior teacher versus subordinate students" philosophy. Freire cautions, "those who use the banking approach, knowingly or unknowingly . . . , fail to perceive that the deposits themselves contain contradictions about reality" (56). Readily acknowledging "contradictions of reality" in our academic system can at least encourage us to inject an improvisational element in our classes, and that is a step toward humanizing our teaching practices. We can encourage improvised "performance engagements" in response to theory, to social situations, and to events (Pineau 13–14). Employing the kind of improvisation that challenges students and teachers is not a renunciation of responsibility. On the contrary, it demands more work, more planning, and more tolerance from all participants; but the possibilities are extensive, and the rewards can be great.

How does performance studies specifically contribute to our understanding of improvising performance? To me, it serves in two important ways, and both involve praxis. First, performance studies scholars lead the way in articulating how our performing disciplines can contribute to the changing complexion of pedagogy in general. Elyse Pineau's work in developing a critical performative pedagogy is particularly insightful in helping us to understand and use what we know in relation to other fields (Worley 137–38). Second, other education studies (Benton; Fuoss and Hill; Harrison-Pepper) reflect and urge the expanding scope of performing classes to include not only those devoted to teaching performance as entertainment/art but also those that teach performance as an innovative method of exploring and interrogating issues and situations, as a performative means of probing theory, as an aesthetic/political praxis.

All the performances studies courses at SMSU offer students the opportunity to study performance and to perform, as do the actor-training courses. Here, however, the emphasis shifts from teaching performance as an aesthetic act to exploring performance as a continuum with art on one end and society on the other. Students are often encouraged to compose their own performance scripts in relation to social issues and events, to improvise their responses to literature and to theory. Students not only improve themselves as performers, they also consciously explore possibilities of choice in their lives and change in the world. They examine ethical considerations of performance and interrogate theory engaging in a performative praxis. Thus, the performance studies classroom provides improvisational space to probe the givens of our work, to question academic, theatrical, and social traditions, to interrogate the accepted norms—not necessarily to subvert but to open and to complement other forms of knowledge and ways of knowing.

Similarly, the performance studies activities at SMSU focus on alternative genres, social contexts, and intercollegiate performance venues. Established in 1993 and stemming, in part, from my own interest in performance and health issues (e.g., Park-Fuller, "Narration"; Conquergood, "Health Theatre"; Corey), the performance troupe Bare-Stage has used improvisational techniques such as theatre of the oppressed, playback theatre, personal narrative, and trigger scripting to address issues of particular interest to students (acquaintance rape, sexual harassment, HIV/AIDS, long-distance relationships). In 1997, the group was granted funding to construct a performance aimed at arousing interest among rural area high school students in health issues and professions. The resulting study found that a forum theatre model was useful in raising student awareness of health issues and needs of rural communities as well as raising interest in health careers (Park-Fuller and Rich 6). In addition to the positive outcome, the process of participating in the study benefited university and community students alike.

Compatible with both theatre arts and theatre studies, performance studies courses and activities bring a unique dimension to the department by providing a vital means of balancing the artistic and the political, the traditional and the alternative, the theoretical and the practical, and students are the richer for the combination. Richard Schechner recommends that theatre departments develop three tracks for students: a broad performance studies track (for most students), a track for appreciating theatre art, and a professional theatre track for selected students (8–9). It seems to me that isolating people from the joys of performing through further specialization and division (of both faculty and students) is not the answer. We need to unite, to integrate, rather to separate. For me, the way to do that is to put our students and faculty together and, at least beyond mandatory degree requirements, let them improvise their own "learning tracks."

At SMSU, degree programs require students to participate in a healthy amount of each type of work, and theatre and performance studies faculty regularly direct productions or perform as well as write. However, we need to find ways to further integrate performance theory with theatre training (e.g., Gainor and Wilson) and to communicate better among ourselves. This process of colleague interaction must be nurtured as carefully as we attend to our individual classes and departmental productions. I believe faculty members can achieve better interaction if we stop thinking of one another as the "resident expert" in this or that "field" (each of which must be jealously guarded) and start thinking of each other as improv partners on whom we depend and with whom we share the struggles and joys of an ensemble improvisational production designed to meet our students' many-sided and ever changing needs.

What do I tell my hypothetical students when they ask me about performance studies? I tell them that it is a postmodern manner of studying performance and performing. I tell them that it is learning how performance functions in the world so we can use it to help ourselves and others, as well as to enrich our souls. And when they ask me how to prepare for a career in performance studies *or* theatre, I recommend that, in addition to learning everything they can about performance, they would do well to adopt the characteristics of the improvisational actor, including a willingness to live in the present, an awareness of and appreciation for one's surroundings, a knowledge of current issues and events, a good vocabulary, a playful attitude toward life, a readiness to change, an ability to see what is appropriate, and a strong sense of intuition and vitality (Fox; Johnstone). I suggest that if they gain expertise in these areas, they will learn to "make up" as well as "find" their jobs; they will be able to use performance to improve society and to help others to do the same, and in the process, they will help to invent a better world. I propose that performance studies courses and activities will help them to learn to improvise in this way.

While it may prove useful, the metaphor of improvisation should not become the only metaphor for what we do. Negative connotations of the term (e.g., lack of preparation, imperfection, or neglect) still prevail among purists and positivists and should be taken into account when promoting our work. Nevertheless, the concept of improvisation provides one way of imaging our work as liberating yet accountable, active and interactive, inclusive yet distinguishing, artistic, and political. Its positive connotations of inspiration, collaboration, spontaneity, freedom-in-structure, and creation-through-performance are still compelling to me as a way to explain "what" it is that I do and teach and love.

We limit our students' potentials if we see performance education solely as "training," apart from "resistance" and "questioning," or if we design programs only to help our students succeed professionally without helping them learn to live lives of fulfillment. We need to nourish both impulses. Moreover, if we can lift our eyes from the terrain of the "fields" long enough to imagine our work as act and agency, we may see that there are no boundaries to cross. There are only potential learning opportunities, opportunities to serve our institutions, coalitions, and supporting associations, opportunities to have fun and to help others. As scholars, as teachers, and as students, we can improvise these opportunities into substantial, tangible, meaningful reality that is yet dynamic, ever tentative, ever evolving. And as we collectively improvise our "performative postdiscipline" into being, so we collectively create a better world.

WORKS CITED

Allison, John M., Jr., and Karen S. Mitchell. "*Textual Power* and the Pragmatics of Assessing and Evaluating 'Powerful' Performances." *Communication Education* 43 (1994): 205–21.

Bateson, Mary Catherine. "Joint Performance Across Cultures: Improvisation in a Persian Garden." *Text and Performance Quarterly* 13 (1993): 113–21.

Benton, Carol L. "Performance Studies Across the Curriculum: Using Performance in Introduction to Women's Studies, a Case Study." Dailey 145–49.

Boal, Augusto. *Games for Actors and Non-Actors.* Trans. Adrian Jackson. New York: Routledge, 1992.

Bowman, Michael S. "Performing Literature in an Age of Textuality." *Communication Education* 45 (1996): 97–101.

———. "Toward a Curriculum in Performance Studies." Dailey 189–94.

Bowman, Michael S., and Cindy J. Kistenberg. "'Textual Power' and the Subject of Oral Interpretation: An Alternate Approach to Performing Literature." *Communication Education* 41 (July 1992): 287–99.

Butler, Judith. "Performative Acts and Gender Constitution: An Essay in Phenomenology and Feminist Theory." *Performing Feminisms: Feminist Critical Theory and Theatre.* Ed. Sue-Ellen Case. Baltimore: Johns Hopkins UP, 1990. 270–82.

Carlson, Marvin. *Performance: A Critical Introduction.* New York: Routledge, 1996.

———. "Theatre History, Methodology, and Distinctive Features." *Theatre Research International* 20.2 (1995): 90–96.

Conquergood, Dwight. "Health Theatre in a Hmong Refugee Camp: Performance, Communication, and Culture." *Drama Review* 32 (Fall 1988): 174–208.

———. "Of Caravans and Carnivals." *Drama Review* 39 (Winter 1995): 137–41.

———. "Rethinking Ethnography: Towards a Critical Cultural Politics." *Communication Monographs* 58 (1991): 179–94.

Corey, Frederick C., ed. *HIV Education: Performing Personal Narratives. Proceedings of a Conference Funded by the U.S. Centers for Disease Control and Prevention and Arizona State University.* Tempe: Speech Communication Dept., Arizona State U, 1993.

Dailey, Sheron J., ed. *The Future of Performance Studies: Visions and Revisions.* Annandale: National Communication Assoc., 1998.

Dolan, Jill. "Geographies of Learning: Theatre Studies, Performance, and the 'Performative.'" *Theatre Journal* 45 (1993): 417–41.

Fox, Jonathan. *Acts of Service: Spontaneity, Commitment, Tradition in the Nonscripted Theatre.* New Paltz: Tusitala, 1986.

Freire, Paulo. *Pedagogy of the Oppressed.* Trans. Myra Bergman Ramos. Rev. ed. New York: Continuum, 1993.

Fuoss, Kirk. W., and Randall T. Hill. "A Performance-Centered Approach for Teaching a Course in Social Movements." *Communication Education* 41 (1992): 78–88.

Gainor, Ellen J., and Ron Wilson. "(Con)Fusing Theory and Practice: Bridging Scholarship and Performance in Theatre Pedagogy." *Theatre Topics* 5 (1995): 69–80.

Gray, Paul H., and James VanOosting. *Performance in Life and Literature.* Boston: Allyn, 1996.

Harrison-Pepper, Sally. "Dramas of Persuasion: Utilizing Performance in the Classroom." *Excellence in College Teaching* 2 (1991): 115–27.

Hill, Randall T. G. "Performance Pedagogy Across the Curriculum." Dailey 141–44.

HopKins, Mary Francis. "Cultural Capital in the Academic Marketplace: The Place of Literature in Performance Studies." *Communication Education* 45 (1996): 89–95.

Johnstone, Keith. *Impro: Improvisation and the Theatre.* New York: Routledge, 1979.

Kendig, Daun. "How to Survive in Hog Heaven: Thoughts for the Next Millennium." Dailey 158–62.

Logan, Christie. "Improvisational Pedagogy." Dailey 181–85.

Long, Beverly Whitaker. "Performance Criticism and Questions of Value." *Text and Performance Quarterly* 11 (1991): 106–15.

Nudd, Donna. "Improvising Our Way to the Future." Dailey 150–55.

Park-Fuller, Linda M. "Narration and Narratization of a Cancer Story: Composing and Performing a Clean Breast of It." *Text and Performance Quarterly* 15 (1995): 330–33.

———. "Towards an Interdisciplinary Performance Studies Course: Process and Politics." Dailey 163–69.

Park-Fuller, Linda M., and Ronald J. Pelias. "Charting Alternative Performance and Evaluative Practices." *Communication Education* 44 (1995): 126–39.

Park-Fuller, Linda M., and Marc Rich. "Interactive Performance: A Tool to Promote Health Awareness in Secondary Schools and to Recruit Students to Health Professions." Unpublished evaluative report of a project sponsored by Southwest Missouri Area Health Education Center and Southwest Missouri State U, Coll. of Arts and Letters, 1997.

Pelias, Ronald J. "Empathy and the Ethics of Entitlement." *Theatre Research International* 16 (Summer 1991): 142–52.

———. *Performance Studies: The Interpretation of Aesthetic Texts.* New York: St. Martin's, 1992.

Pineau, Elyse. "Performance Studies Across the Curriculum: Problems, Possibilities, and Projections." Dailey 128–35.

Roach, Joseph. "Culture and Performance in the Circum-Atlantic World." *Performativity and Performance.* Ed. Andrew Parker and Eve Kosofsky Sedgwick. New York: Routledge, 1995. 45–63.

Schechner, Richard. "Transforming Theatre Departments." *Drama Review* 39 (Summer 1995): 7–10.

Scholes, Robert. *Textual Power: Literary Theory and the Teaching of English.* New Haven: Yale UP, 1985.

Stern, Carol Simpson, and Bruce Henderson. *Performance: Texts and Contexts.* White Plains: Longman, 1993.

Strine, Mary S. "Mapping the 'Cultural Turn' in Performance Studies." Dailey 3–9.

Strine, Mary S., Beverly Whitaker Long, and Mary Frances HopKins. "Research in Interpretation and Performance Studies: Trends, Issues, Priorities." *Speech Communication: Essays to Commemorate the 75th Anniversary of the Speech Communication Association.* Ed. Gerald M. Phillips and Julia T. Wood. Carbondale: Southern Illinois UP, 1990. 181–204.

Stucky, Nathan. "Performing Oral History: Storytelling and Pedagogy." *Communication Education* 44 (1995): 1–14.

———. "Re/Membering Our Future by Re/Searching Our Past: What to Wall In and Wall Out in Performance Studies History." Dailey 93–97.

Taft-Kaufman, Jill. "Embodied Performance." Dailey 195–98.

———. "Other Ways: Postmodernism and Performance Praxis." *Southern Communication Journal* 60 (1995): 222–32.

Taussig, Michael, and Richard Schechner. "Boal in Brazil, France, the USA: An Interview with Augusto Boal." *Playing Boal: Theatre, Therapy, Activism.* Ed. Mady Schutzman and Jan Cohen-Cruz. New York: Routledge, 1994. 17–32.

Worley, David. W. "Is Critical Performative Pedagogy Practical?" Dailey 136–40.

Worthen, W. B. "Disciplines of the Text/Sites of Performance." *Drama Review* 39 (Spring 1995): 13–44.

"I Dwell in Possibility—"

Teaching Consulting Applications

for Performance Studies

14
Cynthia
Wimmer

In the spring of 1998, Elaine Showalter, then president of the Modern Language Association (MLA), addressed fellow educators regarding shrinking employment opportunities for new graduates:

> Solving our problem will demand a radical rethinking of attitudes, programs, and goals in graduate education. . . . The expanding job market for the future lies in what we still revealingly call "alternative careers"—that is, stimulating, well-paid careers in business, government, the media, and technology. . . . Preparing students for these opportunities is not just a matter of repackaging resumes or offering job-placement advice at the end of years of academic apprenticeship. If we really want our students to aspire to broader career horizons, we are going to have to change the culture and climate of expectation in humanities doctoral education. (3)

Other scholars are also demonstrating and analyzing the impact that occurs between their scholarly work and work outside the academy. For example, Cathy Robertson analyzes the place of elocution as training for workplaces outside the academy (such as law courts) where lives are often permanently changed by the performance of texts. Jon McKenzie has done extensive work on the relation of performance paradigms in business and academia. These scholars have taken performance studies as "equipment for living" (as Burke called literature) and extended its range. Such examples, however, indicate moves only by individual members of the academy to broaden the horizons for their skills; those working in most humanities departments still do little to support or prepare their students specifically for such employment opportunities. The move to broaden career horizons in which humanities graduates can find employment is not only vital for ensuring the well-being of some students but also for continuing to assure the viability and, in some cases, even the existence of offerings by graduate and undergraduate programs.

The "radical rethinking" called for by Showalter will, of course, involve modifying attitudes and behavior of individual teachers and students as well as departments, specifically pedagogical and scholarship modification that begins to collapse the boundaries between the academic and nonacademic worlds, as this essay seeks to do. Can performance studies recover the "market value" envisioned by late-nineteenth-century teachers of elocution, such as Thomas Clarkson Trueblood, at the University of Michigan, or Robert McLean Cumnock, who founded the School of Oratory at Northwestern University? As Paul Edwards notes, the teachers of that age envisioned a "use value" aimed at "'the professional-managerial class' as training for certain kinds of business communication" (11). In light of the current employment environment and students' skill sets at the time of graduation, let us look at the reality our students will face and increase our concerted efforts to prepare them for a wider variety of quality career paths.

The purpose of this essay is to investigate specific areas in business, government, and nonprofit organizations (the BGN sectors)[1] where performance studies scholars can find employment using the knowledge and skill sets developed in higher education. My goal is to provide teachers of performance studies with information on marketplace applications for work that could be done by their graduates (or even by themselves full-time or in conjunction with teaching). Proficiency in particular performance studies techniques, perspectives, and analyses are marketable. Furthermore, while I do not hold out hope that the use of performance studies methods will create utopian organizational work environments, I do believe that the humanistic reformations offered by some performance studies consultants have the potential to affect ethical and humanistic changes in BGN sectors and in the individual lives of workers.[2]

Organizational cultures are aware of women's issues, diversity issues, cultural issues, and environmental issues, and some executives and organizations are attempting to address such issues.[3] They are looking for ways to change the structure and culture of their organizations. Jon McKenzie discusses this shift in some depth:

> In recent years . . . organizations have come to stress diversity
> rather than equality and, at the same time, they have begun to
> take a more proactive approach to cultural diversity, attempting
> to create work environments that promote diversity rather than
> simply tolerate it. R. Roosevelt Thomas, Jr. describes this as a
> shift from affirmative action to *affirming diversity*, from controlling differences to managing them. (12)

In the information age, the age of service industries, what is good for business can be what is good for its workers.

A fortuitous blend of the current developmental trends of organizational cultures and the paradigms explored in performance studies
curriculum creates an employment opportunity that is time sensitive. Peter Vaill calls our current destabilized, fluctuating work environment a "permanent white water." [4] Performance studies teachers, like teachers of other disciplines affected by the popularity of ideas, must stay current to the marketability of their students' skills to help students anticipate their working life.

Performance studies and performance training teaches teamwork, cooperation, ingenuity, adaptability, flexibility, imagination, writing, problem analysis, problem solving, project completion, responsibility, and other vital skills. These skills, already being taught in many classrooms, have direct value for employers. The question this essay addresses is how to connect the seemingly disparate worlds of performance studies classrooms and the BGN sectors. Performance studies classrooms have already been laying the groundwork for this connection, but teachers and students (and sometimes potential employers) often do not easily recognize these transferable skill sets. As a consultant to business organizations, I have used performance studies methods with great success; a review of the newest BGN management literature strongly suggests that many organizations are receptive to our ideas and skills in this moment of massive change.

Organizations are not impenetrable monoliths with thousands of workers walking in step. They are complex matrices of individuals working in unique environments. Organizational cultures of the BGN sector are already prepared for the entrance of performance studies scholars as evidenced by the fact that their discourse already includes performance-related paradigms and their leaders covet perspectives in which performance studies scholars have informational and analytical expertise.

"More Numerous of Windows":
The Teaching-Consulting Nexus

A major part of many consulting assignments is teaching. What is also remarkable is that the teaching skills used in performance studies classrooms are similar to those employed by consultants currently working in BGN settings to modify employee behaviors, mental models, and performances.[5]

Performance studies students assimilate teaching practices that use a wide variety of pedagogical methods, as this volume demonstrates. While most of us still lecture to students at some point, we recognize that performance studies pedagogy, with its strategies of "enfleshment," invites our students to learn things that they could not learn and do not learn by "talking-head" pedagogy.[6] A pedagogy of embodiment represents an attempt to recognize life as it is lived, in the body. Our games, exercises, experiments, and frames lead to explorations of perspectives and to recognition of diversity through inhabiting alternative psychic spaces and through embodying another's demeanor, speech, actions, and mental frame. Our body work often reveals cultural, social, and economic imprints and sometimes teaches knowledges for which we have no words. While some BGN clients might resist consultants employing such methods, many others are embracing them.

Graduates who decide to teach in BGN sectors will find that the posture and self-presentation of "teachers" who consult successfully is modified by the BGN settings. In the classroom, we are positioned as experts by the institutional settings in which we teach; often, performance studies pedagogues have to work toward encouraging more free-flowing communication patterns and toward undoing some of the "talking-head" expectations both we and our students tend to inhabit unconsciously. In contrast, consultants have to continuously and consciously maintain their self-presentation as experts while they develop a respectful and at times deferential rapport with employees at all levels. The pedagogical method used by consultants to these sectors needs to be one based on mutual, respectful exchange infused with large doses of tact.

For this next paragraph, try to image yourself as a consultant. When entering a new organizational culture, you are aware you have been hired on the basis of your expertise and are presumed to be "the subject who knows" in your particular area of consulting. You are presumed to be able to contribute to worker job-satisfaction and productivity. But you will need to walk sensitively and delicately to produce the most beneficial self-presentation. If you don't position yourself as enough of an expert, corporate executives will not feel justified in hiring you and will resist cooperating with your methods. However, if you position yourself as too much of an expert and perhaps even attempt to teach in the banking model condemned by Freire,[7] you will meet with resistance from those who are experts in their particular capacities and industries. You are hired as an expert but certainly not as one with the authority to determine the agenda. To be successful, your demeanor needs to be that of someone who is able to guide employees gently and subtly to modify behaviors, by offering appropriately timed proposals and suggestions based on mutually developed experience and knowledge of each particular client's workplace. While confidently employing the pedagogical practices and theories of performance studies, you will need to learn a great deal about the industries and languages of the organizations that hire you, about their challenges, their competitors, their way of doing business, and the government regulations that govern their decisions.[8] As bell hooks has written, "To teach in varied communities not only our paradigms must shift but also the way we think, write, speak. The engaged voice must never be fixed and absolute but always changing, always evolving in the dialogue with the world beyond itself" (11). In other words, consulting is an opportunity to develop another performance of our teaching selves.

Both organizational consultants and performance studies scholars may view themselves as change agents who are primarily motivated by striving for improvement and pressing for social and cultural change. As part of our regular teaching curricula, we could create windows in our regular course material to inform our students about nonacademic sites where they could use the teaching practices they are learning. While teaching a variety of courses through the English department at the University of Maryland, College Park, after having had a career of many years in the business sector, I regularly included information from my former career experiences. By the time I had the opportunity to first teach Performance Theory and Drama during the spring of 1994, inclusion of this subtext in my courses had become habitual. Thus, the pedagogical turn of including such a subtext (only partly discussed in this essay) in a course on performance studies arose during my classroom preparation and during interaction with my students, and it is perhaps their enthusiasm that has confirmed my advocacy.

Most of us who teach are, indeed, overworked and underpaid, and we resist that "one-more-thing" someone is urging us to do. It is to my colleagues who have never worked in the BGN sectors but who recognize the need for broader career horizons for our graduates that I address this piece. While saluting "those who have taken their academic literary training and made it work, nicely, in non-academic realms," Leo Braudy, University Professor and Bind Professor of English at the University of Southern California, calls us:

> to look beyond our antique assumptions about what we know
> and the audiences we serve; we need to explore the pastures new
> that lie all around us. Not as a booby prize but as a goal, not as a
> stop-gap but as an opportunity, and not as a diversion from what
> we were trained for but as an essential part of that mission. (31)

As teachers, we do know ways to transmit information about which we are not experts. We can introduce the concept of BGN employment by referring students to this chapter and its sources or by handing out other materials that discuss ways that specific classroom exercises, practices, methodologies, and applications can be exported from the academy to organizational life. Our teaching practices have been highly successful in imparting self-knowledges and cross-cultural perspectives. We can confidently let our students know that these practices are marketable and that the effect of their use in BGN sectors can bring about positive change in individual lives.

"Superior—for Doors":
Types of Outside and Inside Consulting

Some outside consultants are self-employed, marketing themselves and their expertise and negotiating their own contracts. Self-employed consultants have the luxury of managing their time and responsibilities and of determining how, when, and for whom they will work. However, recent graduates should rarely attempt the self-employed route. To market themselves, consultants must have a proven track record of success, and that is usually best secured while working for either a small or a large experienced consulting firm.[9] Working for an outside consulting firm provides not only a learning opportunity but also security—employee benefits, perks, and a steady income. The downside is that these consultants are told how, when, with whom, and for whom they will work. The larger the firm, the less control they have over these working-life elements. Key considerations in determining whether entry-level consultants should find employment in a large or a small consulting firm have to do with their comfort level with the size of organizations, the area in which they want to develop expertise, and the opportunities any given organization will provide. Many times, these employment opportunities, especially those in larger firms, require that junior consultants be willing and able to travel almost continually and live in various locations around the globe for weeks and months at a time.

Inside consultants are hired by large BGN organizations. They may work through a human resources department, a training and development division, or a consulting team assigned to modify specific types of behavior in several divisions and locations throughout an organization. These consultants have both the benefits and the liabilities of working for any large organization. But as the ones who are to provide critical perspective and effect change, they perhaps have the additional challenge of remaining influential and not becoming the prophet who has little credibility at home. Large organizations, however, also provide the positive possibility of progressive self-improvement that derives from experiences with team synergy and strategic effectiveness.

For the purposes of this essay, I have grouped both outside and inside consultant functions into three broad categories. It should be understood that some of the performance studies theories and pedagogies I have linked with specific job functions could easily be linked with others. I have sought to be suggestive rather than definitive or comprehensive in my linkages. Though there are consultant functions that I have not included here that could potentially be performed by performance studies scholars, I have limited this discussion to those doors to employment that are most readily open to performance studies specialists.

Business Group Performances:
Conventions, Meetings, Team Building

The industry of organizing, designing, promoting, and conducting conventions is one employment sector where graduates, particularly of theatre and speech communication programs, can seek employment. This industry is composed of positions that use such skills as producing, directing, stage management, set design, costuming, lighting, sound production, script writing, and multimedia proficiency. Any performance studies scholar who attends either large or small industry conventions can clearly see the need for an ability to design appropriate rituals and symbols when such extravaganzas are planned. Performance studies graduates who enter the field of convention administration can also apply their knowledge of how spatial configurations will affect levels and types of interaction among convention attendees when choosing the hosting facilities, the particular rooms, and the position of furniture within those facilities.

The weekly meeting is a standard business ritual, it is a continuing social drama, and it is dreaded by nearly all who are forced to attend. A large consulting industry has grown to meet the demand for productive and positive business meetings.[10] Meeting facilitators are often hired for three to six months to train attendees in techniques that are designed to break the traditional meeting matrix and discover new ways that each individual group can meet more effectively together. The ritual of the meeting is its form, but it is the spirit and soul of the group as a whole that determines the quality and effectiveness of such gatherings. It is the job of the meeting facilitator to modify behavior and attitudes to improve the spirit and soul of the group meeting. The working environment causes employees to self-edit their performances much more strictly than they would do in other spaces. Behavior sets have generally been rigorously prescribed and naturalized, and a strong, unspoken imperative proclaims that any deviation from those sets of appropriate conduct may result in loss of income or promotions. All interventions, therefore, must be conducted sensitively and with an awareness of what is at stake for some meeting attendees. Many of the pedagogical strategies discussed in this volume, especially those that interrogate the performance of self, would be very productive in helping people consider alternative behaviors for BGN meeting performances and rituals. Because people self-perform differently in different spaces, enabling meeting attendees to be aware of their self-performances in a specific weekly meeting is one first step to their being able to consciously transform those self-performances in that space. Exercises in which people climb figuratively into other people's skins and perform as another person can allow experimentation with coworkers' ideas and behaviors and bring to light what kinds of performances are going on within the specific BGN space. Discussion of meeting practices where the influences of a whole organizational performance are placed in relation to the small group performance, as well as discussions of how the small group performance reflects and impacts the whole organizational performance, are also useful in creating productive group self-reflection.

Meeting facilitators must often first approach those who lead meetings and persuade them to "buy into" the recommended techniques. Eliciting deep learning or transformative personal responsiveness from corporate executives can be quite challenging. One of the keys to positioning yourself as an expert facilitator who can reach all meeting attendees is to develop such a rapport with the executives you are working with that the desired personal responsiveness begins in them. If the only responsiveness attained is cognitive analysis, rather than personal deep learning, it is unlikely that suggested changes will be integrated into reconstructed small-group performances. However, if you, as an outside consultant, can crack open the layers of entrenched meeting performances, you can often help to create altered mental models of individuals' meeting behaviors that may be effective in transforming meeting rituals.

Team building is often the function of inside consultants. Many industries and individual companies have moved to the team organizational structure and hire team builders to inspire a higher level of performance among team members.[11] One of the great benefits of performance studies scholarship and the techniques it can bring to BGN consulting is that these approaches tend to stimulate imaginative problem solving. To reframe various situations using performance studies paradigms—be they the utilizing of individual performance tools and ideas, the putting together of unlikely components, or the synthesizing and matching of various tasks, skill sets, and elements in new ways—unleashes the imaginations of team members and sets the stage for risk-taking play to begin. When an environment of play is established, team members and team builders can look at "as-if" possibilities; they can begin to imagine scenarios that will enhance their working environment and their individual and team productivity. Instituting an environment where imagination, creativity, and play are honored as appropriate venues for the exploration of organizational solutions and synergistic team possibilities will provide a fertile atmosphere for risk taking and progress. BGN culture as a whole has shown itself to be open to using such techniques. As people switch jobs within a given team or organization, BGN leaders have learned the benefit of having new minds look at old ways of doing things and have seen improvement in on-the-job productivity and greater job satisfaction. Having an atmosphere of play, enjoyment, fun, self-reflection, and experimentation is necessary to keeping an organization's culture lively and vibrant and, therefore, moving toward reaching its goals, even in white water.

Executive Coaching

The industry of executive coaching rests on the premise that executive functions are performances and that these performances are ways of knowing and can be modified and improved through coaching on the performance of self. Performance studies scholars who chose this type of consulting might think in terms of Brecht's *alienation effect.* Their job can often involve drawing their client's attention to naturalized behaviors and at the same time defamiliarizing these behaviors. This act of defamiliarizing everyday practices in order that they may be understood more comprehensively makes them available for modification and for the consultant to bring performance values to bear on clients' self-presentation. The individual attention given by these coaches provides a mirror for their clients, an opportunity for a healthy narcissism, for assessment and adjustment, and for gathering oneself in readiness for forward movement.[12]

I have grouped consultants in this industry into three areas of expertise. These market niches have traditionally been filled by communication consultants. Performance studies specialists can build on their work using techniques that place a greater emphasis on experiential and kinetic learning, on discovering and developing artistic performative sensibilities and abilities of their clients, and on enhancing their clients' understanding of the social organization and cultural values of their audiences. In all three of the arenas discussed below, alba-emoting, everyday life performance (ELP), and neuro-linguistic programming can be useful tools.

Generalized coaching addresses an executive's personal presentation in everyday work situations. Consultants work with individual clients and are hired both by organizations who want to capitalize further on the talents and skills of particular executives and by individual executives who recognize that they need to modify behaviors and self-presentations to achieve their career goals. Situation-specific goals determine the length and course of such consulting assignments. These consultants focus on areas of corporeal style—dress, posture, gesture, vocal quality and articulation, presence, poise—and on tools for better interpersonal skills. The best of these coaches work with executives to develop leadership skills and to help them express their passion for their work, their organization, and its mission in order to inspire dynamic on-the-job performance both from themselves and from others.[13]

Throughout the United States, there is now a large market demand for coaching to a specific purpose and effect. This type of coaching is needed at various levels, from coaching individuals in the basic elements of presentation and public speaking for in-house meetings or larger conventions, to helping prepare executives for major professional life moments, especially in Washington, DC, where I live. Here, I will elaborate with a specific industry situation. Bids for government contracts once took the form of written proposals of many hundreds of pages. Now, an executive may be required to present a bid from his company to government buyers in a fifteen- to thirty-minute live performance. Only those companies whose presentations strike the determining agency panel as viable will have their written proposals read. With government contracts often totaling millions of dollars, the life or death of an organization, the careers of its employees, and the welfare of their families can ride on the success of one presentation. Coaching executives to make presentations involves all the areas of generalized coaching but also may involve assisting with the presentation's content by research and script writing, rehearsing delivery with individual executives, and even participating in determining which executive will actually make the presentation for the company. This kind of consulting is not for the fainthearted.

The final form of executive coaching I discuss will be particularly suitable for some performance studies scholars: consulting with organizations and specific employees to assist them in the adjustments needed for working in an international environment. BGN organizations are already very aware that personnel sent overseas must be familiar with the cultural practices, traditions, and business methods in the countries where they expect to function. Though they may not put the ideas in academic language, companies know that presentations of self—acceptable and unacceptable gestures, posture, speech, movement, and dress—inscribe cultural meanings and map social territories. Teaching such personnel how to walk, stoop, bow, sit, enter and exit rooms, and how to modify demeanor, eye movements, gestures, and personal presence is to teach them to work an entire "other" cultural presentation into their own bodies. These consultants need to provide a safe environment for their clients' learning so clients will be free enough, self-aware enough, that they can comfortably role-play within another culture and develop rapport with their indigenous counterparts through matching their bodies to the mental models of other cultures. Expertise in these cultural elements is desperately needed. Performance studies scholars who have expertise in specific Asian, African, Middle Eastern, and East European cultures can expect to find high-paying consulting assignments to teach personnel to enact another culture through their bodies.

Transforming Organizational Culture and Climate

Since the early 1990s, outside consultant teams, as well as individual consultants, have been hired to change the culture of BGN organizations. Performance studies scholars may recognize the difficulties of such a task, yet some good work has been done in this area.[14] Because talking in terms of transforming an expressive culture depersonalizes the changes that are needed, the work done by cultural consultants may be less threatening to clients than other types of consulting, but it is, ironically, far more extensive and demanding. In the development of modified organizational cultures, two of the key elements that performance studies professionals can advance with their clients are a more continual habit of metaself-consciousness, a consciousness of what is going on in the emotional and spiritual life of the organization, and an organizational self-reflexivity. The idea is to habituate executives to see again and to see a different way.

No organization succeeds financially and socially for very long unless an overarching, visionary, and admirable value system inspires and guides quality performance from employees on the job. Many BGN employees enjoy being encouraged and allowed to seek the higher ground while meeting their personal career goals and their organization's target objective. Developing and expressing this value system provides such employees with inspiration and motivation for daily working life. Outside cultural consultants are often hired to assist top-level executives compose a mission statement that will epitomize their goals and act as a foundation stone for strategic planning. They are looking for that pinnacle, that symbolic language, that vision that will pull together all the elements of an organization into a cohesive, mobilized unit. To craft a lasting, visionary mission statement, the cultural consultant must find ways to discover the higher-purpose values of those who are leading the organization. Many executives have been so preoccupied with their careers that they have not taken enough time for individual and group self-reflection to imagine the relationship between corporate goals and community-building ethics. Many times, executives will think that they are looking for something outside themselves that can be formed into a mission statement. However, for a mission statement to be enacted, to trickle down into everyday corporate performance, that statement must rest upon organic values, values resident in the company's collection of top executives. The completed mission statement has to give meaning to organizational life, meaning above a paycheck. Unless the statement succeeds in creating meaning for goal-directed work actions, it will never affect the culture of an organization. An effective mission statement can reform and retool the belief structures and mental models of work and of employee interaction by shifting their meaning. The crucial issue is not what is said in a mission statement but how what is said is performed in day-to-day business activities.

Consultants can use performance studies skill sets and methodologies to help people who are already leaders find those overarching values, unearth them, elaborate them, embrace them consciously, and transmit them to all the members of their organization. These consultants not only evaluate the arrangement of people and objects in spaces and the corporeal style of employees at all levels but also the salaries, benefits, and class structure within the company. They assess not only company discourse and how it deviates from area to area but also the use and kinds of humor and the spirit and emotional flavor found in various departments.

Cultural consultants also analyze the symbols that permeate every segment of an organization and that embody their existing culture. They listen to how employees at all levels define who they are and what they do in order to understand the character of an organization. They look for the metaphors and signs that define the organization, assess their fit to the developing mission statement, and help to structure an appropriate symbolic frame. They examine the myths that hold the company together and record stories of the organization's heroes and heroines and their daring deeds. They help create new mythological and narrative frames to aid adjustment to a changing organizational ecosystem. They probe the organization's traditions and rituals, such as the conventions and business meetings discussed above or the initiation rites for new employees and the ceremonies that mark promotions and mergers. Cultural consultants manipulate such opportunities, modifying existing traditions and rituals and/or developing new ones that better reinforce the organization's reborn mission and strategic plan. Keys to maintaining a healthy, thriving organization with an ability to contribute positively to our global and social fabric are the adaptability of its culture and its vigilant preservation of ethical and humanistic values.

Change begins at the top, with those most wholly invested in the corporation. If some of the most prominent members of an organization refuse to work to change a cultural climate, there is little hope for change down the line. Few people enjoy the kinds of change needed to modify the culture of an organization. Change itself is work. The process of change causes discomfort. Many times, a consultant has to create desire for change in specific executives, and that involves giving them a vision of how things could be different. To establish rapport, a consultant often has to meet with stakeholders one-on-one to find out their views on pertinent issues, especially the existing attitudes toward the organization itself and toward the project of cultural modification. Experience has shown that one person, with a value system that others can admire and embrace, can lead an organization to success when that value system is expressed frequently and effectively. That person may well be the one who is waiting to step forward to become the company's change agent, and the consultant has to find that individual and work with him or her individually.

A consultant can spend months working with people, meeting with individuals and groups, to analyze different levels of performance and different levels of self-presentation to really get at something that will drive an organization. An assignment to compose a mission statement is far more complex than it may first appear and presents many opportunities for performance studies scholars to be intellectually challenged, creative, and productive.

Perspective

We need to be aware that we can affect the culture of power. We can use our skills to benefit people in our society by changing the environment in which they spend the majority of their working days. Our graduates have skills and perspectives worth exporting to the BGN sectors.

Clearly, opportunities in these sectors exist for performance studies scholars. The same skills that lead to success in graduate school and in teaching are portable and applicable to a wide variety of corporate situations. Theoretical perspectives and paradigms derived from Bertolt Brecht, Richard Schechner, Paulo Freire, Susana Bloch, Augusto Boal, and so many others are marketable assets. Performance studies teachers can not only recognize these opportunities but address them in course curricula. This radical rethinking is in our interest and in the interests of our students.

NOTES

I have chosen the first verse in 657 of Dickinson to frame this essay because of its emphasis on expanding horizons, on multiplying openings and entrances, and on imagining the poetry of life.

1. I have borrowed the acronym BGN from Nerad and Cerny's study of the careers of a group of English PhDs who graduated between July 1982 and June 1985. Although both the graduates working in the academy and those working in BGN sectors expressed high levels of job satisfaction, those surveyed were "highly critical of their doctoral programs for failing to adequately professionalize students and for not supporting them in the difficult job search" (8).

2. The direction the academy is likely to take has been the subject of several recent books. From the business side, see Katz et al. Nelson and Watt

have stirred much controversy both inside and outside the academy itself, proclaiming that "higher education as we know it will be over
within a decade or two" (12).

3. One effort in the Pacific Northwest is Social Venture Partners, founded
by Paul Brainerd, the inventor of PageMaker, and funded by one hundred thirty of Seattle's veterans of the high-tech sector. This nonprofit is
based on a venture capital model and is devoted to issues of children and
education. Brainerd also founded the Brainerd Foundation, which funds
environmental activism. See Lerner for an interview with Brainerd on
this work.

4. The rapidly changing business climate exacerbated by continually changing technological development and unexpected financial reallocations
throughout the global economy has created the demand that decisions
be made much faster. Vaill also calls this "an unpredictable wild river"
and states,

> This image captures the change of context; indeed, it suggests that
> contexts themselves have destabilized to the point where we can no
> longer assume that the basic structure of the context surrounding a
> situation will hold still long enough to make a planned course of ac-
> tion feasible. (3)

5. Examples can be found in many of the books referenced here. For a
quick look, see Farson 74, 132. Also see Bennis and Townsend, which has
exercises at the end of every chapter.

6. In much of his work, McLaren has developed the concept of *enfleshment*,
"in which subjectivity is formed in the temporal archives of the flesh and
the historical moments of lived experience" (282).

7. For Paulo Freire's notion of the banking model, see *Pedagogy of the Oppressed* and works that followed. Freire's work is foundational. But more
important, as McLaren has pointed out,

> What has endeared Freire to several generations of critical educators,
> both in terms of a respect for his political vision and for the way he
> conducts his own life, is the manner in which he has situated his
> work within an ethics of compassion, love, and solidarity. (70)

8. Each industry has its own body of literature. For the technology sector,
Moore is a good example. Reading the *Wall Street Journal* and other investment advisories, as well as watching CNBC, can bring students up-
to-date on the concerns developing in each sector.

9. See, e.g., Goodman.

10. See "Interpersonal and Group Dynamics" in Bolman and Deal; Doyle
and Straus; and Vaill 155.

11. See "Organizing Groups and Teams" in Bolman and Deal.

12. See Drucker; Harkins; and Buckingham and Coffman. Dotlich and Cairo
adds another layer, by teaching consultants to teach organizational executives to become coaches.

13. Volumes on leadership skills abound. See Vaill; Farson; and De Pree, *Leadership Jazz* and *Leadership Is an Art.* Other recommended texts are: Blanchard and Shula (for clients who are into sports); Bennis; Richardson and Thayer; and the popular work by Ziglar.

14. For success stories of cultural transformations, see Kotter and Heskett; Senge et al.; Rosen; and Turner, who describes the steps taken at Xerox to take it from one of the biggest and slowest companies to a fast-moving, adaptable organization.

WORKS CITED

Bennis, Warren. *On Becoming a Leader.* 1984. New York: Addison, 1994.

Bennis, Warren, and Robert Townsend. *Reinventing Leadership: Strategies to Empower the Organization.* New York: Morrow, 1995.

Blanchard, Ken, and Don Shula. *Everyone's a Coach: Five Business Secrets for High-Performance Coaching.* New York: Harper, 1995.

Bolman, Lee G., and Terrence E. Deal. *Reframing Organizations: Artistry, Choice, and Leadership.* San Francisco: Jossey, 1997.

Braudy, Leo. "Doing Public Pedagogy: Speaking Outside the Walls." *Profession 1999.* New York: Modern Language Assoc. of America, 1999. 27–31.

Buckingham, Marcus, and Curt Coffman. *First, Break All the Rules: What the Greatest Managers Do Differently.* New York: Simon, 1999.

De Pree, Max. *Leadership Is an Art.* New York: Bantam, 1989.

———. *Leadership Jazz.* New York: Bantam, 1992.

Dickinson, Emily. *The Complete Poems of Emily Dickinson.* 1890. Ed. Thomas H. Johnson. Boston: Little, 1960.

Dotlich, David L., and Peter C. Cairo. *Action Coaching: How to Leverage Individual Performance for Company Success.* New York: Jossey, 1999.

Doyle, Michael, and David Straus. *How to Make Meetings Work! The New Interaction Method.* New York: Berkley, 1993.

Drucker, Peter. *Management Challenges for the 21st Century.* New York: Harper, 1999.

Edwards, Paul. "Unstoried: Teaching Literature in the Age of Performance Studies." *Theatre Annual: A Journal of Performance Studies* 52 (1999): 1–147.

Farson, Richard. *Management of the Absurd.* New York: Simon, 1996.

Freire, Paulo. *Pedagogy of the Oppressed.* Trans. Myra Bergman Ramos. Rev. ed. New York: Continuum, 1970.

Goodman, Gary Scott. *Six-Figure Consulting: How to Have a Great Second Career.* New York: American Management Assoc., 1997.

Harkins, Phil. *Powerful Conversations: How High-Impact Leaders Communicate.* New York: McGraw, 1999.

hooks, bell. *Teaching to Transgress: Education as the Practice of Freedom.* New York: Routledge, 1994.

Katz, Richard N., et al. *Dancing with the Devil: Information Technology and the New Competition in Higher Education.* San Francisco: Jossey, 1999.

Kotter, John P., and James L. Heskett. *Corporate Culture and Performance.* New York: Free, 1992.

Lerner, Jonathan. "Philanthropy Made Modern." *Hemispheres* Nov. 1999: 48–51.

McKenzie, Jon. *Perform or Else: Performance, Technology, and the Lecture Machine.* Unpublished manuscript, 1999.

McLaren, Peter. *Revolutionary Multiculturalism: Pedagogies of Dissent for the New Millennium.* Boulder: Westview, 1997.

Moore, Geoffrey A. *Inside the Tornado: Marketing Strategies from Silicon Valley's Cutting Edge.* New York: Harper, 1995.

Nelson, Cary, and Stephen Watt. *Academic Keywords: A Devil's Dictionary for Higher Education.* New York: Routledge, 1999.

Nerad, Maresi, and Joseph Cerny. "From Rumors to Facts: Career Outcomes of English Ph.Ds." *CGS Communicator* 32.7 (1999): 1–11.

Richardson, Robert J., and S. Katharine Thayer. *The Charisma Factor: How to Develop Your Natural Leadership Ability.* Englewood Cliffs: Prentice, 1993.

Robertson, Catherine. "Performativity v. Textuality: Some Second Thoughts." *The Future of Performance Studies: Visions and Revisions.* Ed. Sheron J. Dailey. Annandale: National Communication Assoc., 1998. 86–89.

Rosen, Robert H. *The Healthy Company: Eight Strategies to Develop People, Productivity, and Profits.* New York: Putnam, 1991.

Senge, Peter, et al. *The Fifth Discipline Fieldbook: Strategies and Tools for Building a Learning Organization.* New York: Bantam, 1994.

Showalter, Elaine. "Let's Not Go Gentle into That Museum." *MLA Newsletter* 30.1 (1998): 3–4.

Turner, Chris. *All Hat and No Cattle: Shaking Up the System and Making a Difference at Work.* New York: Perseus, 1999.

Vaill, Peter B. *Managing as a Performing Art.* San Francisco: Jossey, 1989.

Ziglar, Zig. *Top Performance: How to Develop Excellence in Yourself and Others.* New York: Berkley, 1986.

Performative In(ter)ventions
Designing Future Technologies Through Synergetic Performance

15

Eric
Dishman

> You will.
>
> —AT&T advertising campaign

> Theatre is a form of knowledge; it should and can also be a means of transforming society. Theatre can help us build our future, rather than just waiting for it.
>
> —AUGUSTO BOAL, *Games for Actors and Non-Actors*

Performance Pedagogy for Product Development

The competition to design the future is currently dominated by technologists and transnational corporations who, armed with a "you will" technological imperative and extraordinary amounts of capital, are barraging consumers worldwide with perpetual announcements of the "next, latest, greatest thing." In the midst of Internet hysteria, we risk being left behind if we stop the online race for even a moment to ask some critical questions. Where is all of this hype taking us? What kind of "new world order" is being imagined for us? And what are we leaving behind as Microsoft asks us, in their omnipresent advertising campaign: "Where do you want to go today?"

Performance studies, largely construed, has much to offer to counteract this hype-driven tendency to focus on the technological props at the expense of the social actors who are supposed to use them. Performative ways of knowing, thinking, and critiquing provide counteractions to the global visions imposed upon us. They provide us with opportunities to contribute to both the invention and intervention of the future.

Since 1993, under the rubric of *informance,* or "informative performance," I have been teaching and doing performance in strange places—in the corporate cubicles and product development "war rooms" of Silicon Valley—to develop new products, services, and businesses from a more human-centered perspective. I will use these experiences from the corporate classroom to describe a performance pedagogy for product development. By rethinking technology design through the lens of performativity theory, we can move beyond the polarizing rhetorics of most hype-or-hate technology discourse. Furthermore, performance practice is a much-needed intervention in the invention process, especially in an age where "thinking outside of the box" is necessary for survival.

This chapter is about involving more players in the cultural competition to design and produce the future. My main task here is to envision a new kind of *performer*-designer, one who can imagine and invent a wide range of performativities in the world, and one whose very existence questions the assumption that technology design belongs only to technologists.[1] Who gets to participate in the design of the infrastructures that will support these imagined futures, and by what claims to legitimacy? Who will *not* be allowed to play at this fortune-telling (and fortune-making) table? Who is the future designed for? And who will be written out, whether by intention or omission, from the next chapter of global-technological history? By what means might we begin to counter these finished and seemingly inevitable visions that leave too many people out of the profit margin?

As I rethink design in terms of performativity theory and performance practice, I also find it necessary to reconceptualize what it means to perform and what it means to teach performance when the pupils are engineers and technologists and when the final product is one that sits on a shelf somewhere for people to buy. Dwight Conquergood writes, "Instead of a stable, monolithic paradigm of performance studies, I prefer to think in terms of a caravan: a heterogeneous ensemble of ideas and methods on the move" (140). What does the "we" of performance studies gain and lose from such cont(r)acts?

It is not just the Microsofts or AT&Ts who are depending on mass media campaigns to usher in the age of the Internet. From grocery stores to garbage services, almost everything is being advertised as "online," "net-powered," or "e-connected." These powerful product narratives do more than advertise the features of some electronic component or service. As Mary Strine argues, "we live in the gravitational pull of stories . . . [that] give shape, direction, and significance to otherwise chaotic existence and, ultimately, inform our sense of who we are" (367). Thus, these commercial stories stake a claim about what society should be and how its infrastructures should be organized to support particular modes of existence and identities. In some sense, the hype becomes our hope.

As I think of my own experiences with teaching performance primarily to communication students, terminal patients, and technology designers, my political agenda has certainly been that of getting people to "break and remake" their performative ties that bind. While performance and cultural studies as academic fields may well have shifted into this more critical and political relationship with performance, my students, design colleagues, and other performers I meet are still mired in the traditional paradigm of mimesis. They are in the grip of the "real." When conducting workshops with performers who are perhaps untrained in the verse of postmodern theory or unaccustomed to examining the ideological infrastructures that support their daily interactions, I have found it most useful to shift between performance modes of mimesis, poiesis, and kinesis—thus, to view performance as a collective and intertextual *synergesis*. As versions of performed action overlap, sometimes reifying, sometimes contradicting, and always "interanimating" one another, as Conquergood puts it, the "outcome" is a holistic, synergetic, and empowering critique of realism—of reality—that is somehow greater than the sum of the individual scenes or performances. In this critical pedagogical process of performance as synergesis, performativity itself can then be seen as a synergetic cultural construction, derived from a variety of socioinfrastructural resources such as languages, technologies, mediated discourses, architectures, bodily dispositions, and interpersonal habits.

Practicing Synergy:
Telerats, Touch, and Telecommunications Design

> Technologies offer new opportunities for creative, interactive experiences and, in particular, for new forms of drama. But these new opportunities will come to pass only if control of the technology is taken from the technologist and given to those who understand human beings, human interaction, communication, pleasure, and pain. It is time for the engineers to go back to engineering. To develop these technologies, we need a new breed of creative individuals, most likely those associated with poetry, writing, and theatrical direction. (Norman ix)

The performativity of technology designers can be characterized, in part, as being too technocentric; their vision is typically myopic in its focus on the machine. Norman's call for artistic input is a response to that lack of humanistic vision. His words come from the foreword to Brenda Laurel's *Computers as Theatre,* in which she argues that computer-human activity is really about "designed experience" and, thus, requires a more artistic and interaction centered approach to design (Norman xvi). Breaking the academic and corporate boundaries that protect the techno-turf, Laurel insists that design be done by a "team of individuals who, like the playwright, director, actors, technicians, and scenery, light, and costume designers in the theatre, will contribute different skills toward the realization of a common vision" (*Art* xiii). These thinkers have opened a door to performance studies and to a performative definition of technology.

In 1993, I started doing qualitative research for a company called Interval Research Corporation, a long-range technology laboratory that is itself a corporate experiment in the redesign of design. Housing scholars and researchers from almost every imaginable field, Interval often blurs traditional boundaries by combining artistic and scientific approaches. David Liddle, the president of Interval, says of artists, "In the first five minutes with a piece of technology, artists push it to the edge of what's possible. That is how you find out what *is* possible. You need unreasonable people doing things for reasons they can't verbalize" (qtd. in Kirkpatrick 78). In this multidisciplinary context, I began developing a synergetic performance pedagogy called *informance design* with an industrial designer named Colin Burns. Informance—"informative performance" but also suggesting "informants"—is an alternative approach to design praxis that uses ethnographic studies, ethnomethodological analysis, and performance to help designers envision and embody the implications of the artifacts that they are designing, as well as to unleash their imaginations from current product paradigms—to get out of their respective boxes. As the technologists experience ethnographic and performance encounters with disruptive "other" performativities, they begin to break out of the typical Silicon Valley mind and body set. They start to use performance to create prototypes of complex, politicized, personalized futures.

In this climate of artistic acceptance and as a continuation of Laurel's improv class for Interval employees, informance began with a traditional mimetic skit called "Marcia's Hairworks."[2] Colin and I reperformed two informants, a small town hairdresser and her client, who, given their expressed technophobia and lack of electronic sophistication, would certainly not fall within the purview of most designers' concerns. By situating and shaping several technology ideas to "Marcia's" values, practices, and preferences, we provided the opportunity to counteract the tendency to discuss only the technologies themselves and moved, instead, to the social and personal implications of those devices. Furthermore, this embodied action produced design knowledge, new modes of creativity, in some radical and compelling ways that we now refer to as *bodystorming*, an important corrective to the term *brainstorming*. We have continued to experiment with performance techniques and theories and to work on pedagogical strategies (such as natural performance) to get engineers and designers to do such ethnographically informed bodystorms for themselves.

In a subsequent informance experiment called "Telerats," we worked with a group of students in the Computer-Related Design department at the Royal College of Art in London. This week-long workshop was part of a project called Fields and Thresholds led by designers Anthony Dunne and Fiona Raby, who wanted to arrive at some of the complexities of face-to-face interaction in their designs of "virtual" telecommunication spaces but without imposing face-to-face contact as a constant and necessary overlay for these imagined kinds of interaction. They hoped that performance might help them "to investigate design ideas and qualities that could only be explored through experiential methods" (Dunne and Raby 16). From Judith Butler to Augusto Boal, from parody to productions of realism, we experimented with multiple modes of performance. These experiential exercises provided a grounded space for me to explore further the notions of synergetic performance praxis, interaction infrastructures, and a performative definition of technology.

Boal uses various warm-up exercises to "undo" the performers' muscular infrastructures (128), to unhinge what Bourdieu refers to as the bodily "hexis." Boal claims that workplaces are major sites of what McLaren calls "enfleshment" (63) and that the first order of business in performance work is to liberate one's body from those structures of enfleshment. Given the alien nature of such activities to novice performers, these "defleshment" techniques should not be thought of as mere warm-ups on the margins of the "real" performance work. Even simple stretches in the middle of the day were a shocking intervention in the designer-students' embodied routines. Their hexis is one of sedentary thought, where the predominant motion is a mouse click at a computer workstation. Their creativity is channeled into on-screen software prototypes, meaning that the students are most often bound by a televisual view of the interactions they are imagining/imaging. Everything of the body and of interactivity in their design concepts has to be translated, flattened, into software routines for their high-resolution monitors. It is an enfleshment of impoverishment and inactivity.

Equally shocking to the students were various blindfold exercises used to jar them out of their normal ways of "seeing" the world. With only the touch of a partner's hand to go by, then blindfolded and scattered around the room in silence, they had to find their partners by touching only the crooks and crannies of hands. This simple exercise provoked a lengthy debate about the gendered modalities of touch— an awareness that was crucial to understanding how new telecommunication devices, new modes of expressive touch, may reify or defy those sociocultural norms. Two male participants in particular were deeply embarrassed, when the blindfolds came off, to discover that each other were male, after they both had been so sure that the other's hand belonged to a woman. The rest of the group deconstructed their stereotypic assumptions of soft, small hands as feminine. Then we began to explore the cultural differences of handshakes, kisses on the cheek, hugs, and hand-holding, and the group members suddenly found themselves to be fractured along several axes of cultural difference, even as they had come into that room assuming homogeneity as European designers. These microstructures of touch, sometimes different and sometimes the same across contexts, revealed to us that design for one's own subjectivity is a limiting and impoverishing endeavor, given that it smoothes over important cultural affordances and considerations that should be part of a designer's understanding.

Moving from these fun-and-games to performing in front of each other produced no lack of anxiety for the designers, but various forms of mimetic natural performance proved useful in overcoming that anxiety and in demonstrating to the students that they perform, often quite differently, from one social context to another. I asked them to reperform five minutes of our having first convened together that morning. On the first take, they dropped immediately into parody and nervous laughter, but by the second and third tries, they were producing realistic reperformances of that social interaction. As they played the scene over and over again, the iterations encouraged them to deconstruct aspects of the scenes that had not been "real" or "believable." This inaugurated an analysis of the most microscopic details to see what components of our interaction infrastructure—of speech, action, emotion, props, attitude, and bodily disposition—were needed, and in what predictable combinations, to produce *realism* within that reperformance as well as *reality* in that first instance of our early morning greeting. Again, the consequences for technology design were profound. Having witnessed the complex structures enabling greetings, the students bodystormed about how to orient to the importance of openings and closings of "conversations," whether face to face, on the phone, in an email chat, or through some yet unimagined media channel.

From mimetic reperformances, we moved to what Boal calls *image theatre*, where one performer "sculpts" an image using the bodies of the other performers (135). I asked each person to create an image that represented current issues in the design of telecommunications. One of the most striking was of a person thrown at the feet of all the other performers, who pointed accusingly down at him. During the discussion afterwards, its creator said, "I'm tired of the technology blaming *us* all of the time—you just feel accused all of the time. Even the teller machine tells me it's *my* fault when something goes awry." Another performer created a parody of AT&T's "reach out and touch someone" campaign. Her image consisted of the rest of the cast standing close, almost touching one another, but unable to really join hands and feel anything. She painted looks of horror, disgust, and pain on their faces, as they were tempted but unable to reach out and touch anyone. Boal suggests that once you have "a grouping of 'statues' accepted by all as representative of a real situation, each one is asked to propose ways of changing it" (135). The students moved to create images of the future that counteracted this nightmarish vision. These images produced themes of intimate contact, new forms of sharing presence across distances, escaping from communicability altogether, expressing privacy concerns, making technology available to all people, and even abandoning the Internet to have real personal contact instead. Many of these controversial themes, enacted, practiced, and politicized in Image Theatre, became the major design challenges addressed throughout the rest of the week as we built prototype concepts.

These still images emerged into parodic improvisations without prompting when several students started performing subversive parodies of both American and British high-tech advertisements. Jumping fluidly in and out of performance and subsequent discussion, they had moved into performance as kinesis—breaking and remaking the images of the future fed to them by utopia-peddling advertisers. "Who would want to live life like that?" "Who is AT&T to tell me what *my* future is gonna' be?" "Who the hell is going to be able to buy any of this crap?" "Can't we come up with something better than that?" I was surprised that these students in particular, who were being groomed for jobs in the likes of AT&T or Microsoft or Phillips Electronics, were so eager to vent their criticisms of those popular culture visions. Their parodies, as Butler suggests, exposed the advertising ideologies at work and unpacked the social implications of the latent performativities proposed by such commercial media *(Gender Trouble; Bodies)*.

Later in the week, we moved out of our sometimes claustrophobic performance space and into the streets of London to practice what Boal calls "invisible theatre," or what I think of as "garfinkeling," after Harold Garfinkel's exercises described below:

> Procedurally it is my preference to start with familiar scenes and ask what can be done to make trouble. The operations that one would have to perform in order to . . . produce disorganized interaction should tell us something about how the structures of everyday activities are ordinarily and routinely produced and maintained. . . . I have found that [procedures of "making trouble"] produce reflections through which the strangeness of an obstinately familiar world can be detected. (37–38)

Into the pubs, elevators, libraries, grocery stores, and tube stations we went, disrupting the social process to determine what that process is and what interaction infrastructures support it. Many of these performances had quick payoffs for the participants by contributing both to their specific design issues as well as to their general critical consciousness about human interaction, technological objects, and social space. These studies in performativity yielded insights into many patterns of interaction that proved relevant to the design of a telecommunications environment, such as the nuances of waving between familiars and strangers, violations of personal space, limits of eavesdropping on the conversations of strangers, trajectories of movement along sidewalks, propriety of elevator behavior, zones of appropriate eye contact upon the body, and the gendered function of the gaze as a kind of contact and solicitation.

Perhaps the most consequential scene for our telecommunications endeavors involved two female performers who went into a crowded pub and began "hogging" the social space of complete strangers. They observed that many of the bar patrons tended to territorialize their space by placing objects such as umbrellas, coats, lunch trays, and newspapers (though placed quite specifically so as not to be confused with a "public" copy available for anyone to browse) in microspecific configurations of symbolic meaning. By playing around with these protocols of proxemics, the Telerats designers, using the world as a laboratory, began to develop an appreciation for spatial negotiation. By taking on the roles of two drunk, obnoxious women, they tested the limits of those social boundaries to discover the corrective strategies by which barroom patrons sanctioned their offending actions. These observations of present-day interactions surfaced issues that informed the design of a particular kind of human future and provoked many critical questions. How will we design and represent finely nuanced zones within a telecommunicative space? What will the construction of *virtual* proxemics entail? Should current patterns of sociality serve as templates for the future? What are the implications of power, gender, class, ethnicity, and appearance within such a space? What are the micropolitics of interaction in an Internet world?

There were numerous other performance modalities used during the informance workshop, too many to cover here, but I turn to one called "Party, Party, Party" as a final example, because it reveals the power of a synergetic performance praxis to move novice performers into a space of profound cultural observation, critique, and reinvention. During our workshop, the faculty sponsored a party to celebrate the collaboration between RCA and Interval and to display some of the students' informance and telecommunications work to various London designers, engineers, and academics. In anticipation of the big event, I had the cast perform the party as they envisioned it would be, using an improvisatory style similar to Boal's tag-team approach in forum theatre (139). We conducted both realistic and parodic iterations of this anticipatory performance. Then, we "performed" and videotaped the actual party, with some amount of invisible theatre going on to spark certain (re)actions. After briefly analyzing these interactions on the tape, especially to see how the partygoers managed entrances and exits in the different social groups that had splintered, we reperformed the event as faithfully as possible, though frequently switching identities. Finally, we carried out a futuristic party performance to incorporate some of the designs we had been working on during the week.

To produce meaningful, intelligible action within each of these laminations taught us much about the ideological productions of reality. No academic theory was needed to prove to the students that reality is socially constructed or contingent. The complex infrastructural connections between bodies, identities, discourses, spatialities, and technologies became prominent, critiqueable, and inspiring to our imaginations of what else might be possible. The anticipatory versions—the preparty—surfaced our individual assumptions about the nature of cocktail party performativity, but when compared to the videotaped and reperformed versions, they were overly simplistic and interactionally impoverished. Having studied the microstructures of the real event, we were able to situate our future designs within believable scenarios that explored both the negative and positive consequences of those techno-in(ter)ventions. As these various informance design approaches collapsed in upon one another, playfully and politically, we found ourselves less technocentric and more liberated from the futuristic visions spoon-fed to us by televisions, magazines, and books. Instead, we were able to imagine, embody, and put into practice alternative interaction infrastructures that would offer us new obstacles and opportunities—and that would, we hoped, afford a wider range of future performativities, an expanded (re)definition of what it means to "be" and "do" human.

Synergetic Futures and Performative Potentials

> When it becomes a program, hopelessness paralyzes us, immobilizes us. We succumb to fatalism, and then it becomes impossible to muster the strength we absolutely need for a fierce struggle that will create the world. . . . [H]ope is necessary, but it is not enough. Alone it does not win. But without it, my struggle will be weak and wobbly. We need a critical hope the way a fish needs unpolluted water. (Freire 8)

Whether the utopian dreams of AT&T's Tomorrowland or the dystopian warnings of unemployment wars, these polarizing visions, I have argued, produce a pervasive cultural hopelessness that must be overcome somehow. For at the heart of these fatalistic "futurologies" is an existential argument about the definition of society itself—about what it means to be human in a certain place and time. Previous definitions have much linguistic and conceptual gravity from which to escape; we are fettered by our own current understandings and invisible interpretations of what is right, natural, and possible. Of course, there are large, powerful, and complex infrastructures in place to reproduce those norms—those ideological centers that hold. They also tend to reify the very hopelessness that keeps us from counteracting them. But performativity theory and performance praxis can help us to render those structures visible and mutable. These tools of situated, embodied criticism enable us to release, albeit temporarily and in limited ways, the shackles of our current subjectivities so as to invent new notions of humanity. In those performative moments of invention and intervention, we can also find hope for the future.

A synergetic performance praxis is an empowering pedagogy of hope, one that can promote innovative intervention in both the practices of performance studies and design. As a multimodal, iterative, improvisatory, and complexifying process, performance as synergesis suggests a kind of theatrical rap. It appropriates, "samples," methods and moves from a range of performance traditions, popular media, and points of view to create a politicized, personalized, and powerful critique of cultural taken-for-granteds. Homi Bhabha writes:

> What is theoretically innovative, and politically crucial, is the need to think beyond narratives of originary and initial subjectivities and to focus on those moments or processes that are produced in the articulation of cultural differences. These 'in-between' spaces provide the terrain for elaborating strategies of selfhood—singular or communal—that initiate new signs of identity, and innovative sites of collaboration, and contestation, in the act of defining the idea of society itself. (1–2)

Synergetic praxis puts performers in those in-between spaces, in those encounters and articulations of/with cultural difference. It thrives on realisms (the plural is important here) in an age of cultural theory that often trumpets the death of the real, perhaps forgetting that realism, as a cultural production with great rhetorical force, can be a powerful political weapon. And it aspires with critical hope to innovate those new strategies of selfhood.

Informance design, as a particular experiment in synergetic theory, prompts performer-designers to explore the performative implications of their techno-productions. It provokes a politicization of engineering, which reveals to designers their ideo-authorial power and responsibility to their cultures as understood through ethnographic encounters with "real users" and self-reflective reperformances. The goal is to imagine, embody, and "test drive" a technologized future that actually cares for these real people—these flesh and blood citational sources. As we face the development of a new social contract, asking who its authors are and who will be left in its margins, informance evokes the politicizing, empathic, and synergetic powers of performance in the hope that our new social machinery can be designed so that it does not come back to haunt us like some Frankensteinian monster.

I have argued here that the design of technology figures largely into the cultural processes that create our contingent selfhoods and perfor- mativities as well as the strategies of practice by which they are main- tained. We are surrounded by technologies—mechanical, electronic, discursive—that enable and constrain the ways we think, act, move, and perceive. And every new technology, whether guided in its design by profit motives or by social responsibility, has performative conse- quences both intended and unintended. While I believe that synergetic performance has much to offer to *consumers* of technologies to pro- mote awareness and understanding of those consequences, I also be- lieve that it can reshape the very ways in which these products are imagined, produced, and marketed. The synergetic potential and risk of multiple performance modalities brought together to interrogate various sociotechnological dilemmas is vast but underpracticed and undertheorized. This chapter is a baby step in that direction. As we, in Conquergood's apt phrase, put "performance studies in motion," where will we go, and what will we leave behind? How will the perfor- mativity of performance scholars be redefined by new technology, by new collaborations, by a new academy, and by moving to new loca- tions? How do we climb out of the hopelessness often brought on by all of that newness? The answers to these questions lie only in a con- tingent and, thankfully, contestable future.

NOTES

Portions of this chapter were presented at the 1994 Speech Communication Association convention in New Orleans and at the 1997 Northwest Com- munication Association convention in Coeur d'Alene, Idaho. I wish to thank Dr. Bonnie Johnson of Interval Research Corp. for enabling this re- search. Also, I thank Ashley Armstrong for her helpful suggestions with this chapter.

1. Norman Fairclough predicts that "discourse analysts and linguists will increasingly be expected to act as, or make available the results of their research to, discourse technologists" (216). His fear seems to be that the technologization of discourses threatens to give even more power of control to hegemonic corporate interests. I argue, however, that the transformation of languages and discourses into technologies them- selves, while risky for a project of critical pedagogy, means that those linguistic tools are thus usable and deployable by the "oppressed" as much as by the "powerful."

2. For more on Marcia's Hairworks, see Burns et al. Also see Kirkpatrick for a brief description and photo of some other informance activities.

WORKS CITED

Bhabha, Homi K. *The Location of Culture.* New York: Routledge, 1994.

Boal, Augusto. *Theatre of the Oppressed.* Trans. Charles A. McBride and Maria- Odilia Leal McBride. New York: Theatre Communications Group, 1985.

Bourdieu, Pierre. *The Logic of Practice.* Trans. Richard Nice. Stanford: Stanford UP, 1990.

Burns, Colin, Eric Dishman, William Verplank, and Bud Lassiter. "Actors, Hairdos, and Videotape—Informance Design." *Human Factors in Computing Systems: CHI '94 Conference Companion, Boston, 24–28 April 1994.* Boston: Addison, 1994. 119–20.

Butler, Judith. *Bodies That Matter: On the Discursive Limits of "Sex."* New York: Routledge, 1993.

———. *Gender Trouble: Feminism and the Subversion of Identity.* New York: Routledge, 1990.

Conquergood, Dwight. "Of Caravans and Carnivals: Performance Studies in Motion." *Drama Review* 39.4 (1995): 137–41.

Dunne, Anthony, and Fiona Raby. "Fields and Thresholds": A Record of Experiments Carried Out at the Royal College of Art, London, for Stiching Het Nederlands Vormgevingsinstituut. Unpublished report, 1994.

Fairclough, Norman. *Discourse and Social Change.* Cambridge: Polity, 1992.

Freire, Paulo. *Pedagogy of Hope: Reliving "Pedagogy of the Oppressed."* Trans. Robert R. Barr. New York: Continuum, 1995.

Garfinkel, Harold. *Studies in Ethnomethodology.* Englewood Cliffs: Prentice, 1967.

Kirkpatrick, David. "A Look Inside Allen's Think Tank." *Fortune* 11 July 1994: 78–80.

Laurel, Brenda, ed. *The Art of Human-Computer Interface Design.* New York: Addison, 1990.

McLaren, Peter. *Critical Pedagogy and Predatory Culture: Oppositional Politics in a Postmodern Era.* New York: Routledge, 1995.

Norman, Donald A. Foreword. *Computers as Theatre.* By Brenda Laurel. New York: Addison, 1991.

Strine, Mary S. "Of Boundaries, Borders, and Contact Zones: Author(iz)ing Pedagogical Practices." *Communication Education* 42 (1993): 367–76.

Theatre of the Oppressed with Students of Privilege

Practicing Boal

in the American College Classroom

16

Bruce
McConachie

In spring 1995, I taught a new course at the College of William and Mary entitled Empowerment Through Theatre. My eighteen students ranged from senior theatre majors with some education in the techniques of Augusto Boal to freshmen for whom any kind of performing was a new, somewhat frightening experience. Sixteen were white, two were black, males slightly outnumbered females, and nearly all were upper middle class. Although nonacademic workshops on theatre of the oppressed (TO) abound, there have been few attempts to offer courses for college credit centered on Boal's ideas and techniques. As I will demonstrate, however, modest progressive work centered on the goals and strategies of Boal can occur in academic settings if one can negotiate the immense gap between Boal's Marxist assumptions about oppression and the students' lack of experience of oppressive situations. To make this argument, I will draw from my notes and syllabi, student journal entries and essays (with authors' permissions), and literature about teaching Boal.

The goal of the course, as I announced it in the syllabus, read as follows: "By exploring the political and theatrical ideas and techniques of Augusto Boal, students will learn ways of empowering themselves and others." I divided the three-hour-per-week, fourteen-week course roughly into quarters, with the first quarter for warm-ups, trust exercises, and image theatre, the next for invisible theatre, and the final two for forum theatre. For texts, we used Boal's *Games for Actors and Non-Actors* and most of the essays in *Playing Boal: Theatre, Therapy, Activism*, edited by Mady Schutzman and Jan Cohen-Cruz.

Before proceeding, let me provide some quick definitions of Boalian techniques drawn from the glossary in Schutzman and Cohen-Cruz:

> Image theatre (IMT) is a series of wordless exercises in which participants create embodiments of their feelings and experiences. Beginning with a selected theme, participants "sculpt" im-

ages onto their own and others' bodies. These frozen images are then "dynamized," or brought to life, through a sequence of movement-based and interactive exercises.

Invisible theatre (INT) is a rehearsed sequence of events that is enacted in a public, non-theatrical space, capturing the attention of people who do not know they are watching a planned performance. It is at once theatre and real life, for although rehearsed, it happens in real time and space and the "actors" must take responsibility for the consequences of the "show." The goal is to bring attention to a social problem for the purpose of stimulating public dialog.

Forum theatre (FT) is a TO technique that begins with the enactment of a scene (or anti-model) in which a protagonist tries, unsuccessfully, to overcome an oppression relevant to that particular audience. The Joker [a facilitator] then invites the spectators [Boal calls them spect-actors] to replace the protagonist at any point in the scene that they can imagine an alternative action that could lead to a solution. The scene is replayed numerous times with different interventions. This results in a dialogue about oppression, an examination of alternatives, and a "rehearsal" for real situations. (236–37)

To do them thoroughly, each of these TO techniques would require six to ten weeks of intensive work. I knew that I was attempting too much for a semester-long course. I also knew, however, that nowhere else in their experience at William and Mary would my students be able to practice and analyze interactive political theatre.

Although much of Boal's current work is now aimed against internal, psychological forms of oppression, he continues to practice and advocate the standard genres of TO that he perfected in the 1960s and 1970s to fight oppressive external forces in South America. In planning the course, I deliberately omitted Boal's newer "rainbow of desire" techniques rather than turn students primarily toward the contradictions of their own privilege and away from the massive realities of social and economic oppression of others.

Like many introductory classes at William and Mary, Empowerment Through Theatre was to be a "writing-intensive" course. In fact, I had won approval from a theatre faculty skeptical about Boal and his kind of theatre because the college was requiring us to teach several writing-intensive "seminars" oriented mostly to freshmen. This meant, in our case, a daily journal, plus short essays, scenarios, and character profiles, with the opportunity to revise and resubmit everything except the journal. In planning the course, I had been concerned that the kind of work we would be doing would not logically generate the amount and variety of writing I had to assign. My concern was misplaced; the students used their writing to plan and revise their projects, analyze their processes and results, and explore the wider implications of their work. In their journals and papers, they frequently turned to the essays in *Playing Boal* to critique and/or reinforce their own understandings. Learning to be Boalian facilitators requires several theatrical skills, the sensitivity of a good counselor, and careful sociopolitical analysis. The writing assignments helped the students to work through the complex demands of their projects and apply their learning to their next undertakings. In retrospect, the course could not have succeeded without its strong writing component.

Envisioning how I might teach Boal, I struggled to overcome one of the major contradictions that bedevil instructors of social workers, grade school teachers, and other professions in which the best learning occurs through structured interaction with the public. I wanted my students to experience "real world" situations, but I was also determined not to use oppressed people as "guinea pigs" for student learning. Of course, I planned to have students begin by working on themselves, exploring situations in which others had exerted illegitimate power over them; starting with your own life is a commonplace of Boalian instruction. The goal of the course, however, was also to help students learn ways of empowering others. For their invisible theatre projects, the "others" would be other students at William and Mary, but I wanted my students to consider populations outside the academy so that they might begin to come to terms with their social isolation and privilege and also discover possibilities for cross-class (also cross-gender and cross-race) coalitions.

Since there was no ethical way to do this directly, I decided that their forum theatre project would be focused on a significant sociopolitical issue beyond the immediacies of student life but relevant to most student citizens. Further, I required that the students role-play spect-actor members of an oppressed population in one of their forum theatre projects. By the end of the semester, I reasoned, the students would have become adept at improvisatory role-playing; so why not have them improvise both spect-actor and performer participation on two different FT projects (we did three in all)? This pedagogical strategy had the further benefit of underlining the "all-of-life-is-a-theatre" metaphor that is an important foundation of Boal's work. For the most part, the strategy was successful. In one of our FT projects, student role-playing of oppressed spect-actors led to some of the best learning in the semester.

The theatre games, trust exercises, and image theatre work of the first third or so of the course, plus copious reading, oriented the students toward the goals and strategies of TO and also generated student solidarity. What began as a very disparate group of kids—freshmen fearful of upper-class domination, "insider" theatre majors suspicious of interlopers, plus the usual tensions generated by differences in race, gender, and sexual orientation—soon became a friendly and flexible support system as the students experienced each others' strengths and vulnerabilities through their bodies. I encouraged several of the students with extensive experience in improvisational theatre to coach those fearful of performing. Many a timid first-year student, in turn, later came up with some of the best ideas for group projects; one emerged as a leader of the class. Several of the freshmen took time in their journals to discuss the importance of this initial bonding as a necessary foundation for our later work.

We began our image theatre work with simple exercises modeling emotions and rather quickly moved to more challenging tasks. Alistair Campbell's wheel exercise, in which students take turns sculpting each other, provided a nonthreatening way to discover and begin to elaborate a shared language of the body (53–63). Soon, the students were modeling in groups; one striking image centered on a depressed student pulled in several directions by parents, professors, and friends. We ended with group images contrasting a real situation to an ideal one and then encouraging the spect-actors to explore strategies to move the sculpted figures from the first pose to the second. In one exercise, the spect-actors explored family dynamics to transform a dysfunctional family into an ideal one. The most pointed group project, though unfortunately not the most successful, was a satire on recent productions at the William and Mary Theatre. The students sculpted some of the stereotypical characters and bored spectators they had recently witnessed and then transformed them, depicting a much more interactive relationship between complex characters and animated spectators.

I would like to be able to report that the class glided smoothly from image to invisible theatre techniques, but INT was a baptism by fire in Boalian activism for many of the students. Suddenly, they had to leave the warm cocoon of classroom relationships and use their knowledge and theatrical skills to try to change the world! Knowing the ethical dilemmas that INT involves, I had given the students the option of doing a different assignment, but none of them took it. Most were eager to construct and enact scenarios that would confront their fellow students with a social problem on campus. Their initial plans explored a range of issues for group action, from fraternity hazing to campus discrimination against homosexuals.

One group, hoping to expose the contradictions of the college honor code, ran into faculty opposition when a psychology professor told them that INT was unethical because it experimented on people without their consent; he refused to give a fake pop quiz in one of his courses that would have provided the context for the students' scenario. This led to a heated discussion in our class on the "reality" of improvised theatre and the ethics of manipulating others for what some social activists might consider the greater good. No consensus was reached, but the discussion challenged the students to think clearly about political ethics and the price they might be willing to pay to violate liberal norms of individual freedom and choice. Boal's problematic use of INT in Brazilian politics was a frequent touchstone in our classroom controversy. The morality of INT continued to trouble several students and became the focus of a few final papers.

Most in the class decided that they would try INT for themselves before making up their minds about its ethics. One relatively successful animation centered on male sexism. A student on crutches had been studying with his girlfriend in a lounge at the library. In the midst of a petty argument, she announced that she was leaving to walk home alone. He became upset and insisted she call the escort service at the college because he could not accompany her. She reluctantly agreed, and the escort soon appeared, a large woman. Seeing this, the boyfriend became upset, their argument about gender roles intensified, and the female escort left. Finally, a male escort arrived, and all three left the room, the girl in tears and the boy hobbling along to continue the argument. There was laughter, relief, and a buzz of conversation from the rest of the two dozen or so students in the study lounge. Three undercover animators guided the discussions to gender stereotypes and relationships, but there was little need for prompting. Everybody knew what was at stake in this conflict, and the lounge bubbled with diverse opinions.

Another of our three INT groups wanted to animate their fellow students to examine what they took to be the problem of free speech versus the right of privacy, especially as it relates to the expression of religious beliefs. At William and Mary, a vocal minority of students "witness" for Christ in public spaces. Six students in the class put together a scenario in which one of them would begin preaching in a crowded lunchroom cafeteria, and then two others would get into an argument about whether the evangelist had a right to speak freely in such a situation. Other animators in the crowd would then take up the question with those seated nearby. The plan had clear theatrical potential, but the students worried that the reputation of their classmate doing the witnessing would suffer. I, too, was concerned and questioned the student who would be playing an evangelist about the risk. He explained that he would be witnessing for his own religious beliefs and that he was willing to endure the ridicule he knew he might encounter. So, the group performed as planned and kicked up some of the controversy they had hoped for. Afterward, the born-again student in the group reported that others in his residence hall were treating him differently, but he remained adamant about the correctness of his own participation.

Other students in the class, however, pointed to the limitations of INT on a campus the size of William and Mary. One concluded in her journal that the believability of INT was problematic in a setting where some of the spect-actors were acquainted with the performers—and furthermore knew that the performers did not usually take controversial stands on difficult issues. Another said, "In Sweden or Spain or wherever Boal does this form of theatre, the community is large enough that one could perform in this manner and not have his/her reputation suffer for it." One student suggested that the class go off-campus for INT projects. "We learn in a very encapsulated environment and that does not allow us to find out about many different parts of society," he added. In our class discussion, we concluded that INT was nearly impossible at William and Mary. While the students recognized that some of the projects had succeeded, they agreed that none of them had been truly "invisible." What we had been doing instead, they concluded, was "opaque" theatre, or perhaps, as one suggested in her journal, "translucent."

Another problem gained significance in the INT projects, one that had occurred earlier but that had not been adequately addressed: Many of the students were politically naive about the issues they were attempting to define and animate in their scenarios. Because this was the first time many of them had performed in public—not to mention doing a kind of theatre that was morally problematic and potentially damaging to one's reputation—there had been more immediate problems to discuss, and I had shelved my political concerns. Nonetheless, part of the shortcoming of the project centered on lunchroom evangelists, for example, was insufficient political analysis. While many students were annoyed at the Bible-thumpers, there was no free-speech versus right-to-privacy issue here: No one can claim privacy in a public space. Nor has anyone at William and Mary really tried to circumscribe the freedom of evangelists or their opponents to argue with each other in lunchrooms. In short, many students had difficulty understanding oppression and how it affects their lives.

This difficulty became more pronounced as we moved into our work with forum theatre. To prepare the students to envision anti-model scenarios in which a protagonist struggles, unsuccessfully, against her or his oppressors, I invited them to improvise situations from their own lives when they had felt others oppress them. By this time, they had read Lib Spry's "Structures of Power" in *Playing Boal*, which helpfully redefines personal oppression as an ongoing situation in which others have illegitimate "power over" you. They had also read

Julie Salverson's "The Mask of Solidarity," which explains that TO workers must explore their own moments of oppression so that they can feel a bond with the oppressed people in their workshops. Without it, TO techniques too easily devolve into "us" trying to help "them," rather than building on common experience and the search for mutual liberation.

Still, many of the students had difficulty thinking of incidents of recurrent oppression from their past. We improvised one situation in which an older man had tried, unsuccessfully, to bully a student because of his youth. Another student remembered feeling oppressed by a store owner who suspected her of shoplifting, and the class played that out. But in neither incident had the adult actually succeeded in gaining illegitimate power over the student. Although other situations enacted by the class were more relevant to the assignment—situations involving sexism and racism—it was apparent that many William and Mary students lacked a clear experiential basis for understanding oppression. One student would later write in her final paper that the assignment to think about oppression in her own life "froze [her] mind." She stated:

> It's hard to let go of the white, middle-class attitudes that are instilled in us from such an early age. Society teaches us that we should feel guilty about all the oppression others feel, and that we are selfish if we think of our situations as oppressive.

This comment sums up the double bind most William and Mary students experienced with this assignment. Because they knew they were privileged, they could not admit that they might have been oppressed. Any solidarity in oppression they might feel with those who lacked their advantages made them feel guilty. If it was not "us" helping "them," the students could not be sure of their own social identities.

Some students simply expanded the concept of oppression to encompass situations in which others disagreed with them but where there were no acts of illegitimate power. One student, for example, wrote in his journal that he has felt very oppressed by political correctness. He worked up an FT scenario in which the majority of students at a local high school mocked a group of school-prayer advocates. One FT scenario that was finally performed, despite my attempts to alter it, involved a majority of people at a party, including the boy's father, ganging up on him to get him to take steroids so he could win a college athletic scholarship. Even after I pointed out that this was simply a "just-say-no" scenario, with a relatively easy moral choice at its center, the students wanted to define the high school boy's situation as oppressive. Their confusion was not accidental or surprising, of course. Having grown up in the 1980s, when politicians and pundits encouraged middle-class Americans to see themselves frequently as victims and to misperceive the genuine oppression of others, many of my students were simply playing out the anxieties of their culture.

On the whole, however, the forum theatre exercises helped the students to alter their perceptions of oppression, to see instances where power touched their lives, and to identify with oppressed others. This began to occur as soon as the students worked up their ideas for scenarios. FT, like all good improv, demands that its practitioners translate abstractions such as "power" and "oppression" into embodied actions; real people have to exert illegitimate power over others through believable behavior in FT scenarios. As the students discussed each others' planned improvs, the scenes that focused on conflicts between genuine oppressors and victims tended to emerge as the best choices for the groups to pursue. The responsibility to consider the needs of the spect-actors in FT—those who would later become participants in the event—also pulled the students toward a sharper understanding of the dynamics of oppression. By asking, "What could the spect-actors do to alter this situation?" the students had to think in terms of physical and vocal action to counter oppression. In the essays by Campbell, Fisher, and others in *Playing Boal,* they had read that this occurred, but now they knew it by having to come to terms with it themselves.

Two of the three student groups put together and enacted scenarios that grappled believably with oppressive situations. In one, inner-city gang members threatened and manipulated the mother of a young boy the gang wanted to enlist. His older brother had been killed by a rival group, and now the gang sought to bring the kid into their brotherhood to avenge the death. The scenario centered on a tug-of-war between the mother and three gang members over the boy's affection and loyalty. The students designed this scenario to be performed before a group of inner-city parents whose children had been or were at risk of being involved in gangs.

In discussions about their FT plans, I cautioned the students to avoid the clichés that the media had pasted onto gangs. The writing requirement for the assignment, which asked them to research their scenario and draw up socially credible profiles of the characters they were performing, helped me to insist on careful social analysis. The students playing the spect-actors, too, had to write a three-page paper on who they were and what they wanted, based on reliable evidence and persuasive reasoning. What emerged was not simply a conflict between traditional family values and gang violence but a complex situation with no easy answers. The students might have gone further, but I was relieved that they had created a situation of genuine oppression and were able to identify with several of the protagonists and antagonists within it.

While their scenario and their acting were insightful, the response of the spect-actors sparked the best learning to come out of this improvisation. Cast as a support group of parents concerned about their childrens' involvement in gangs, it became, as one spect-actor put it in her journal, "the most hostile support group I can imagine." The parents disagreed about child-raising strategies, and their arguments escalated into mocking and even threatening behavior. One spect-actor, a gentle mother urging love instead of strict discipline, started crying. With little time left, the parents finally settled their differences and acted together to support two interventions that resulted in genuine progress for the protagonist-mother in the scene. In the class discussion and journal writing that followed, some students found fault with the parents for too much talking and too little action, while others praised the believability of that behavior, pointing out, accurately enough, that most adults would rather talk than act. Similarly, some blamed the Joker-facilitator of the forum for allowing spect-actor participation to disintegrate, while others praised his forbearance. Frankly, I was delighted that the spect-actors and the Joker-facilitator identified with their roles to such an extent that they could stay with the problem long enough to resolve it believably. In part because it was completely unanticipated, this process of fighting out the issues was the most exhausting and exhilarating improv witnessed by the class. To me, it fit Boal's definition of FT as a rehearsal for reality.

The second successful FT group explored the dynamics of rape among college acquaintances. Having worked on an improvised play about date rape on campus a couple of years before, I was able to help the students shape a believable and workable anti-model scenario. But most of the success of this piece was due to the careful planning, writing, and facilitating of its leader, a first-year woman with no prior theatre experience. Drawing on the essays by Schutzman, Spry, and Salverson in *Playing Boal*—as well as the ideas and skills of her group and her own strengths—she fashioned an FT exercise that substantially changed the attitudes of her spect-actors, a group of incoming freshmen, to rape. As she explained in her final essay, she sought to overcome the social problem of "silent witnesses," a common situation that casts many Americans "in the role of isolated witness to daily crimes of inhumanity" (Schutzman, "Brechtian" 144). She noted, following Spry, that many Americans are unaware of the sexist attitudes they hold, even though these often conflict with other values. Thus, when students witness acts against women, the resulting inner turmoil often paralyzes their will to respond.

To counter this, she created an anti-model in which both the protagonist and the spect-actors were silent witnesses when a college woman reported she had been raped just a few minutes before by a male student she thought was her friend. The leader planned to tell the freshman spect-actors that their goal was to help the protagonist assist her raped friend. She would not tell them, however, that the best long-term assistance they could give would be to convince her friend to go to the hospital and report the crime to the police; the spect-actors had to discover that for themselves. In working toward that end, of course, they would have to confront or at least neutralize the actions of the other characters, who either denied that a rape had occurred or passed it off as unimportant. They also had to overcome their own victim-blaming prejudices. The leader had designed the scenario, she stated, so that "the spect-actors' understanding of the power structure sur-rounding victim-blaming was essential to ending the oppression of the victim. . . . The liberation of the victim was tied to the self-liberation of the spect-actor from social and sexual prejudices."

As the Joker for the production, the leader began with some warm-ups involving both performers and spect-actors. Moving to image the-atre, she asked everyone to sculpt themselves into a pose expressing how they would feel if they had been raped. Anticipating that this would draw a mixed response, she asked the participants to notice the differences between male and female images; the women looked more hurt and withdrawn. After the initial run-through of the scenario, which left the rape victim crying in a corner by herself and the protag-onist angry but impotent, the Joker invited spect-actor substitutions. Because they had difficulty identifying with the victim, the spect-actor-protagonists started by arguing with the characters, urging them to change their attitudes toward the victim. That got them nowhere, of course, and only increased the isolation of the victim. Slowly, the spect-actors learned from each other to comfort the victim, separate her from the taunts of the other characters, and finally make a phone call that brought the police. The last spect-actor as protagonist ex-plained to the police what her friend had reported, insisted she be taken to the hospital, kept the other characters at bay, and then ac-companied her friend to the waiting squad car.

Those of us who had witnessed the hour-and-twenty-minute exer-cise were quick to congratulate the performers, spect-actors, and espe-cially the Joker for their perseverance and insight. I pointed out that their creative role-playing had enabled them to work through a prob-lem they had been struggling with all semester; they had recognized a massive but hidden form of oppression and identified with one of its victims. The students casually acknowledged this but pressed on to dis-cuss other forms of sexism on campus. As is often the case with new knowledge learned inductively, most of the students treated it as though it had always been a part of their understanding. I took this as success and enjoyed their discussion.

The first-year leader of the forum, on the other hand, understood the difficulty of her achievement. She wrote:

> The main goal of this forum was the liberation of both the victim and the spect-actor, one being necessary for the other. The frustrations and oppressions felt by the spect-actor in forum theatre can be broken through by seeking out their origins. . . . [The spect-actors] were able to come to the understanding that they were both the victims of unconscious oppression from society and perpetrators of oppression themselves. This knowledge resulted in their desire to change themselves, the key to their liberation.

In transforming "silent witnesses" into helpful citizens within the improv, the student had provided the entire class with a rehearsal for life.

This rehearsal of the techniques of forum theatre with upper-middle-class college students differs in crucial ways from Boal's teaching of FT to New York University undergraduates in 1989 and the modified structure for forum theatre that grew out of it. Significantly, the differences hinge on the dramatic role of the silent witness. As Mady Schutzman reports, the NYU students, like their counterparts at William and Mary, had little direct experience of oppression but often felt powerless as bystanders witnessing social evils. To speak to these anxieties, Boal and his students substituted the "silent witness" for the oppressor in the oppressor/oppressed binary that powers FT. In one FT dealing with the problem of homelessness, for instance, the scene consisted of an improv between a silent witness and a homeless beggar; no figure representing the oppressive forces causing homelessness was present. According to Schutzman, this alteration of FT allowed the NYU students to "share [their] impotence" and "identify and embody oppressive territory rather than the more dichotomous oppressors and oppressed." She reports that this modified FT, now apparently the thrust of much Boalian work done at the Brecht Forum in New York City, helps the participants "in the more personal arena—in one's sense of self, in one-to-one relationships, or perhaps in one's family or work situation" ("Brechtian" 144, 145).

I can understand that this mode of therapy could provide its workshop participants with a way of mollifying their feelings of impotence, anxiety, and rage as they witness acts of oppression against others in their daily lives. But appropriate therapy does not always work in conjunction with good education. The NYU students above, for instance, apparently felt better about how to handle their guilt and what to do in "oppressive territory" (is there any territory on the globe that is not oppressive?), but what did they learn about housing and poverty in the United States? Why must the temporary shelving of social activism lead students to think that they can make no effective changes in the future? Much college education, after all, is premised on the belief, or at least the hope, that well-educated graduates can make a progressive difference in the world over time. This hope may be misplaced for the majority of students, but it is certainly less naive than the exploded assumption that revolution is just around the corner, if only enough lefties rehearse for radical change. In short, to turn FT into therapy for the privileged can continue to mystify the sources of oppression in society and undermine the broader purposes of a progressive education.

Certainly, the first-year William and Mary student in Empowerment Through Theatre who led us all through her acquaintance-rape scenario sensed the progressive potential of FT. After reading Schutzman's reports of the NYU workshops, she adapted the "silent witness" character to the more traditional structuring of FT that my assignment had called for. That is, she used FT to transform silent witness spectactors into active agents for change. Unlike Boal's silent witnesses at NYU, her's learned how to confront the oppressors of a rape victim and worked improvisationally to improve the social environment for women. Since taking the course, she told me later, she has become a hall counselor and has found many other opportunities to merge her therapeutic and her educational interests.

Our modest success with conventional FT points to an important moral: Students can still learn much by dividing the world between oppressors and oppressed. This strategy runs some risks, of course. As participants in a 1991 roundtable discussion among Canadian practitioners of Boalian work noted, most of them do not use the term *oppression* in their workshops. For them and their clients, the connotations of the word were too "political," too "flaky," too "dark, difficult, troubling"—"when you hear oppression . . . you don't think entertaining." These words also characterize the initial response of most William and Mary undergraduates. Then, following this initial antagonism, they jumped too easily into the belief that they themselves were as systematically oppressed as any third-world subaltern. Schutzman reports that this occurred with the NYU students as well: "What happened was that several of the white, middle-class students wanted to get in touch with the ways in which they too felt oppressed. In a way, it almost became a glorification of the whole concept—I'm oppressed too!" ("Canadian" 212, 213, 214). For the educator, of course, the challenge is to facilitate situations in which students can learn that oppression comes in many forms and varies significantly in degree. *Oppression* may shift from being threatening to being glorious for many American college students, but when they have imaginatively experienced its innervating range in their own bodies—from sharp stab to mundane grind—the term can help privileged undergraduates to figure out how the world works for most of its inhabitants.

At least, how it works some of the time. The implicit structure of FT is melodramatic Marxism; spect-actors are drawn into a situation in which they must finally confront the old agitprop question, "Which side are you on?" Much has been made of Boal's similarity to Brecht, but conventional FT works within a less complex understanding of power and history. Boal schematizes characterization in such a way as to make impossible the divided figures of Brecht's mature plays who struggle against themselves as well as an oppressive power structure. In FT, on the other hand, such characters must be completely split in two; the form can only accommodate villains and victims who struggle to become heroes. Spect-actors may feel pulled in contrary directions, like Mother Courage, but finally they must intervene on the side of the angels if the improvised scenario is to have a hopeful ending. Any sense of the ongoing contradictions of their situation receives less emphasis than the possibilities of a short-term solution.

Nonetheless, I believe that the melodramatic schematization of FT is also its chief strength in educating college students. Students need to recognize that the binary of oppressor/oppressed does fit many situations in the real world today—especially situations centering on conflicts over race, class, and gender that involve them in the wider contradictions of our society. The challenge for educators is not to abandon the binary but to guide students toward choosing appropriate FT scenarios in which Boal's melodramatic Marxism can open up possibilities for insight and action. Ironically, the gray area of interpersonal relationships—the area in which FT is often deployed today—is generally less appropriate for the agitprop schematics of the conventional FT structure. Students need an arena in which they can imaginatively experience the dynamics of oppression and work to redefine themselves and others as agents rather than victims.

WORKS CITED

Boal, Augusto. *Games for Actors and Non-Actors*. Trans. Adrian Jackson. New York: Routledge, 1992.

Campbell, Alistair. "Reinventing the Wheel: Breakout Theatre-in-Education." Schutzman and Cohen-Cruz, *Playing Boal* 53–63.

Fisher, Bernice. "Feminist Acts: Women, Pedagogy, Theatre of the Oppressed." Schutzman and Cohen-Cruz, *Playing Boal* 185–97.

Salverson, Julie. "The Mask of Solidarity." Schutzman and Cohen-Cruz, *Playing Boal* 157–70.

Schutzman, Mady. "Brechtian Shamanism: The Political Therapy of Augusto Boal." Schutzman and Cohen-Cruz, *Playing Boal* 137–56.

———. "Canadian Roundtable: An Interview." Schutzman and Cohen-Cruz, *Playing Boal* 198–226.

Schutzman, Mady, and Jan Cohen-Cruz. Glossary. Schutzman and Cohen-Cruz, *Playing Boal* 236–37.

———, eds. *Playing Boal: Theatre, Therapy, Activism.* New York: Routledge, 1994.

Spry, Lib. "Structures of Power: Toward a Theatre of Liberation." Schutzman and Cohen-Cruz, *Playing Boal* 171–84.

Performance Studies, Neuroscience, and the Limits of Culture

17
John
Emigh

Jokes can be seductive. In 1993, while mired in the usual long, dark wait for the tedious and teasing entrance of a New England spring, I was engaged in assessing the next year's curricular offerings in Brown's Theatre, Speech, and Dance Department. Stepping down from chairing the department and faced with the luxury of teaching a new course, I was asked by my colleagues what that course would be. I replied, jokingly, and to my own surprise, that I'd like to teach a seminar in theatre and neuroscience. This attempt at self-deprecating humor provoked, I thought, more laughter in the room than was healthy. The joke became a challenge.

My remark had been prompted in part by recent conversations I'd had in my duty as concentration adviser. Two sophomores I had talked to expressed a desire to double major in theatre arts and neuroscience. Both students, it struck me, spoke as though embarrassed, almost apologizing for an aberration in character, and both assumed there was no way to effect such a bizarre combination. This seemed an unfortunate example of the cultural divide between the humanities and the sciences. Out of whatever combination of pride, intellectual curiosity, and foolhardiness, I did eventually teach a course called Theatre and Neuroscience. What follows is an account of how that course was put together, some notes on what I encountered while teaching it (three times now), and comments on possible connections between the concerns of performance studies and recent findings in the domains of neural and cognitive sciences.

As I thought more about the real possibilities of offering a course linking the concerns of theatre and performance with perspectives from neuroscience, it struck me that the two fields really have a great deal in common. However different the means of inquiry, both are, of necessity, concerned with the manipulation of attention and arousal, with perception and deception, with the play between figure and ground, and with the interaction of cognitive systems and emotional ones. Both deal with the construction of meaning through symbolic representation. One of the hallmarks of postmodernism is a foregrounding of the unstable process of constructing meaning from signification. This clearly involves the brain and its workings; yet, oddly, there seems to be remarkably little attention given in recent critical literature to emergent paradigms in the cognitive and neurosciences. How could the study of the actual brain as it monitors and precipitates understanding and action be irrelevant? What little reading I had done gave me hope that there were people out there who were now able to understand, at least a little better, the workings of the mind as embodied in the brain, and that we were therefore at a point where processes central to making and enjoying performances could be better understood, or at least understood in a slightly different way.

The tendency in the post-humanist humanities has been to see all as social construction (with varying degrees of attention paid to the individual artist/reader/observer), while at the same time, it seemed to me, the sciences were suggesting that our parameters of choice are severely restricted by our biological makeup (see, e.g., Konner; Pinker). I remembered Lévi-Strauss's remarking somewhere that the human mind was the uninvited guest at the anthropological banquet (cited in Gardner 32); and Victor Turner's apology, in the last essay of his extraordinarily productive life as a scholar, as he turned his attention to the then current findings of neuroscience and wondered how deeply he might be undermining the presumptions of cultural construction at the heart of anthropological discourse ("Body"). If performance, as Peggy Phelan remarked at the 1997 Performance Studies Conference in Atlanta, "exists as a negotiation between biology and culture," then studying some of the relevant concerns and findings of neuroscience in relation to those of performance theory and practice seemed an appropriate way to provide a reality check on the rhetoric of performance studies and, perhaps, to help mediate the wide gulf between the humanities and the sciences that was frustrating my students.

I had brushed up against the edges of scientific writing enough to compose a sort of wish list of connections to investigate, stressing: (1) jokes, dreams, creativity, and neural activity; (2) the psychobiology of emotion as performed on and off the stage; (3) trance, shamanic imagery, healing, and neural activity; and (4) iconography, archetypes, and neural maps of the body. And I was able to justify my interest in these broad areas of inquiry well enough to secure a small grant from an indulgent dean (herself a cognitive scientist). One of the conditions of the grant was that I first conduct an exploratory seminar in addition to my usual course load. Five students signed up for this extremely informal "course," all of them (fortunately) with more substantial backgrounds in the relevant sciences than myself. We sent out an open call to professors in the neural and cognitive sciences and followed that up with specific invitations. The response from the scientists was extraordinarily generous. Though several were initially dubious about the project (and some perhaps remain so), for a semester the students and I met with one or two professors from the sciences each week for two to three hours at a time, discussing a wide range of issues: the use of actors in experiments on the biology of emotion, studies of brain states during trance, studies in face recognition and preference, the hows and whys of optical illusions, the role of kinesis in cognition. One neural engineer started to sit in on a regular basis. Others would call from time to time about a new connection or a book that came to mind. As books and articles were mentioned, they were parceled out among the students and myself for review. Gradually, and in a somewhat chaotic fashion, a working bibliography was formed.

I quickly learned that consensus concerning the things I cared most about was not yet at hand; instead, there was an exciting range of theories and findings, some pointing to very different possibilities. While I confess to initially being on my guard against a naive biological determinism, I also quickly learned that those studying the biology of the brain, no less than those working from a phenomenological, semiotic, or linguistic base, were intrigued by the tenuous relation of the worlds we construct to the worlds that exist outside of our percepts; they were not about to offer facile reductive solutions to complex mysteries. The seminar afforded what, for me, was a unique, almost utopian luxury within the academy: a semester of free exchange in uncharted waters. I still treasure it and the generosity of the students and scientists participating.

A formal course was offered in the following year. By that time, I had been able to audit some neuroscience seminars, and I was able to secure the services of two advanced undergraduates in neuroscience as peer teaching assistants. Sixteen students enrolled, approximately half identifying themselves as primarily science students and half identifying themselves as primarily from the arts and humanities. I asked all the students to fill out a questionnaire that not only assessed their backgrounds and expectations for the course but that also inquired if there were outcomes that they feared in studying performance theory and practice in relation to findings from cognitive and neuroscience. Some of the theatre students predictably foresaw becoming lost in a sea of impenetrable scientific prose; they feared feeling irrelevant and incompetent. Less predictable to me, some of the science students feared losing a precious sense of mystery and wonder in their experience of performances. Neither of those fears proved justified: the arts and humanities students found that they had plenty to offer and became fully engaged in the scientific discourse (though class discussions admittedly tended to move rather quickly from specific findings and models to speculations about "the great so what"); and of course, at the end of our studies, there was plenty of mystery left, and all the more to induce wonder. I have never so clearly felt that I was enabling students to do in the future what I was not equipped to do myself.

When, a few years later, I taught the course again, a notable change had taken place: almost all of the twenty students eventually taking the course had substantial backgrounds in *both* cognitive/neural sciences *and* in some aspect of performance. The "two cultures" seemed to be already converging, and the conversations in class were far more apt to include rigorous assessments of scientific hypotheses and models.

In setting up a class syllabus and in recently retooling it, I wanted to preserve some of the freedom of initiative in the original, exploratory seminar, while proceeding in a more comprehensive and orderly fashion. For this reason and to allow maximum play to the specific interests of a divergent student population, I asked the students to pick, in rank order, three of the broad topics I had selected for study in each half of the course. The peer assistants and I then composed teams of three to four people so that "science" and "arts/humanities" students would work with each other (a practice maintained in the most recent go-round, though the difference had become more one of degree than of kind). After an initial three weeks covering general introductory readings in both neural science and performance theory, each topic was presented by one of these teams, with each student serving as a part of two presentation teams over the course of the semester. Working with one of the peer advisers and myself, each team prepared a packet of readings with a maximum of one hundred pages to be read in advance by the entire class. Lesson plans, including hypotheses to be discussed, were handed in by the teams on the day of discussion, and a summary and assessment of the class was handed in the week after.

In the most recent offering of the course, these were the topics addressed:

A. Jokes, Dreams, and Creativity: Bisociation and Cortical Activity. How do we understand and respond to jokes? And why? What might this activity suggest about the way in which we organize information? And how might this affect performance?

B. Synesthesia. Does performative art deliberately work to confuse or blend the sensory signals in ways distinct from our everyday perception? How might this be done?

C. Trance and the Brain. How and why are sensory deprivation and overload used as theatrical devices? How do performances engage and encourage altered modes of consciousness? How might this relate to studies of "split brain" patients and conjectures on the evolution of the brain?

265
*Performance
Studies,
Neuroscience,
and the Limits
of Culture*

D.   The Brain and the Detective Story. Is there an inherent pleasure in revisiting old facts and finding new meanings (e.g., *Oedipus Rex*)? What might current theories and empirical evidence about the workings of the brain and its feedback systems suggest about how narratives are constructed and comprehended?

E.   Complexity and Attention. What factors control attention? How does this relate to theatricality and performativity? Why is art so complicated? How might this be pleasurable? And when does complexity cease to be enjoyable?

F.   Memory as Performance/Memory and Performance. What is the role of memory in attending to and "understanding" a performance? How do performances themselves become encoded in memory?

G.   Biology, Emotion, and Theatre Training. Why are emotions so prominent in considerations of the theatre? How do actors access emotions? What might studies of the brain tell us about this process and actors' procedures suggest as to the workings of the brain?

H.   Audience and Empathy. How does the spectator recognize and respond to emotional cues? What is the physiological basis for empathy, and what is its role in performance? What is the role of memory in this process?

I.   Archetype and Neurobiology. Why do certain specific "archetypal" treatments of the face reassert themselves in performance cultures around the world? What might the brain's structure and workings have to do with this phenomenon?

The classes themselves were an eclectic mix of presentations using video clips from programs on the brain and its workings, discussions of scientific findings and theories, and readings from the humanities and social sciences that seemed either to dovetail or to be at odds with those findings in interesting ways, all supplemented and challenged by examples of live and filmed performance gathered with a wide net. Along with readings from Richard Cytowic and from Wassily Kandinsky, clips from Disney's *Fantasia* and selections of field tapes on Balinese dance were used to show how the performing arts may create a sort of false synesthesia by conflating and confusing the recognition of sensory cues; manuals on writing mystery stories and clips from Laurel and Hardy movies and *Deep Space Nine* episodes were combined with Paul Ricoeur's writings on the hermeneutics of narrativity and Daniel Dennett's and Erich Harth's conjectures on how the mind makes multiple drafts and puts them to the test; examples from joke books and instances of unintentional humor were combined with various works by Freud, Arthur Koestler, George Lakoff, and Gerald Edelman on laughter, creativity, and the construction and disruption of categories; Viktor Shklovsky's and Eugenio Barba's complementary observations on "enstrangement" in literature and "extra-daily" uses of the body in performance were set beside the works of Michael Gazzaniga and Howard Gardner and clips from documentaries on the brain; Joseph Ledoux's discussion of the physiological basis for emotion in the brain was considered alongside the practical work and writings of Lee Strasberg, Michael Chekhov, Susana Bloch, Paul Ekman, and Bharat-muni. While some of these combinations panned out better than others, all provided ample food for thought.

At the end of the semester, either individually or in self-selected groups, students presented a final project/paper that had both a performative and a written aspect. These ranged widely, from self-parodying demonstrations on comedy and the brain to slide shows on animal display. The proportion of writing to presentation was deliberately allowed to vary from project to project.

After going through this process twice since the original seminar, I'm ready to offer some observations on ways that studying aspects of neuroscience may help address issues at the heart of understanding the hows and whys of performance. A few caveats may be in order. There is little in what follows that is brand-new; often, this study has helped me to reassess the importance of older materials and experiences. The paradigms of consciousness and cognition coming out of neuroscience are still very much in flux, and quite possibly, I have a more than healthy taste for snake oil in my hurry to find significance. Still, I am convinced that there is much to be learned in bringing these two fields together; perhaps my notes will be helpful in indicating directions that others may pursue more fully.

One quickly acquires a sense of wonder at the magnitude of difficulty in studying the brain and its workings. The sense of scale is staggering. Ten billion or so neurons populate the human neocortex, with an estimated ten trillion synaptic connections formed among and between them. In studying the ways these connections work and how they relate to the cognition of performance, it makes some sense to begin with the visual system. The visual system in the brain occupies a disproportionate amount of space and has received by far the most attention in studies of perception, while a theatre, after all, by etymology (*theatron*) and by tradition, is a place where one watches—acutely, attentively. As Dennett (101–38) has persuasively pointed out, whether in the theatre or out of it, we are constantly making multiple drafts of what we see, with specialized areas of the brain converting information about shape, color, movement, and texture/depth into data to be reclaimed as an image; that image is in turn open to multiple interpretations, and by shifting attention, we can often see things in different ways, literally and metaphorically. A relatively simple and well-known instance of this capability—one that allows us to observe the mind in the act of creating multiple drafts—is the famous line drawing that can be viewed as either opposing faces or a central vase. Intriguingly, we are not able to perceive both images at once, though, with a little practice, we can alternate these views, or drafts, at will.

The mechanisms for exerting executive control in the shifting of attention from draft to draft is not well understood (Posner), but it is tempting to extrapolate this pattern onto the juggling of alternative meanings that has become familiar as the hermeneutic circle, in which a series of competing interpretations are framed, altered, sometimes reclaimed, and then altered again when subjected to new information. A relatively simple instance of this phenomenon is the series of alternate narratives that an audience member creates in trying to follow a "who-done-it." It is difficult to keep more than one of these possibilities fully "in mind," or at least in full consciousness; rather, they are tested, rejected, and revived turn and turn about as new information is brought forward. This pattern of forming and testing drafts seems to be intrinsic to cognitive operations of the brain; and the tracking of alternative narratives, supported or put into doubt by the accumulation of data, seems to be central not only to scientific method but to what Langer long ago pointed to as the "form in suspense" of a dramatic illusion.

In the simple visual teaser of vase and faces, two lines are sufficient for us to perceive the shifting borders between figure and ground and to create two realms of possible "meaning." This raises another issue. As one studies the way in which form is decoded in the visual system, with the excitation of center/surround cells playing a crucial role in creating a percept of form, one realizes just how crucial the detection of borders is to understanding. Indeed, tests often show that subjects decode abstract line drawings of a shape more quickly than photographic images of similar objects (Ramachandran and Hirstein 24, 32). Again, it is tempting to extrapolate from these findings. Roach has recently reminded us of Mikhail Bakhtin's observation that "the most intense and productive life of cultures takes place on their boundaries" (qtd. in Roach 63). This is literally true of the visual system. It/we are drawn to borders, for borders provide the essential cues to form, to category, to meaning. For the brain, as for societies, borders are where the action is, or at least the identification of borders stimulates much of that action. The enduring popularity of cartoons and animated features and their particular appeal to children may depend on this principle. So, too, may common practices in mask making; simple masks are often most effective, the inessential cues having been stripped away.

Of course, most cognitive acts are more complex than decoding a simple line drawing, even an ambiguous one. As you read and find significance in the essays of this book, synaptic connections among neuron groups are being established, abandoned, and reformed, with some of these connections being reinforced and groups of neurons being encoded in ways that will allow you to recall and work with this information. We commonly refer to these activities as "mental," but they are, of course, physical in nature. We are, in a literal sense, what we think, what we imagine, what we can remember. "To change one's mind" is more than a figure of speech; it denotes a transformative biological act. In staging a performance, one can, to a degree, control this process, or at least influence it as percepts change and agents execute new actions in new scenes. The words appearing on a blackboard during Richard Foreman's early *Sophia (Wisdom): The Cliffs*, "as the naked woman appears," come to mind: "Think harder" (*Plays* 114). I recall laughter, and a younger but not young-looking Richard Foreman is hunched over a sound system somewhere in my mind's Greenwich Village.

Early work on the visual system stressed the peculiarities of the inverted image on the retina and the work of the rods and cones in collecting and encoding bits and pieces of visual information. But we now know that what happens in the retina is the beginning and not the completion of the process of image formation (Zeki; Kosslyn). Fully a third of the brain's mass is involved in constructing visual images, and other areas are also brought into play through analogy and association as "meaning" is ascribed and images are stored. Data constituting the visual image — or at least subject to interpretation as a visual image — are sent on to specialized areas (primarily but not exclusively in the occipital lobe at the back of the head) through two relay stations in the thalamus, one for the left field of vision, the other for the right: the lateral geniculate nuclei, or LGN. Different specialized colonies of neurons in identifiable sections of the brain will then search for information about color, form, motion, and texture/depth. As this information is brought back together, chains of associative memories will also be brought into play, and with these memories, the traces of accompanying emotions will be reawakened in the limbic system. Further connections are made to the excitatory system of the brain stem through the LGN: the picture of an ice-cream cone or a dripping beer can on a hot day may make us long for the physical sensation of the thing itself (the advertising industry depends on this).

Neuroscientists know a great deal about how the data of visual percepts are broken down and parsed for information. They know relatively little about how this information is put back together again. This is known as "the binding problem." Somehow, the information about color, shape, motion, and texture/depth is put back together into a single visual image, selecting the most persuasive of many possible drafts. Though there are still many questions about how this is accomplished, a system of reentrant loops drawing upon information generated by many of the brain's specialized systems and connecting back to the LGN is involved, and these loops may be thought of as forming a complex and demanding optimizing system.

But the brain's optimization process is constructive as well as corrective. The prominence of higher-level analysis of visual material in the formation of "meaningful" images may be indicated by the striking fact that the axon bundles of the neurons coming back from the neocortex of the brain to the LGN take up four times as much space as the axon bundles carrying information out to the neocortex. In this ongoing construction of image and meaning, there is no terminus, no end station for the hermeneutic circles, but only cessation, and even that may be only a falling off of attention as the mind moves on to its next image-making task.

Harth, describing this optimization network, makes an observation that has important implications for performance. Proposing an alternative to Dennett's vision of a helter-skelter, "pandemonium" process of cognition (253–54), Harth suggests we think of the LGN as a sort of "sketch pad" (70–76). Perhaps, as Kosslyn suggests, this "sketch pad" constitutes but one of a series topographic maps of the visual image being formed (188–89); but the most important point Harth makes is not dependent on the accuracy of his surmises about the LGN. However and wherever the "binding" together of information into a "meaningful," coherent image (or series of competing images) takes place, humankind seems to be unique in the ability to exteriorize this internal process. Of all animals, the human species is the only one that can make maps, blueprints, drawings, or paintings that represent a coherent mental image and therefore make that image open to social debate and judgment.

To think of shaping performances as a special form of sketch making that mimics the process of image formation in the brain is to stress the usefulness of performance as a focus for individual and group reflection. The progression of images and words offers a sketchlike version of what it is like to be alive and conscious in the mode of performed behavior. That version is offered synecdochically to a group of onlookers for contemplation and discussion. Does it resonate with their separate and shared experiences of life? Does it resonate with their individual and shared banks of images, memories, and emotional traces? Is it a memorable and significant addition to the narratives and images that life and art have already offered?

Crucial to judgments of the analogical power of a performance is the employment of memory; and "memory," as Edelman points out, "is the ability to repeat a performance" (102). Memory is a performance by dedicated specialists among myriad neuron groups, performed for the benefit of what Minsky has termed "the society of the mind"—a contentious society, as it turns out, composed of specialized groups of neurons interacting with other groups of neurons with only partially predictable results. Edelman stresses that this repetition, this recall, is—like "live" performances elsewhere—unstereotypic; there are always differences in the associations brought into play, and encountering or engaging the same stimulus twice will result in different constellations of images and phrases being recalled. In this sense, the mind works more like a piece of improvised theatre or a variety show than like a computer, or even a film or a scripted and well-rehearsed play.

Memories are created through changes in synaptic populations and are themselves subject to alterations in synaptic strength. The categorical circuits that memory depends upon are in flux, then, and subject to change, some more quickly than others (Edelman 99–110). We accept—happily or not—the changes of face and form in the mirror as we grow older, while still maintaining the ability to recognize our "selves." When an arm or a leg is lost, phantom limbs linger and hurt; but, gradually, these phantoms become foreshortened and lose their power. Memory, as this last example makes painfully clear, is grounded in the body's performed experience. Indeed, the systems that control memory, emotion, and decision making within the brain are all linked up to and informed by the somatosensory system of the brain, which monitors touch, temperature, pain, and the internal movements of our musculature.

Damasio suggests these linkages make the brain a captive audience of the body (xv). Our consciousness of a "self," he suggests, is first and foremost the result of an awareness of the continuity of the body's integrity, of the brain's constant monitoring of the body's limits in its interface with the "not-self" around us, and this sense of integrity and continuity is further reinforced by memories of recurring values and emotions that have been associated with the body's life in its shifting contexts (223–44). We are, perhaps, particularly drawn to observing human bodies, or (in the case of films, animations, and puppet shows) simulacra and abstractions of human bodies, because of the ceaseless and essential monitoring of our own physical selves as they move and push up against the world outside. This is one explanation for why the semiotician's reduction of the body to "the stage figure" fails to account for the body's phenomenological power in performance. Our memories of body awareness and our capacity to extrapolate from our own bodily experience—our own life performances—may be essential in allowing us to identify with the performed activities of another, providing the basis for empathy as well as self-identification.

Returning to Harth's suggestive metaphor, there is more to be said of the particular kinds of "sketches" that constitute artistic works, and specifically performances, that are framed as art. Unlike blueprints and maps, artistic creations in general have no obvious purpose. With the important exception of rituals that are viewed as efficacious in changing status, in healing the sick, or in placating the dead, the "performing arts" are composed of strips of bodily performance (including the utterance of speech) that, Brechtian polemics aside, seem to be superfluous to events outside of the performance, however richly they may reference those events. Indeed, its seeming superfluousness is one of the distinguishing characteristics of theatre. "The theatre, i.e., an immediate gratuitousness provoking acts without use or profit," writes Artaud (24); and Turner reminds us that the word *entertainment* etymologically signifies that which is "held-in-between"—that which is temporally and physically set apart from what is usually regarded as purposive (*Ritual* 114).

Yet, what performative play lacks in overt effectiveness it often makes up for in complexity; these seemingly purposeless activities are so structured as to demand a great deal of attention and effort to "understand." The mimetic play with life's potential actions that takes place in these betwixt and between times is characterized by confusions of ontological status, by ambiguity, by tricks of illusion and deception, by excessive or insufficient sensory information, by the contemplation of beauty in unlikely places, by surprising turns of plot, by the sadness of death remembered, and by the laughter at life reclaimed.

In an effort to understand how and why so much affect and intellectual puzzlement might be packed into moments where nothing is "really" at stake, I have found it useful to return to the psychoanalytic literature on jokes and laughter and have reread Freud's seminal work *Jokes and Their Relation to the Unconscious* and Koestler's lucid expansion of Freud's essay into a general theory of creativity *(Act; Janus)* with particular interest. Intuiting a link between dreams and jokes, and interested in the tendentious nature of joke making as it eludes taboos around the expression of hostile, obscene, cynical, and skeptical impulses, Freud theorized that the sudden bisociation of categorical fields (especially when in the service of these tendentious goals) could lead to a sort of mental short circuit, a sudden economizing of energy, creating a seemingly innocent joking "envelope" for the delivery of these tendentious impulses, thereby releasing laughter. Koestler elaborated on Freud's observations, with less emphasis on the tendentious content of jokes and a more acute interest in their use of bisociation. Edelman's Theory of Neural Group Selection provides a sophisticated model of what might be going on in the brain as latent synapses are engaged, arching across weakly connected or previously disconnected constellations of neuronal groups through a leveraged selection.

Koestler points out that poetic works and scientific breakthroughs share the sudden snapping into form of previously disassociated phenomena associated with the involuntary burst of laughter. Compare Zeami's description of the moment in viewing a *Noh* play when the eyes and ears of the spectator "open": "The deep sensations inherent in the play are suddenly experienced in one moment of profound exchange. . . . Understanding and sensation will be unified, producing a moment when the entire audience will be moved" (158). Freud's observation that a "tendentious" joke—one related to hostile, obscene, cynical, or skeptical ends—tends to elicit a stronger reaction than an "innocent" one troubles the seeming purposelessness of comic action, but the question remains: What is the inherent fun of connecting the unconnectable that gives license even (or especially) to attacks on taboos?

Why these pyrotechnics of neural firings? Why the pleasure in so much work? Why, as Shklovsky asked (15–16), is art so difficult? Why does Shakespeare write in verse, why does Tolstoy use such convoluted plots? What is so engaging about angels falling from the ceiling as Mormon wives and dying queens collide? Why the fascination with performances of "other cultures"—forms that have been constructed without regard for "our" liking? Why the complex reworking of emotional states, the endless variations on, and subversions of, the "who-done-it"? Why the manic persona-shifting of a Robin Williams or the radical attack on social constructs of race and gender of an Anna Deavere Smith or a Kate Bornstein? To make the stone stony, as Shklovsky noted, to reinvest the world with wonder, to move men and women to action, as Brecht hoped. No doubt. But most of all, I suspect, and as a prelude to all of these worthy aims, it is to exercise our sensory and cognitive faculties in a situation where we are freed from decisions that may affect lives and livelihoods, where nothing seems to be at stake, and in that purchased or stolen time between times, to give our categorical precepts a good workout and to keep our responses alert and working. To use all our mental capacities while monitoring the bodies of others in action. To do this for enjoyment because, owing to sensory and cognitive systems that have evolved, no doubt, for very different purposes, this activity makes wonderful use of everything that the body-minded brain does best. *Performance, I am suggesting, is a busman's holiday for the brain.*

What is the role and what are the limits of "culture" in this process?

Surely, the relative strength of taboos and the strength of binaries used in categorical construction vary from place to place and from time to time. There may even be ways in which the brain accommodates cultural patterns in its assigning of functional areas in early childhood: Shore has recently argued for a reassessment of the ways in which "cultural models" embodied in cognitive patterns encourage "a significant overlap [among individuals] within a community as to how novel experiences will be reconstituted as memory" (372). "Cultures," though, are not static enmities but contested terrains. Insofar as they are things at all, they exist as shared sets of concerns, images, and categories—some of these contradictory, some more entrenched than others, and all subject to change.

273
*Performance
Studies,
Neuroscience,
and the Limits
of Culture*

Ultimately, cultural constructions must exist as constellations of neuron groups in the brains of individuals; they may be viewed as predispositions to relate images and ideas, to construct categorical groupings of neurons, to use the mind by invoking well-exercised pathways. It may prove useful to thus locate the symbolic webs of culture as more or less fragile constructions within the contested consciousness of the body-minded brain. Envisioning cultural constructions in this manner may provide a way of understanding their staying power, as well as their vulnerability. Making and viewing performances seems to be among the more productive and, potentially at least, the more pleasurable ways of giving form to these values as well as contesting their worth in a relatively safe space.

To be sure, clichés and stereotypes can be perpetuated through performance; but the cognitive system cries out for the pleasure of new ways of putting things together, new associations among neuron groups, new sets of images, new memories. Challenge and novelty are welcome, as long as they generate a richness of associations, a resonance with memories of other images taken from the "sketchpads" encoding life and art as memory, and the possibility of enjoying life's possibilities in a refreshing way. The role of performance as art may be not so much to provide a momentary stay against confusion but to provide a shaking up of overdetermined thought patterns. One of the scientists I met with in the initial seminar at Brown noted with some awe that the things he values most—the human capacity to make art among them—seem to have no evolutionary advantage. One of my students once expressed his skepticism of any shared human trait that did not serve to keep the saber-toothed tigers at bay. But what could be more useful than keeping the brain ready and responsive by giving it some good, hard exercise in situations that are relatively removed from risk?

The findings of neuroscience—in their multiple and competing drafts—promise to provide a useful means of reminding us of the ways we are alike, as well as the ways in which, in constructing our own multiple drafts, we can be at odds: between cultures and within our selves. Bracketing strips of behavior as performance—as somehow "re-presented" outside of the driven flow of causally chained actions and responses that constitute (or seem to constitute) everyday life—provides a way of externalizing the internal process by which disparate cues are assigned and reassigned meanings. These cues, given new significance by their selection and presentation to the view of others as percepts destined for signification, set off complex chain reactions of electrical and chemical activities dashing about axons and dendrites, catching meanings in margins, and through both predictable and unpredictable bisociative connections, enforcing and breaking apart categorical constructions, looping back into memory, provoking bursts of laughter or fleeting moments of comprehension, and, ultimately, changing both the ways in which we can view the world and the configuration of the neurons that must make sense of the viewing.

Perhaps, our small but growing comprehension of how the mind works will span the two academic cultures. Or maybe, at the least, it will serve to cut the trope of culture down to size while we agree to disagree—with each other, with ourselves, with the past, and with the other fortunate or unfortunate souls who essentially share our mental architecture. Performances serve to project the mind's sketching and paradigm-making abilities out beyond the confines of the individual being, where other minds can assess the persuasiveness and power of our fleeting, embodied visions—affirming and denying, remembering and forgetting, assimilating them into old categories, forging new ones, blending fantasy and reality in fragile images made of our very biological selves, shifting storage areas, strengthening weak synaptic connections and making new ones, rededicating neurons used to store information that has fallen into disuse, and maybe, if we are very, very lucky, using this process as a way to live better, or at least to enjoy the passage of our time here more fully.

NOTE

The research for this essay was funded in part by a Brown University course development grant. The thoughts in this essay have been developed through presentations for conferences of Performance Studies International, the American Society for Theater Research, the Société d'Ethnoscénologie (Paris), the Indira Gandhi National Center for the Arts (New Delhi), and Tufts University. While they should not be held accountable for my errant thoughts, I am indebted to my colleagues in the sciences at Brown who helped to nurture my interests, especially Sheila Blumstein, James Anderson, Jerry Daniels, Phil Lieberman, James McIlwain, Michael Paradiso, Jerome Sanes, and Bill Warren. Among theatre colleagues, Jean-Marie Pradier, Donnalee Dox, John Erickson, Spencer Golub, Joseph Roach,

Arthur Sabatini, and Phillip Zarrilli have been especially supportive. The greatest debt is to the students who have shared the journeys described, especially Eric Hazen, Yann Montelle, Mindy Sobota, and Noah Raizman, who have served as teaching assistants.

WORKS CITED

Artaud, Antonin. *The Theatre and Its Double.* 1938. Trans. M. C. Richards. New York: Grove, 1958.

Barba, Eugenio. *The Paper Canoe: A Guide to Theatre Anthropology.* London: Routledge, 1995.

Damasio, Antonio R. *Descartes' Error: Emotion, Reason, and the Human Brain.* New York: Putnam, 1994.

Dennett, Daniel. *Consciousness Explained.* Boston: Little, 1991.

Edelman, Gerald M. *Bright Air, Brilliant Fire: On the Matter of the Mind.* New York: Basic, 1992.

Foreman, Richard. *Plays and Manifestos.* Ed. Kate Davy. New York: New York UP, 1992.

Freud, Sigmund. *Jokes and Their Relation to the Unconscious.* 1909. Trans. James Strachey. New York: Norton, 1960.

Gardner, Howard. *Art, Mind, and Brain: A Cognitive Approach to Creativity.* New York: Harper, 1982.

Harth, Erich. *The Creative Loop: How the Brain Makes a Mind.* Reading: Addison, 1993.

Koestler, Arthur. *The Act of Creation.* New York: Hutchinson, 1964.

———. *Janus: A Summing Up.* New York: Vintage, 1979.

Konner, Melvin. *The Tangled Wing: Biological Constraints on the Human Spirit.* New York: Holt, 1982.

Kosslyn, Stephen M. *Image and Brain: The Resolution of the Imagery Debate.* Cambridge: MIT P, 1994.

Langer, Susanne. *Feeling and Form.* New York: Scribners, 1953.

Minsky, Marvin. *The Society of Mind.* New York: Simon, 1985.

Pinker, Steven. *The Language Instinct: How the Mind Creates Language.* New York: Morrow, 1994.

Posner, Michael I. "Attention in Cognitive Neuroscience: An Overview." *The Cognitive Neurosciences.* Ed. Michael S. Gazzaniga. Cambridge: MIT P, 1995.

Ramachandran, V. S., and William Hirstein. "The Science of Art: A Neurological Theory of Aesthetic Experience." *Journal of Consciousness Studies* 6 (1999): 15–51.

Roach, Joseph. *Cities of the Dead: Circum-Atlantic Performance.* New York: Columbia UP, 1996.

Shklovsky, Viktor. *Theory of Prose.* 1929. Trans. Benjamin Sher. New York: Dalkey, 1990.

Shore, Brad. *Culture in Mind: Cognition, Culture, and the Problem of Meaning.* New York: Oxford UP, 1996.

Turner, Victor. "Body, Brain and Culture." *The Anthropology of Performance.* New York: PAJ, 1986. 156–78.

———. *From Ritual to Theatre: The Human Seriousness of Play.* New York: PAJ, 1982.

Zeami. *On the Art of Noh Drama: The Major Treatises of Zeami* [c. 1400]. Trans. J. Thomas Rimer and Yamazaki Masakazu. Princeton: Princeton UP, 1984.

Zeki, Semir. *A Vision of the Brain.* Oxford: Blackwell, 1993.

John
Emigh

Contributors

William O. Beeman is an associate professor of anthropology and theatre, speech, and dance at Brown University. He has conducted research on traditional performance forms in the Middle East, Japan, India, and the United States. He is the author of *Culture, Performance, and Communication in Iran* and *Language, Status, and Power in Iran* as well as a coauthor of *The Third Line: The Opera Performer as Interpreter*. He has published numerous scholarly articles on performance theory and practice. A professional singer, he also appears regularly as an opera performer.

Michael S. Bowman teaches performance studies at Louisiana State University, Baton Rouge, where he is an associate professor and the director of graduate studies in the Department of Communication Studies. His teaching and research interests are in the areas of performance pedagogy and performance and cultural studies, with a particular emphasis on tourism and travel. He has served as the chair of the Performance Studies Division of the National Communication Association and as an associate editor for several scholarly journals.

Ruth Laurion Bowman is an associate professor in the Department of Communication Studies at Louisiana State University, Baton Rouge, where she teaches performance studies and manages the Performance Studies Mary Frances HopKins Black Box theatre. Her teaching and research interests are in nineteenth-century US cultural history, performance historiography, and theories of performance practice.

Eric Dishman is a senior researcher and manager of People and Practices Research at Intel Labs in Hillsboro, Oregon, where he uses and teaches performance, ethnography, and interaction analysis for the design of new products, businesses, and services. Using innovative human-centered approaches to product development, he continues to evolve this body of work called "informance design," which he started at Interval Research Corporation in Palo Alto, California, in 1993. He is completing his doctorate in the Department of Communication at the University of Utah with a dissertation on informance design and innovation through performance.

John Emigh is a professor in the Theatre, Speech, and Dance Department at Brown University and is the author of *Masked Performance: The Play of Self and Other in Ritual and Theatre*. He has directed more than sixty plays, and his own performances have been documented in the *Drama Review* and the *Asian Theatre Journal*. He was the founding chairperson of the Association for Asian Performance.

Craig Gingrich-Philbrook is a performance artist who has appeared at Dixon Place in New York, Sushi Gallery in San Diego, and elsewhere. He teaches performance studies at the Department of Speech Communication at Southern Illinois University Carbondale, having previously taught at Hofstra University. His work has been published in *Text and Performance Quarterly*, *Communication Theory*, and *Cultural Studies*.

Judith Hamera is a professor of communication studies and theatre arts and dance at California State University, Los Angeles. She received her doctorate in performance studies from Northwestern University. Her work examining issues of form, gender, and culture as these emerge in classical and contemporary dance has been published in a variety of journals. She is a former editor of *Text and Performance Quarterly*.

Joni L. Jones is an associate professor of performance studies in the Department of Theatre and Dance and the associate director of the Center for African and African American Studies at the University of Texas at Austin. She teaches performance of literature and history of African American theatre to undergraduates and teaches performance ethnography, performing black feminisms, and performance and activism to graduate students. Her most recent work examines the use of a jazz aesthetic in theatrical productions.

Michelle Kisliuk is on the faculty of the McIntire Department of Music at the University of Virginia. She holds a doctorate in performance studies from New York University and specializes in performance theory, ethnographic writing, and ensemble music (bluegrass, African performance). Since 1986, she has researched the ensemble music and dance of the forest people (BaAka) from the Central African Republic. She is the author of *Seize the Dance! BaAka Musical Life and the Ethnography of Performance*.

Bruce McConachie is the director of graduate studies in the Department of Theatre and Performance Studies at the University of Pittsburgh. His publications include *Interpreting the Theatrical Past*, edited with Thomas Postlewait, and *Melodramatic Formations: American Theatre and Society, 1820–1870*. In addition to teaching and working in theatre history and performance theory, he facilitates community-based theatre in the Pittsburgh area.

Linda M. Park-Fuller currently teaches performance studies at Arizona State University. She holds a doctorate in performance studies from the University of Texas at Austin. A past chairperson of the National Communication Association's Performance Studies Division, she has published numerous articles in such publications as *Literature in Performance* and *Text and Performance Quarterly*. She also tours her one-person performance "A Clean Breast of It," a personal narrative based on her experiences with breast cancer.

Elyse Lamm Pineau is an associate professor of speech communication at Southern Illinois University Carbondale, where she conducts research and teaches performance studies pedagogy, gender and performance, and autoethnography. She holds a doctorate in performance studies from Northwestern University and has published in *Text and Performance Quarterly, American Educational Research Journal*, and *Critical Perspectives on Communication Research and Pedagogy*.

Joseph Roach is the Charles C. and Dorathea S. Dilley Professor of Theater at Yale University. He has chaired the Department of Performing Arts at Washington University in St. Louis, the Department of Performance Studies at New York University, and the interdisciplinary doctoral program in theatre at Northwestern University. He is the author of *Cities of the Dead: Circum-Atlantic Performance*.

Arthur J. Sabatini is an associate professor of performance studies in the interdisciplinary arts and performance program at Arizona State University West. He holds a doctorate from the Department of Performance Studies, New York University, and has received two National Endowment for the Humanities fellowships. His essays have appeared in *Discours social/Social Discourse, Bucknell Review*, and other publications. He is currently writing a book on composer Robert Ashley.

Nathan Stucky is an associate professor and the chair of the Department of Speech Communication at Southern Illinois University Carbondale, where he teaches courses in performance studies. From 1995 to 2001, he edited *Theatre Annual: A Journal of Performance Studies*. He has served as the chair of the Performance Studies Division of the National Communication Association and on the executive board of

Performance Studies International. His research on conversation analysis, performance, and pedagogy has appeared in *Literature in Performance, Text and Performance Quarterly, Journal of Pragmatics, Speech Communication Teacher, Journal of Language and Social Psychology,* and *Communication Education.*

Richard F. Ward is an associate professor of preaching and performance studies at the Iliff School of Theology in Denver. In addition to courses in preaching, he teaches a drama workshop, storytelling, and the performance of texts. He is the author of *Speaking from the Heart: Preaching with Passion* and *Speaking of the Holy: The Art of Communication in Preaching.* At Yale Divinity School, he held the first Clement-Muehl Chair in Communication Arts. He holds a doctorate in performance studies from Northwestern University and is an ordained minister in the United Church of Christ.

Cynthia Wimmer has had careers in both academia and business. While completing her Ph.D. in English at the University of Maryland, College Park, she originated courses in playwriting and performance theory. She has been a guest lecturer at the Folger Shakespeare Library, and her interview with playwright Beth Henley was published in *The Playwright's Art: Conversations with Contemporary American Dramatists.* She served on the Governing Council of the Association for Theatre in Higher Education for three years and helped to develop its Performance Studies Focus Group. In her business career, she has been a consultant for change management, operations management, performance improvement, project management, public relations, and culture modification and is chair of the board of Wimmer Solutions, a bicoastal consulting and staffing firm.

Phillip B. Zarrilli is internationally known for training actors through Asian martial arts and for directing the plays of Samuel Beckett. He runs the Tyn-y-parc C.V.N. studio/kalari in Wales. A professor of drama at the University of Exeter in the UK, he is the author of *Kathakali Dance-Drama: Where Gods and Demons Come to Play* and *When the Body Becomes All Eyes* and the editor of *Acting (Re)Considered: Theories and Practices.*

Index

Theater in the Americas

The goal of the series is to publish a wide range of scholarship on theater and performance, defining theater in its broadest terms and including subjects that encompass all of the Americas.

The series focuses on the performance and production of theater and theater artists and practitioners but welcomes studies of dramatic literature as well. Meant to be inclusive, the series invites studies of traditional, experimental, and ethnic forms of theater; celebrations, festivals, and rituals that perform culture; and acts of civil disobedience that are performative in nature. We publish studies of theater and performance activities of all cultural groups within the Americas, including biographies of individuals, histories of theater companies, studies of cultural traditions, and collections of plays.